TALES FROM THE ARABIAN NIGHTS

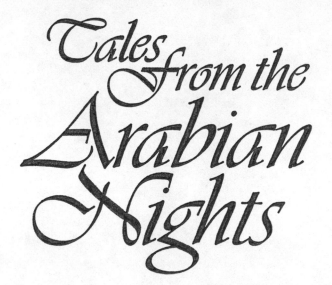

Tales from the Arabian Nights

Retold from the Original Arabic by
N. J. Dawood

Illustrated by Ed Young

Doubleday & Company, Inc.
GARDEN CITY, NEW YORK

This version follows Macnaghten's Calcutta edition of *The Thousand and One Nights* (1839–42) but the first Bulaq edition (1835) has also been consulted wherever the Macnaghten text appeared faulty. "Aladdin and the Enchanted Lamp" follows Zotenberg's text (Paris, 1888).

Library of Congress Cataloging in Publication Data

Dawood, N J
Tales from the Arabian nights.
SUMMARY: Presents a retelling of traditional tales
from the Middle East.
1. Fairy tales, Arab.   2. Tales, Arab.   [1. Fairy
tales.   2. Folklore, Arab]   I. Young, Ed.
II. Arabian nights.   III. Title.
PZ8.D198Tal   398.2
ISBN 0-385-12365-5
Library of Congress Catalog Card Number 77–16886

To Juliet, Richard, Norman,
and Andrew

Contents

Foreword

Ever since they were introduced to the Western world by the French Orientalist Antoine Galland at the beginning of the eighteenth century, the tales of *The Thousand and One Nights* (perhaps better known as *The Arabian Nights*) have enjoyed such fame and have entertained so many generations in Europe and America that they have virtually become part of the cultural heritage of the West.

Although the book of *The Nights* is outside the body of classical Arabic literature, on account of its ungrammatical language and vernacular style, it has attained the status of a classic through translation; and despite its uninhibited candor and unorthodox morality it has, equally paradoxically, been seized upon as ideal material for childhood reading. For by their imaginative richness, their colorful portrayal of both the mundane and the marvelous, and their ever-soaring inventiveness, these tales remain unrivaled among the short stories of all time.

Almost every generation of children has had its own version of *The Nights*. Most of these, whether in print or in pantomime, on television or on the cinema screen, have come to bear such little resemblance to the original stories that it is now time to go back to the authentic source. This volume, unlike any other children's edition before it, presents modern boys and girls with a straightforward but not over simplified version containing the finest stories *retold directly from the original Arabic*. A number of tales in this edition, such as "Maaruf the Cobbler," "Khalifah the Fisherman," and "The Dream," have never before been included in a children's version of *The Nights*.

The idiom is of today, without being colloquial, and the style attempts to preserve the oriental flavor without recourse to archaisms. The only Arabic words used in this book are those that have been assimilated into the English language, such as *Caliph*, *vizier*, and *cadi*.

N.J.D.

TALES FROM THE ARABIAN NIGHTS

The Tale of King Shahriyar and His Brother, Shahzaman

Once upon a time, there ruled over India and China a mighty King, who commanded great armies and had numerous courtiers, followers, and servants. He left two sons, both famed for their horsemanship—especially the older, who inherited his father's kingdom and governed it with such justice that all his subjects loved him. He was called King Shahriyar. His brother was named Shahzaman and was King of Samarkand.

The two brothers continued to reign happily in their kingdoms, and after twenty years King Shahriyar longed to see Shahzaman. He ordered his vizier to go to Samarkand and invite Shahzaman to his court.

The vizier set out promptly on his errand and journeyed many days and nights through deserts and wildernesses until he arrived in Shahzaman's city and was admitted to his presence. He gave him King Shahriyar's greetings and told him of his master's wish to see him. King Shahzaman was overjoyed at the thought of visiting his brother. He made ready to leave his kingdom, and sent out his tents, camels, mules, servants, and retainers. Then he appointed his vizier as his deputy and set out for his brother's dominions.

At midnight, however, he suddenly remembered a present which he wished to give his brother but which he had left at the palace. He returned alone to fetch it. Entering his private chamber, he was outraged to find his beautiful queen, whose affection he had never doubted, entertaining a palace slave.

"If this can happen when I am scarcely out of my city," he thought, "what will this wicked woman do when I am far away?"

He drew his sword and slew them both. Then he rejoined his courtiers and journeyed on until he reached his brother's capital.

Shahriyar rejoiced at his coming. He went out to meet Shahzaman, took him in his arms, and welcomed him affectionately. But as they sat chatting, he noticed that Shahzaman, who was brooding over his wife's disloyalty, looked pale and sullen. Shahriyar said nothing about this, thinking that his brother might be worrying over the affairs of the kingdom he had left behind. Day after day Shahriyar tried to distract him, but all to no avail. At last he invited him to go hunting, hoping that the sport might cheer his spirits, but Shahzaman refused, and Shahriyar had to go to the hunt alone.

Meanwhile, Shahzaman sat at a window overlooking the royal garden, and saw one of the palace doors open and twenty women and twenty slaves appear. In their midst was his brother's Queen, a woman of rare beauty. They made their way to the fountain and sat down on the grass, each slave choosing a woman for his companion. Then the King's wife called out, "Come, Masood!" and a slave at once ran up to her and sat down beside her. There they all remained, feasting together, till nightfall.

"By Allah," said Shahzaman to himself, "my misfortune was nothing beside this."

He was no longer unhappy, but ate and drank, being hungry after his long abstinence.

When Shahriyar returned from the hunt he was surprised to see his brother restored to health and good spirits.

"How is it, brother," he asked, "that when I last saw you, you were so pale and sad, and now you look well and contented?"

"As for my sadness," Shahzaman replied, "I will now tell you the reason. Know that after I had received your invitation I made preparations for the journey and set out from my capital; but I had forgotten the pearl that was my present for you, and went back to the palace for it. There in my room I found my wife in the company of a slave. I killed them both. Then I came on to your kingdom, though my mind was troubled with unhappy thoughts."

When he heard this, Shahriyar was curious to know the rest of the story, upon which Shahzaman related to him all that he had seen that day from the window.

"I will not believe it," Shahriyar exclaimed, "unless I see it with my own eyes!"

"Then let it be known that you intend to hunt again," suggested his brother. "But hide with me here, and you will see what I saw."

And so King Shahriyar announced his intention to set out on another expedition. Soldiers, with their tents, left the city, and Shahriyar followed them. As soon as they had encamped, he gave orders to his slaves that no one was to be admitted to the King's tent. Then, disguising himself, he returned unnoticed to the palace, where his brother was waiting for him. They sat together at one of the windows overlooking the garden. It was not long before the Queen and her women appeared with the slaves and thus King Shahriyar saw that what his brother had told him was true.

Crazed with anger, he put his Queen to death, together

with all her women and the slaves. And after that he made it his custom to marry a young girl every day and kill her the next morning. This he continued to do for three years, until an outcry arose among the people, and some of them left the country with their daughters.

At last a day came when the King's vizier searched the city in vain for a wife for his master. Finding none, and dreading the King's anger, he returned home with a heavy heart.

Now, the vizier himself had two daughters. The older was called Shahrazad, and the younger Dunyazad. Shahrazad was both beautiful and accomplished: she knew the works of poets and the legends of ancient kings.

Shahrazad noticed her father's anxiety and asked what made him so sad. The vizier told her the reason. "Dear Father," she said, "give me in marriage to the King. Either I will die a martyr's death, or I will live and save my countrymen's daughters."

Her proposal filled the vizier with horror. He warned her how dangerous it would be; but she had made up her mind and would not listen to his advice.

"Beware," said the vizier, "of what happened in the fable of the donkey who did not mind his own business."

The Fable of the Donkey, the Ox, and the Farmer

There was once a rich farmer who owned many herds of cattle. He understood the language of beasts and birds. In one of his stables he kept an ox and a donkey. At the end of each day the ox came to where the donkey was tied and found the stall well swept and watered. The manger was plentifully supplied with straw and barley, and the donkey lying at his ease, for his master seldom rode him.

It happened one day that the farmer heard the ox say to the donkey, "How lucky you are! I am worn out with hard work, but you lie here in comfort. The corn you eat is well prepared and you lack nothing. Our master hardly ever rides you. But for me life is one long stretch of painful labor at the plow and the millstone."

The donkey answered, "Let me advise you. When you go out into the field and the yoke is placed upon your neck, pretend to be ill and drop down on your belly. Do not rise even if they beat you; or, if you do rise, fall down again immediately. When they take you back to the stable and put fodder before you, do not eat it. For a day or two eat very little. If you act in this way you will be given a complete rest."

Remember, the farmer overheard this.

So when the plowman brought his fodder, the ox ate hardly any of it. And when the plowman came the following morning to take him out into the field the ox appeared to be far from well. The farmer said, "Take the donkey and use him at the plow all day!"

The day's work being finished, the donkey returned to the stable. The ox thanked him for his kind advice, but the donkey made no reply, bitterly repenting his rashness.

Next day the plowman took the donkey again and made him labor until the evening, so that he returned utterly exhausted, with his neck chafed by the rope. Again the ox thanked him and complimented him on his shrewdness.

"I wish I had kept my wisdom to myself," thought the donkey.

Then an idea came to him.

Turning to the ox, he said, "I heard my master say to his servant just now, 'If the ox does not recover soon, take him to the slaughterhouse and get rid of him.' My fear for your safety, dear friend, obliges me to make this known to you before it is too late."

On hearing the donkey's words, the ox thanked him and said, "Tomorrow I will work willingly." He ate all his fodder and even licked the manger clean.

Early the next morning the farmer went with his wife to visit the ox in the stable. At the sight of his master the ox swung his tail and frisked about in all directions to show how ready he was for the yoke. He was taken to work by the plowman. And so was the donkey.

"Nothing will change my mind, Father," Shahrazad said at the end of the story. "I am resolved."

So the vizier arrayed his daughter in bridal garments,

decked her with jewels, and made ready to announce her wedding to the King.

When she said good-by to her sister, Shahrazad gave her these instructions: "After I have been received by the King I shall send for you. When you come, you must say, 'Tell us, sister, some tale of marvel to pass the night.' Then I will tell you a tale which, if Allah wills, shall be the means of our deliverance."

So the vizier went with his daughter to the King. And when the King had taken Shahrazad to his chamber she wept and said, "I have a young sister to whom I dearly wish to say a last farewell."

The King sent for Dunyazad, who came and threw her arms around her sister's neck and sat down beside her.

Then Dunyazad said to Shahrazad, "Tell us, sister, a tale of marvel so that the night may pass pleasantly."

"Gladly," she answered, "if the King permits me."

The King, who was troubled with sleeplessness, gave her leave and eagerly listened to Shahrazad's story:

The Fisherman and the Jinnee

Once upon a time, there was a poor fisherman who had a wife and three children to support.

He used to cast his net four times a day. It chanced that one day he went down to the sea at noon and, reaching the shore, set down his basket, rolled up his sleeves, and cast his net far out into the water. After he had waited for some time, he pulled on the cords with all his strength, but the net was so heavy that he could not draw it in. So he tied the rope ends to a wooden stake on the beach, took off his clothes, dived into the water, and set to work to bring up the net. But when he had carried it ashore he found that it contained only a dead donkey. "What a strange catch!" cried the fisherman, disgusted at the sight. He freed the net and wrung it out, then waded into the water and cast it again. On trying to draw it in, he found it even heavier than before. Thinking he had caught some enormous fish, he fastened the ropes to the stake, dived in again, and brought up the net. This time he found a large earthen vessel filled with mud and sand.

Angrily the fisherman threw away the vessel, cleaned his net, and cast it for the third time. He waited patiently and, when he felt the net grow heavy, pulled it in, only to find it full of bones and broken glass. In despair, he lifted up his arms and cried, "Heaven knows I cast my net only four times a day. I have already cast it for the third time and caught no fish at all. Surely Allah will not fail me again!"

So saying, the fisherman hurled his net far out into the sea. This time his catch was an antique bottle made of copper. The mouth was stopped with lead and bore the seal of King Solomon, who was renowned for his great skill in magic and his power over spirits and demons. The fisherman rejoiced and said, "I will sell this in the market of the coppersmiths. It must be worth ten pieces of gold."

Shaking the bottle, which he found rather heavy, he thought, "I must break the seal and see what there is inside."

With his knife he removed the lead and again shook the bottle; but scarcely had he done so when there burst out from it a great column of smoke that spread along the shore and rose so high that it almost touched the heavens. Then the smoke took shape and formed itself into a jinnee of such colossal height that his head touched the clouds. His legs towered like the masts of a ship. His head was a huge dome and his mouth as wide as a cavern, with teeth ragged as broken rocks. His nostrils were two inverted bowls, and his eyes, blazing like torches, made his face terrible indeed to look upon.

The sight of the jinnee struck fear into the fisherman's heart; his limbs trembled, his teeth chattered, his tongue dried, and his eyes bulged.

"There is no god but Allah, and Solomon is his Prophet!" cried the jinnee, taking the fisherman for the magician-king, his old master. "I beg you, mighty prophet, do not kill me! I swear never again to disobey you."

"What on earth are you talking about?" the fisherman cried. "Solomon has been dead these eighteen hundred years, and we are now nearing the end of time. But what is your story, and how did you come to be imprisoned in this bottle?"

The jinnee seemed very pleased to hear that Solomon was dead. He burst out laughing, then said sarcastically, "Fisherman, rejoice. I bring you good news!"

"What news?"

"News of your death, horrible and instant!" the jinnee answered.

"Ungrateful wretch!" the fisherman cried. "Why do you wish my death? What have I done to deserve it? Have I not brought you up from the depths of the sea and released you from your imprisonment?"

But the jinnee commanded, "Choose the manner of your death and the way that I shall kill you. Come, waste no time!"

"But how have I wronged you?"

"Listen to my story, and you will know the reason," the jinnee answered.

"Be brief, then, I beg you," the fisherman pleaded, "for you have wrung my soul with fear."

"Know," the giant began, "that I am one of the rebel demons who rose up in arms against King Solomon. The King sent to me his commander in chief, who captured me, despite my power, and led me in fetters before his master. Invoking the name of God, Solomon ordered me to embrace his faith and pledge him absolute obedience. I refused, and he imprisoned me in this bottle, and set upon it a seal of lead bearing the name of the Most High. Then he sent for several of his faithful demons, who carried me away and cast me into the middle of the sea. In the ocean depths I vowed, 'I will bestow eternal riches on him who sets me free!' But a hundred years passed away and no one freed me. In the second hundred years of my imprisonment I said, 'For him who frees me I will open up the buried treasures of the earth!' And yet no one freed me. Whereupon I flew into a rage and swore, 'I will kill the man who sets me free, allowing him only to choose the manner of his death!' Now it was you who set me free; therefore prepare to die and choose the way that I shall kill you."

"Oh, wretched luck, that I should be the one to free you!" the fisherman exclaimed. "Spare me, mighty jinnee, and Allah will spare you; kill me, and so will Allah destroy you!"

"You have freed me," said the jinnee; "therefore you must die."

"Noble jinnee, will you repay good with evil?"

"Enough of this babble! Kill you I must."

At this point the fisherman thought to himself, "Though I am only a helpless human being and he is a powerful jinnee, I may yet have sense enough to outwit him." To the monster he said, "Before you kill me, I beg you in the Name of the Most High, engraved on Solomon's seal, to answer me one question truthfully."

The jinnee trembled at the mention of the Name, and, when he had promised to answer truthfully, the fisherman asked, "How could this bottle, which is scarcely big enough to hold your hand or foot, ever contain your entire body?"

"Do you doubt that?" the jinnee roared indignantly.

"I will never believe it," the fisherman replied, "until I have seen you enter this bottle with my own eyes."

Upon this the jinnee shook from head to foot and dissolved into a column of smoke, which gradually wound itself into the bottle and disappeared within. At once the fisherman snatched up the leaden stopper and thrust it into the mouth of the vessel. Then he called out to the jinnee, "Now you must choose the manner of your death and the way that

I shall kill you. Upon my life, I will throw you back into the sea, and warn all men against your treachery!"

When he heard the fisherman's words, the jinnee struggled hard to get out, but the magic seal held him back. He now altered his tone and, assuming a humble air, said that he had been jesting, and begged to be freed. But the fisherman paid no attention to his cries and took the bottle down to the seashore.

"What are you going to do with me?" whimpered the jinnee.

"I am going to throw you back into the sea!" the fisherman replied. "You have lain in the depths for eighteen hundred years, and there you shall remain till the Last Judgment! Did I not beg you to spare me so that Allah might spare you? But you took no pity on me, and he has now delivered you into my hands."

"Let me out," the jinnee begged, "and I will give you fabulous riches!"

"Faithless jinnee," the fisherman answered, "you deserve no better fate than that of the King in the tale of Yunan and the doctor."

"What tale is that?" asked the jinnee.

The Tale of King Yunan and Duban the Doctor

It is said (the fisherman began) that once upon a time there reigned in the land of Persia a rich and mighty King called Yunan. He had great armies and a numerous following of noblemen and courtiers. But he suffered from a leprosy that his physicians, for all their skill and knowledge, could never cure.

One day a venerable old doctor named Duban came to the King's capital. He had studied books written in Greek, Latin, Arabic, and Persian and was deeply read in the lore of the ancients. He was master of many sciences, knew the properties of plants and herbs, and, above all, was skilled in astrology and medicine. When this physician heard of the King's leprosy and of his doctors' vain attempts to cure him, he put on his finest robes and went off to the royal palace. After he had kissed the ground before the King and invoked blessings upon him, he told him who he was and said, "Great King, I have heard about your illness and have come to heal you. Yet will I give you no medicine to drink, nor any ointment to rub upon your body."

The King was astonished at the doctor's words.

"How will you do that?" he asked. "If you cure me, I

will heap riches upon you, and your children's children after you. Anything you wish shall be yours for the asking, and you shall be my companion and friend. But when is it to be? What day, what hour?"

"Tomorrow, if the King wishes," came the reply.

The King gave Duban a robe of honor and other presents, and the doctor took leave of him. Hastening to the center of the town, he rented a little house to which he carried his books and his drugs and other medicaments. Then he prepared the cure and poured it into a hollow polo stick.

Next morning Duban went to the royal palace, kissed the ground before the King, and asked him to ride into the field and play a game of polo with his friends. The King rode out with his ministers and his chamberlains, and when he had entered the playing field the doctor handed him the hollow club and said, "Take this and grasp it firmly. Strike the ball with all your might until the palm of your hand and the rest of your body begin to sweat. The cure will penetrate your palm and run through your veins and arteries. When it has done its work, return to the palace, wash yourself, and go to sleep. In this way you will be cured; and peace be with you."

The King took hold of the club and, gripping it firmly, struck the ball and galloped after it with the other players. Harder and harder he hit the ball as he dashed up and down the field, until his palm and his body perspired.

Duban saw that the cure was working, and he ordered the King to return to the palace. The slaves hastened to make ready the royal bath and to prepare the linens and the towels. The King bathed, put on his night clothes, and went to sleep.

Next morning the physician went to the palace. When he was admitted to the King's presence he kissed the ground before him and wished him peace. The King quickly got up to receive him, threw his arms around the physician's neck, and seated him by his side.

For when the King had left his bath the previous evening, he had looked upon his body and rejoiced to find no trace of the leprosy; his skin had become as pure as virgin silver. And so the King entertained the physician liberally again all the day. He also bestowed on him robes of honor and other gifts and, when evening came, gave him two thousand pieces of gold and mounted him on his own favorite horse. So thrilled was the King at the extraordinary skill of his doctor that he kept repeating to himself, "This wise physician has cured me without drug or ointment. By Allah, I will load him with honors and make him my companion and trusted friend." And that night the King lay down to sleep in an ecstasy of bliss, knowing that he was clean in body and cured of his disease.

Next day, as soon as he was seated upon his throne, with the officers of his court standing before him and his lieutenants and ministers on either side, the King called for the physician, who came up and kissed the ground before him. The King rose and seated the doctor by his side. He feasted him all day, gave him a thousand pieces of gold and more robes of honor, and talked with him until nightfall.

Now, among the King's viziers was a wicked old man, an envious, spiteful villain. Seeing the King make the physician his favorite friend and lavish on him high dignities and favors, the vizier began to plot the doctor's ruin. So, on the following day, when the King entered the council chamber and was about to call for the physician, the vizier kissed the ground before him and said, "Your Majesty, my duty prompts me to warn you against an evil that threatens your life; nor would I be anything but a traitor if I held my peace."

Troubled at these ominous words, the King ordered him to explain what he meant.

"Your Majesty," the vizier went on, "there is an old proverb that says: 'He who does not weigh the consequences of his acts will never prosper.' Now, I have seen the King bestow favors and shower honors upon his enemy, a murderer who is secretly plotting to destroy him. I greatly fear for the King's safety."

"Who is this man whom you suppose to be my enemy?" asked the King, turning pale.

"I speak of Duban the doctor," the vizier answered.

"He is my friend," replied the King angrily, "dearer to me than all my courtiers; for he has cured me of my leprosy, an evil that my own physicians could not remove. Surely there is no other man like him in the whole world, from East to West. How can you say these monstrous things of him? From this day I will appoint him my personal doctor, and give him every month a thousand pieces of gold. Even if I gave him half my kingdom, it would be only a trifling payment for his service. Your advice, my vizier, is born of jealousy and envy. Would you have me kill my savior and repent of my rashness, as the King in the story repented after he had killed his falcon?"

The Tale of the King and the Falcon

Once upon a time (King Yunan went on), there was a Persian King who was a great lover of riding and hunting. He had a falcon which he himself had trained with loving care and which never left his side for a moment. Even at nighttime he carried it perched upon his wrist, and when he went hunting he took it with him. Hanging from the bird's neck was a golden bowl from which it drank. One day the King ordered his men to make ready for a hunting expedition and, taking his falcon with him, rode out with his courtiers. At last they came to a valley where they laid the hunting nets. A gazelle fell into the snare, and the King said, "I will kill the man who lets her escape!"

They drew the nets closer and closer around the animal. On seeing the King, the gazelle stood on her haunches and raised her forelegs to her head as if she wished to salute him. But as he bent forward to lay hold of her she leaped over his head and fled across the field. Looking around, the King saw his courtiers winking at one another.

"Why are they winking?" he asked his vizier.

"Perhaps because you let the beast escape," answered the other, smiling.

"On my life," cried the King, "I will chase this gazelle and bring her back!"

At once he galloped off in pursuit of the fleeing animal. When he had caught up with her, his falcon swooped upon the gazelle, and the King struck her down with a blow of his sword. Then he dismounted and hung the carcass on his saddlebow.

It was a hot day and the King, who by this time had become faint with thirst, went to search for water. Presently he saw a huge tree, down whose trunk water was trickling in great drops. He took the little bowl from the falcon's neck, filled it up, and placed it before the bird. But the falcon knocked the bowl with its beak and tipped it over. The King once again filled the bowl and placed it before the falcon, but the bird knocked it over a second time. At this the King became very angry; he filled the bowl a third time and set it before his horse. But the falcon sprang forward and knocked it over with its wings.

"Vile creature!" the King exclaimed. "You have prevented yourself from drinking, and the horse too."

So saying, he struck the falcon with his sword and cut off both its wings. But the bird lifted its head as if to say, "Look into the tree!" The King raised his eyes and saw an enormous serpent spitting its poison down the trunk.

The King was deeply sorry for his action. Mounting his horse, he hurried back to the palace. No sooner had he sat down, with the falcon still perched on his wrist, than the bird gave a violent gasp and dropped down dead.

The King was stricken with sorrow and remorse for killing the bird that had saved his life.

When the vizier heard King Yunan's story he said, "I assure Your Majesty that my only concern is for your safety. I beg leave to warn you that if you put your trust in this physician, it is certain that he will destroy you. Did he not cure you by a device held in the hand? And might he not cause your death by another such device?"

This convinced the King. "You have spoken wisely, my faithful vizier. Indeed, it is quite probable that this physician has come to my court as a spy to destroy me. And since he cured my illness by a thing held in the hand, he might as cleverly poison me with something different, such as the scent of a perfume. What should I do, my vizier?"

"Send for him at once, and when he comes, strike off his head. Only in this way will you be safe from his designs."

Thereupon the King sent for the doctor, who hurried to the palace with a joyful heart, not knowing what lay in store for him.

"Do you know why I have sent for you?" the King asked.

"God alone knows the unspoken thoughts of men," the physician answered.

"I have brought you here to kill you," said the King.

The physician was thunderstruck at these words.

"But why should you wish to kill me?" he cried. "What is my crime?"

"It has come to my knowledge," replied the King, "that you have been sent here to cause my death. But you shall die first."

Then he called in the executioner, saying, "Strike off the head of this traitor!"

"Spare me, and Allah will spare you!" pleaded the unfortunate doctor. "Kill me, and so will Allah kill you!"

But the King turned a deaf ear to his entreaties.

"Never will I have peace again," he said, "until I see you dead. For if you cured me by a thing held in the hand, you will doubtless kill me by the scent of a perfume, or by some other foul device."

"Is it thus that you repay me?" the doctor protested. "Will you thus repay good with evil?"

But the King said, "You must now die; nothing now can save you."

When he saw that the King had made up his mind to have him put to death, the physician bitterly repented the service he had done him. The executioner came forward, bandaged the doctor's eyes, and, drawing his sword, held it in readiness for the King's signal. But the doctor continued to plead. "Spare me, and Allah will spare you! Kill me, and so will Allah kill you!"

Moved by the man's lamentations, one of the courtiers interceded for him.

"Spare the life of this man, I pray you," he said to the King. "He has committed no crime against you; rather has he cured you of an illness that your physicians had failed to remedy."

"If I spare this doctor," the King replied, "he will use his devilish art to kill me. Therefore he must die."

Once more the doctor repeated, "Spare me, and Allah will spare you! Kill me, and so will Allah kill you!"

Realizing that the King was firmly fixed in his resolve, he said, "Your Majesty, if you must kill me, I beg you to grant me a day's delay, so that I may go home and wind up my affairs. I want to say good-by to my family and my neighbors, and instruct them how to arrange my burial. I must also give away my books of medicine, among which there is one precious volume that I would offer to you as a parting gift, that you may preserve it among the treasures of your kingdom."

"What may this book be?" the King asked.

"It holds secrets and devices without number, the least of them being this: that if, after you have struck off my head, you turn over three leaves of this book and read the first three lines upon the left-hand page, my severed head will speak and answer any questions you may ask it."

The King was astonished to hear this, and at once ordered his guards to escort the physician home. That day the doctor put his affairs in order, and the next morning returned to the King's palace. There he found, already assembled, the ministers, the chamberlains, and all the chief officers of the realm. With their colored robes the court seemed like a garden full of flowers.

The doctor bowed low before the King; in one hand he held an ancient book, and in the other a little bowl filled with a strange powder. Then he sat down and said, "Bring me a platter!"

A platter was instantly brought in, and the doctor sprinkled the powder on it and smoothed it over with his fingers. Then he handed the book to the King.

"Take this book," he said, "and set it down before you. When my head has been cut off, place it upon the powder to stop the bleeding. Then open the book."

At the King's order, the executioner cut off the physician's head with a single blow of his sword. Then the King opened the book and, finding the pages stuck together, put his finger to his mouth and turned over the first leaf. After much difficulty he turned over the second and the third, moistening his finger with his tongue each time, and tried to read. But there was no writing there.

"There is nothing written in this book," cried the King.

"Go on turning," replied the severed head.

The King had not turned six pages when the venom—for the leaves of the book were poisoned—began to work in his body. He fell backward in an agony of pain, crying, "Poisoned! Poisoned!" and in a few moments he was dead.

"Now, faithless jinnee," the fisherman went on, "had the King spared the physician, he in turn would have been spared by Allah. But he refused, and Allah brought about the King's destruction. And as for you, if you had been willing to spare me, Allah would have been merciful to you, and I would have spared your life. But you sought to kill me; therefore I will throw you back into the sea and leave you to perish in this bottle!"

"Let me out! Let me out!" the jinnee cried. "Do not be angry with me, I pray you. If I have done you evil, repay me with good and, as the saying goes, punish me with kindness. Do not do as the farmer did to the baker."

"What is their story?" the fisherman asked.

"This bottle is no place to tell stories in," exclaimed the jinnee, writhing with impatience. "Let me out, and I will tell you all that passed between them."

"Never!" the fisherman replied. "I will throw you into the sea, and you shall remain imprisoned in your bottle till the end of time!"

"Let me out! Let me out!" moaned the jinnee in despair. "I swear I will never harm you, and promise to render you a service that will enrich you!"

At last the fisherman accepted the jinnee's promise, made him swear by the Most High Name, and then opened the bottle with trembling hands.

At once the smoke burst out, and in a twinkling took the shape of a colossal jinnee, who with a triumphant kick sent the bottle flying into the sea. When the fisherman saw the bottle disappear, he was overcome with terror.

"This is a bad sign," he thought; but, quickly hiding his anxiety, he said, "Mighty jinnee, you have both promised and sworn that you would deal honorably with me. If you break your word, Allah will punish you. Remember that I said to you, as the physician said to the King, 'Spare me, and Allah will spare you!'"

At this the jinnee laughed loud and long.

"Follow me!" he bellowed.

Still dreading the jinnee's intent, the fisherman followed him out of the city gates. They climbed a mountain and at length descended into a vast, barren valley in the middle of which there was a lake. At the shore of this lake the jinnee stopped in his tracks and bade the fisherman cast his net. The fisherman saw white fish and red fish, blue fish and yellow fish sporting in the water. Marveling at the sight, he cast his net into the lake, and when he drew it in, rejoiced to find in it four fish, each of a different color.

"Take these fish to the King's palace," said the jinnee, "and he will give you gold. In the meantime, I must beg you to pardon my ill manners, for I have dwelt so long at the bottom of the sea that I have forgotten the refinements of men. Come and fish in this lake each day—but only once a day. And now, farewell!"

So saying, the jinnee stamped his feet on the earth, which instantly opened and swallowed him up.

The fisherman went home, marveling at all that had happened to him. He filled an earthen bowl with water, placed the fish in it, and carried it on his head to the King's palace, as the jinnee had instructed.

When he had gained admission to the King's presence, the fisherman offered him the fish. The King, who had never seen their like in size or color, marveled greatly and ordered his vizier to take them to the cookmaid. The vizier took the fish to the slave girl and asked her to fry them. Then the King ordered his minister to give the fisherman four hundred pieces of gold. The fisherman received the coins in the lap of his robe, scarcely believing his good fortune. He bought bread and meat, and hurried home to his wife and children.

Meanwhile, the slave girl cleaned the fish, put them in the frying pan, and left them over the fire. When they were well cooked on one side, she turned them over; but scarcely had she done so when the wall of the kitchen suddenly opened and through it entered a beautiful young girl. She had dark eyes with long lashes, and smooth, fresh cheeks. She wore jeweled rings on her fingers and gold bracelets around her wrists, and her hair was wrapped in a blue-fringed kerchief of the rarest silk. The girl came forward and thrust into the frying pan a wand that she carried in her hand.

"Fish, fish, are you still faithful?" she asked.

At the sight of this apparition the slave fainted, and the young girl repeated her question a second and a third time. Then the four fishes lifted their heads from the pan and replied in unison, "Yes, yes, we are faithful!"

Upon this the strange visitor overturned the pan and went out the way she had come, the wall of the kitchen closing behind her. When the slave girl came to her senses, she found the fish burned to cinders. She set up a great screaming and hurried to tell the vizier all that had happened. Amazed at her story, he sent immediately for the fisherman and ordered him to bring four other fish of the same kind. So the fisherman went off to the lake, cast his net, and caught four more fish. These he took to the vizier, who carried them to the slave girl, saying, "Get up now and fry these in my presence."

The slave cleaned the fish and put them in the frying pan; but scarcely had she done so when the wall opened as before and the girl reappeared, dressed in the same way and still holding the wand in her hand. She thrust the end of the wand into the pan and said, "Fish, fish, are you still faithful?"

The four fish raised their heads and replied, "Yes, yes, we are faithful!" And the girl overturned the pan with her wand and vanished through the wall.

"The king must be informed of this!" cried the vizier. He hurried to his master and recounted all that he had seen.

"I must see this myself," said the astonished King.

He sent for the fisherman and ordered him to bring four more fish. The fisherman again hastened to the lake and promptly returned with the fish, for which he received four hundred pieces of gold. Then the King commanded his vizier to cook the fish in his presence.

"I hear and obey," the vizier replied.

He cleaned the fish and set the pan over the fire; but scarcely had he thrown them in when the wall opened and there appeared a great giant. He held a green twig in his hand and, as soon as he set eyes on the pan, roared out, "Fish, fish, are you still faithful?"

The four fish lifted their heads and replied, "Yes, yes, we are faithful!"

Then the giant overturned the pan with his twig and disappeared through the chasm in the wall, leaving the four fish burned to black cinders.

Confounded at the sight, the King cried, "I must find the answer to this riddle. No doubt these fish have some strange history."

He sent again for the fisherman and asked him where he obtained the fish.

"From a lake between four hills," replied the fisherman, "beyond the mountain that overlooks this city."

"How many days' journey is it?" asked the King.

"It is barely half an hour's walk, Your Majesty," he answered.

The King set out for the lake at the head of his troops, accompanied by the bewildered fisherman, who led the way, muttering curses on the jinnee as he went. At last they came to the mountain and, after climbing to the top, descended into a great desert. They all marveled at the mountains, the lake, and the fish of different colors that swam in it. The King asked the troops if any of them had ever before seen a lake in that place, but they all replied that they had not.

"I swear I will never again enter my city or sit upon my throne," he said, "until I have solved the mystery of this lake and these colored fish."

He ordered his troops to pitch tents for the night and summoned his vizier, who was a wise counselor and a man of deep learning.

"Know," he said to him, "I have decided to go out alone tonight and search for the answer to the mystery of the lake and the fishes. I order you to stand guard at the door of my tent and tell anyone who may wish to see me that I am ill and cannot receive him. Above all, you must keep my plan secret."

At nightfall the King disguised himself, girt on his sword, and slipped out of the camp unnoticed by his guards. All that night and throughout the following day he journeyed on, stopping only to rest awhile in the midday heat. Early the next morning he sighted a black building in the distance. He rejoiced and thought, "There perhaps I will find someone who can explain the mystery of the lake and the fishes."

When he drew near, he found that this was a towering palace built of black stone with iron. He went up to the great double door, one half of which was wide open, and knocked gently once, twice, and again, but heard no answer. The fourth time he knocked hard, but still received no reply. Supposing the palace to be deserted, he summoned up his courage and entered, calling out at the top of his voice,

"People of this house, have you any food for a weary traveler?" This he repeated again and again, and, getting no answer, passed to the center of the building. The hall was richly carpeted and hung with fine curtains and splendid tapestries. In the middle of the inner court a beautiful fountain, resting on four lions of red gold, spurted forth a jeweled spray, and about the fountain fluttered doves and pigeons under a golden net stretched above the courtyard.

The King marveled greatly at the splendor of all he saw, but grieved to find no one in the palace who could explain the mystery to him. As he was loitering thoughtfully about the court, however, he suddenly heard a low, mournful voice that seemed to come from a sorrowful heart. The King walked in the direction of the sound and presently came to a doorway concealed behind a curtain. Lifting the curtain, he saw a handsome young man, dressed in a gold-embroidered robe, lying on a bed in a spacious marble hall. His forehead was as white as a lily, and there was a black mole on his cheek.

The King was very glad to see the young man, and greeted him, saying, "Peace be with you!" But the young man, whose eyes were sore with weeping, remained motionless on the bed and returned the King's greeting in a faint voice.

"Pardon me, sir, for not rising," he murmured.

"Tell me the story of the lake and the fishes," said the King, "and the reason for your tears and your solitude."

At these words the young man wept even more bitterly.

"How can I refrain from weeping," he replied, "condemned as I am to this unnatural state?"

So saying, he stretched out his hand and uncovered himself. The King was astonished to see that the lower half of his body was all of stone, while the upper half, from his waist to the hair upon his head, remained that of a living man.

"The story of the fishes," said the youth, "is indeed a strange tale. It is also my story, and the story of the fate that overtook this city and its people. I will tell it to you."

The Tale of the Enchanted King

Know that my father was the King of a beautiful city that once flourished around this palace. His name was Mahmoud, and he was Lord of the Black Islands, which are now four mountains. He reigned for seventy years, and on his death I succeeded to the throne of his kingdom. I married my cousin, the daughter of my uncle, who loved me so passionately that she could not bear to part with me even for a moment. I lived happily with her for five years. It chanced one day, however, that my wife left the palace to visit the baths and was absent so long that I grew anxious for her safety. But I tried to dismiss my fears, and lay down on my couch, ordering two of my slave girls to fan me as I slept. One sat at my head and the other at my feet; and as I lay with my eyes closed I heard one say to the other, "How unfortunate is the young King our master, and what a pity it is that he should have married our mistress, that hateful creature!"

"Allah's curse upon all enchantresses!" replied the other. "This witch who spends her secret hours in the company of thieves and highwaymen is a thousandfold too vile to be the wife of our master."

"And yet he must be blind not to see it," said the first slave.

"But how should he suspect her," returned the other, "when every night she mixes in his cup a powerful drug that so affects his senses that he sleeps like the dead until morning? How can he know what she does and where she goes? After he has gone to sleep, she dresses and goes out of the palace, returning only at daybreak, when she wakes her husband with the aroma of an incense."

When I heard this, my blood ran cold and I was dazed with horror. At dusk my wife came back to the palace, and we sat for an hour eating and drinking together as our custom was. At length I asked for the final cup that I drank every night before retiring. When she handed it to me, I lifted the cup to my lips but, instead of drinking, poured it quickly into the folds of my garments. Then I lay down on my bed and pretended to fall asleep.

Presently I heard her say, "Sleep, and may you never wake again! Oh, how I despise you!"

She then dressed, tied my sword around her waist, and left the palace. I got up, put on a hooded cloak, and followed her. She stole away through the winding streets of the town and, on reaching the city gates, muttered a magic charm. Suddenly the heavy locks fell to the ground and the gates swung wide open. Without a sound I followed her out of the city until she came to a desolate wasteland and entered a ruined hovel topped by a dome. I climbed up to the roof and crouched over a chink in the ceiling. I saw her draw near an evil-looking ruffian who, judging by his appearance, could only have been a fugitive slave. When I saw them exchange greetings I was unable to control my rage. I jumped down from the roof, snatched the sword from my wife's belt, and struck the villain through the neck. A loud gasp shook his body. Thinking that the blow had killed him, I rushed out of the house and ran straight to the palace, where I tucked myself in bed and lay quite still. By and by, my wife returned and lay down quietly beside me.

Next morning I saw that my wife had cut off her tresses and dressed herself in deep mourning.

"Husband," she said, "do not be angry with me for wearing these clothes. I have just heard that my mother has died, that my father has lost his life in the holy war, that one of my brothers has been bitten to death by a serpent, and the other killed by the fall of a house. It is but right that I should weep and mourn."

Showing no sign of anger, I replied, "Do as you think fit. I shall not prevent you."

She went in mourning for a whole week, and at the end of this time she had a dome built in the grounds of the palace. She called it the House of Grief, and to this monument she had her lover carried; for he was still alive, though dumb, and crippled in every limb. Every day, early and late, my wife took to him wine and stews and broths, and fell to wailing under the dome.

One day I entered her room and found her weeping and beating her face. Out of my mind with rage, I drew my sword and was about to strike her when she sprang to her feet and seemed suddenly to realize that it was I who had wounded her accomplice; she muttered a mysterious charm. "Now, Powers of Magic," she exclaimed, "let half his body be turned to stone!"

At that moment I became as you see me now, neither alive nor dead. Then she bewitched my entire kingdom, turning its four islands into mountains with a lake in their midst and transforming all my subjects—Moslems, Jews, Christians, and heathens—into fishes of four different colors. Nor was she satisfied with this, for every day she comes to torture me; she gives me a hundred lashes with a leather thong and puts a shirt of haircloth on my wounds, all over the living part of my body.

When he had heard the young man's story, the King said to him, "My son, your tale has added a heavy sorrow to my sorrows. But where is this enchantress now?"

"With her lover in the monument, which you can see from the door of this hall."

"By Allah," cried the King, "I will do you a service that will be long remembered, a deed that will be recorded for all time."

At midnight the King got up and, as the secret hour of sorcery was striking, stole away toward the monument with his sword unsheathed. Inside, he saw lighted lamps and candles, and braziers in which incense was burning. Before him lay the slave. Without a sound he stepped forward and struck him a mighty blow with his sword. The man fell dead upon the instant; and the King stripped him of his clothes, carried him on his shoulder, and threw him down a deep well in the grounds of the palace. Then he returned to the monument, put on the wretched man's clothes, and sat down with the sword hidden in the folds of his robe.

Shortly afterward the woman came into the monument carrying a cup of wine and a bowl of hot soup. As soon as she entered, she said, weeping, "Speak to me, my master; let me hear your voice!"

Rolling his tongue in his mouth, the King replied in a low voice, "There is no power or majesty except in Allah!"

When she heard the voice of her supposed friend, who had for so long been silent, the young witch uttered a joyful cry.

"Praise to the Highest!" she exclaimed. "My master is restored!"

"Woman," said the King in the same low voice, "you are not worthy that I should speak to you!"

"Why, what have I done?" she asked.

"You have deprived me of all sleep," he answered. "Day after day you whip that husband of yours, so that his cries keep me awake all night. If you had had more thought for my comfort, I would have recovered long ago."

"If it be your wish," she replied, "I will instantly restore him."

"Do so," said the King, "and give me some peace."

"I hear and obey," answered the witch, and leaving the monument, hastened to the hall where the young man was lying. There she took a bowl filled with water, and, bending over it, murmured some magic words. The water began to seethe and bubble as if in a heated caldron; then she sprinkled it upon her husband and said, "Now, Powers of Magic, return him to his natural state!"

A quiver passed through the young man's body and he sprang to his feet, shouting for joy, and crying, "There is no god but Allah, and Mohammed is his Prophet!"

"Go," shrieked his wife, "and never return, or I will kill you!"

The young man hurried from her presence, and she came back to the monument.

"Rise up, my master," she said, "that I may look upon you!"

In a feeble voice the King replied, "You have removed one part of the evil. The root cause still remains."

"What may that be, my master?" she asked.

"The people of this enchanted city and the Four Islands," he replied. "Night after night, the fish raise their heads from the lake and call down curses upon us both. I will not be cured until they are delivered. Free them, and return to help me from my bed, for by that act I will be saved!"

Still taking him for her friend, she answered joyfully, "I hear and obey!"

She hurried to the lake, and took a few drops of water in her palm; then she muttered some secret words. The spell was broken. The fish wriggled in the water and, raising their heads, changed back into human shape. The lake was turned into a bustling city, with people buying and selling in the market place; and the mountains became four islands.

Then the witch ran back to the palace and said to the King, "Give me your hand, my master. Let me help you to your feet."

"Come closer," he murmured.

She drew near, and the King lifted his sword and thrust it into her breast, so that she fell down lifeless.

The King found the young man waiting for him at the palace gates. He congratulated him on his escape, and the youth kissed his hand and thanked him with all his heart. Then the King asked, "Do you wish to stay in your own city or will you return with me to my kingdom?"

"Sir," replied the youth, "do you know how far your kingdom is from here?"

"Why, it is two and a half days' journey," the King answered.

The young man laughed and said, "If you are dreaming, Your Majesty, then you must wake. Know that you are at least a year's journey from your capital. If you came here in two days and a half, that was because my kingdom was enchanted. . . . But I will never leave you again, even for a moment."

The King cried, "Praise be to Allah, who has brought us together in this way. From now on, you shall be my son, for I have no child of my own."

Then the King opened the book and, finding the pages stuck together, put his finger to his mouth and turned over the first leaf.

The two Kings embraced one another and rejoiced.

Returning to his palace, the younger King told his courtiers he intended to set out on a long journey. When all preparations were completed, the King set forth from the Black Islands, together with fifty slaves and fifty mules laden with priceless treasure. They journeyed for a whole year, and when at last they reached the capital, the vizier and the troops, who had abandoned all hope of the King's return, went out to meet their master and gave him a joyful welcome.

Seated upon the throne in his own palace, he summoned the vizier and his other courtiers, and told them about his adventure from beginning to end. Then he bestowed gifts on all who were present and said to the vizier, "Send for the fisherman who brought us the colored fishes."

The fisherman, who had been the means of freeing the enchanted city, was brought into his presence, and the King vested him with a robe of honor and asked him about his manner of life and whether he had any children. The fisherman replied that he had one son and two daughters. The King took one of the daughters in marriage and the young Prince wedded the other, while the fisherman's son was appointed royal treasurer. The vizier became Sultan of the Black Islands, and departed thither with fifty slaves and robes of honor for all the courtiers of that kingdom.

And so the King and the young Prince lived happily ever after. The fisherman became the richest man of his day, and his daughters were the wives of Kings until the end of their lives.

Aladdin and the Enchanted Lamp

Once upon a time, there lived in a certain city of China a poor tailor who had an only son called Aladdin.

From his earliest years, Aladdin was a disobedient, lazy boy. When he was ten, his father wanted him to learn a trade; but as he was too poor to have the boy taught any other business than his own, he took him into his shop to teach him tailoring. Aladdin used to pass his time playing in the streets with other idle boys, and never stayed in the shop a single day. Whenever his father went out, or was attending to a customer, he would run off to the parks and gardens with little ruffians of his own age. He thus persisted in his senseless ways until his father fell ill with grief and died.

Seeing that her husband was dead and her son good for nothing, Aladdin's mother sold the shop with all its contents and took to cotton-spinning in order to support herself and her child. But the young rascal, no longer restrained even by the fear of a father, grew wilder than ever before. The whole day, except for meals, he spent away from home. And thus he carried on until he was fifteen years old.

One day, as he was playing in the street with his companions, a foreign-looking old man who was passing by stopped and watched Aladdin attentively. This stranger, who had come from the remotest parts of Morocco, in Africa, was a mighty enchanter, skilled in the science of the stars. He could, by the power of his magic, uproot a high mountain and hurl it down upon another. Having looked closely into Aladdin's face, he muttered to himself, "This is the boy I have been seeking."

He took one of the boys aside and asked him Aladdin's name, who Aladdin's father was, and where Aladdin lived. Then he went up to Aladdin and led him away from his friends.

"My child," he said, "are you not the son of Hassan the tailor?"

"Yes, sir," Aladdin replied, "but my father has been dead a long time."

At these words the magician threw his arms around the boy's neck and kissed him again and again, with tears running down his cheeks.

"Why do you weep, sir?" asked Aladdin in bewilderment. "Did you know my father?"

"How can you ask such a question, my child?" the magician replied in a sad, broken voice. "How can I help weeping when I suddenly hear of my own brother's death? I have been traveling the world these many years, and now that I have returned in the hope of seeing him, you tell me, alas, that he is dead. But when I first saw you, your blood cried out that you were my brother's son. I recognized you at once, although when I left this land your father was not yet married. But alas, no man can escape his fate. My son," he added, taking Aladdin again into his arms, "you are now my only comfort; you stand in your father's place. Does not the proverb truly say: 'He that leaves an heir does not die?'"

With that the magician took ten pieces of gold from his

purse, gave them to Aladdin, and asked him where his
mother lived. When the boy had directed him to the house,
the magician said, "Give this money to your mother, my
dear brother's wife, with my kindest greetings. Tell her your
uncle has returned from abroad and will visit her tomorrow.
Say that I long to greet her, to see the house where my
brother lived, and to look upon his grave."

Aladdin was very glad to receive the money. He kissed
the magician's hand and ran home to his mother, arriving
there long before suppertime.

"Good news, Mother!" he cried, bursting into the
house. "My uncle has come back from his travels and sends
you his greetings."

"Are you making fun of me, my child?" she answered.
"Who may this uncle be? And since when have you had a
living relative?"

"How can you say I have no uncle or relations?" Aladdin protested. "The man is my father's brother. He embraced me and kissed me, and wept bitterly when he heard
that my father was dead. He has sent me to tell you of
his arrival and of his wish to come and see you."

"It is true, my son, that your father had a brother.
But he is dead, and I never heard your father speak of any
other."

Next morning the magician left his lodgings and wandered about the town in search of Aladdin. He found him
playing in the streets with his companions. Hurrying up to
him, he embraced and kissed him as before and gave him
two pieces of gold.

"Run along to your mother," he said, "and give her this
money. Bid her prepare something for supper, and say that
your uncle is coming to eat with you this evening. And
now, my boy, show me the way to your house again."

"Gladly, sir," Aladdin replied; and after pointing out the road, he took the gold to his mother.

"My uncle is coming to have dinner with us this evening," he told her.

Quickly she went to the market and bought all the food she needed. Then she borrowed pots and dishes from her neighbors and began to cook the meal. When evening came, she said to Aladdin, "Dinner is ready, my son. Perhaps your uncle does not know his way about the town. Go out and see if you can find him in the street."

Although Aladdin had pointed out to the magician the exact whereabouts of his mother's house, he was nevertheless very willing to go; but at that moment there came a knocking on the door. He ran to open it and found the magician standing on the doorstep and, with him, a porter laden with fruit and drink. Aladdin led him into the house, and after the porter was dismissed the magician greeted the boy's mother and begged her, with tears in his eyes, to show him where her husband used to sit. She showed him the place. He knelt down before it and kissed the ground.

"Alas, my poor brother!" he lamented. "Oh, my sorrowful loss!"

His weeping convinced the woman that he really was her husband's brother. She helped him gently from the ground and spoke comforting words to him. And when all three were seated the magician began:

"Good sister, do not be surprised at not having seen or known me when my late brother was alive. It is now forty years since I left this land and began my wanderings in the far-flung regions of the earth. I traveled in India, Sind, and Arabia; then I went to Egypt and stayed for a short time in the city of Cairo, the wonder of the world. Finally I journeyed into the deep interior of Morocco, and there I dwelt for thirty years. One day, as I was sitting all alone, I began to think of my native land and my only brother, and I was seized with a great longing to see him. I resolved to travel back to the country of my birth. I said to myself, 'Perhaps your brother is poor, whereas, thank God, you are a man of wealth. Go, visit him, and help him in his need.'

"I got up at once and made preparations for the journey. After saying my prayers, I mounted my horse and set forth. I experienced many hardships and perils before the Almighty brought me to this city. When I saw Aladdin my heart leaped for joy, for I recognized my nephew. But when he told me of my poor brother's death I nearly fainted from grief."

Noticing that the poor woman was much affected by his words, the magician now changed the subject and, pursuing his plans, turned to the boy.

"Aladdin, my son, what trade have you learned? What business do you follow to support yourself and your mother?"

Aladdin hung his head.

"Oh, do not ask about Aladdin's trade!" his mother replied. "By Allah, he knows nothing at all, nor have I ever seen a more worthless child. He wastes all his days with the young vagabonds of the streets. It was he who sent his poor father to his grave, and I myself shall follow him soon. Day and night I toil at the spinning wheel to earn a couple of loaves for us. Why, he never comes home except for meals! That is all I see of him. I have a good mind to turn him out of doors and leave him to fend for himself; for I am getting old and have not the strength to wear myself out as I used to do."

"That is not right, my boy," the magician said; "such conduct is unworthy of a fine young man like yourself. It does you little credit to let your mother work to keep you, when you are old enough to support yourself. Learn a trade so that you will have the skill to earn a living. Perhaps you did not like your father's trade; choose another that you fancy, and I will do all I can to help you."

Aladdin remained silent, and the magician, realizing that he still preferred his idle life, went on, "Very well, my boy. If you have no mind to learn a trade, there is no harm in that. I will open a shop for you in the town and furnish it with silks and linens, so that you soon become a respected merchant."

Aladdin was pleased with the prospect of being a merchant dressed in splendid clothes. He smiled at the magician and nodded his head in approval of this plan.

"Now, nephew," the magician went on, "tomorrow I will take you, God willing, to the market and buy you a fine merchant's suit. Then we will look for a suitable shop."

Deeply impressed by all the good things the magician promised to do for her son, Aladdin's mother thanked him heartily. She begged the boy to mend his ways and show obedience to his uncle. Then she got up and served the meal. As the three ate and drank, the magician chatted with Aladdin about trade and business affairs. When the night was far advanced, the magician departed, promising to return next morning.

Aladdin could scarcely sleep for joy. In the morning there was a knocking on the door and Aladdin ran out to meet the magician. He greeted him and kissed his hand, and they went off together to the market place. Entering a shop, stocked with clothes of every description, the magician asked to be shown the most expensive suits and told Aladdin to choose the one he fancied. The boy picked out a magnificent outfit, for which the magician paid without haggling. From there they went to the city baths, and after they had washed and refreshed themselves, Aladdin put on his new clothes and rejoiced to see himself so finely dressed. Beaming with delight, he kissed his uncle's hand and thanked him with all his heart.

Then the magician led Aladdin to the merchant's bazaar, where he saw the traders buying and selling in their stores.

"My son," he said, "as you are soon to be a merchant like these men, it is but proper that you should frequent this market and get acquainted with the people."

He showed him the sights of the city, the great buildings and the mosques, and at midday took him to an inn, where they were served a meal on plates of silver. They ate and drank until they were satisfied; and then the magician took Aladdin to see the Sultan's palace and the surrounding parks. After that he took him to the foreign merchants' inn where he himself was staying, and invited a number of his friends to dinner. When they came he introduced Aladdin to them as his brother's son.

At nightfall he took him back to his mother. The poor woman was transported with joy when she saw her son dressed like a merchant, and called down a thousand blessings on the magician.

"Brother," she said, "I do not know how to thank you for your kindness. May Allah prolong your life for both our sakes."

"Dear sister-in-law," the magician replied, "I have done nothing to deserve your thanks. Aladdin is my son; I am in duty bound to be a father to him. He is no longer a child but a man of sense. It is my dearest wish that he should do well and be a joy to you in your old age. I am very sorry, however, that, tomorrow being Friday, the market will be closed and I will not be able to open a shop for him as I promised. But, God willing, we shall do that the day after. I will come here tomorrow to take Aladdin with me and show him the parks and gardens beyond the city."

The magician then said good-by and went back to his lodgings.

Aladdin thought of his good fortune and the delights that were in store for him. For he had never been out of the city gates before, or seen the countryside beyond. Next morning he got up early, and as soon as he heard a knocking on the door, he ran to receive his uncle. The magician took him into his arms and kissed him.

"Today, dear nephew," he said, "I will show you some fine things, the like of which you have never seen in all your life."

Hand in hand they walked along until they came out of the city gates and reached the fine parks and tall palaces that lay beyond. Aladdin exclaimed for joy as they came in sight of each different building. When they had walked a long way from the city and were tired out, they entered a beautiful garden and sat down to rest beside a fountain of crystal water, surrounded by bronze lions as bright as gold. Here the magician untied a bundle that hung from his belt and took out of it various fruits and pastries.

"Eat, nephew, for you must be hungry," he said.

After they had eaten and rested they walked on through the gardens until they reached the open country and came to a high mountain.

"Where are we going, uncle?" asked Aladdin, who had never walked so far in all his days. "We have now passed all the gardens, and there is nothing before us except that mountain. Please let us go home, for I am worn out with walking."

"Be a man, my boy," the magician replied. "I want to show another garden more beautiful than any you have yet seen. No king has the like of it in the whole world."

And to engage Aladdin's attention, he told him strange stories, until they reached the goal that the magician had set himself. To see that spot he had come all the way from Morocco to China.

"Here I am going to show you strange and wondrous things such as the eyes of man have never seen before," he said to Aladdin.

He allowed the boy to rest awhile and then said to him, "Rise now and gather up some dry sticks and fragments of wood so that we may light a fire. Then you shall see the marvel that I have brought you here to witness."

Wondering what his uncle was about to do, Aladdin forgot how tired he was and went into the bushes in search of dry twigs. He gathered up a great armful and carried them to the old man. Presently the magician set fire to the wood and, when it was ablaze, opened a small box he had with him and threw a pinch of incense from it into the flame, muttering a secret charm. At once the sky was overcast with darkness and the earth shook and opened before him, revealing a marble slab with a copper ring fixed in the center. The boy was terrified at these happenings and wanted to run away; but the magician, who could never hope to achieve his aim without Aladdin's help, caught hold of him and, raising his fist, gave him a mighty blow on the head that almost knocked out some of his teeth. Aladdin fell back fainting; nor did he recover his senses until the magician revived him by magic.

"What have I done to deserve this, uncle?" Aladdin sobbed, trembling in every limb.

"I struck you to make a man of you, my child," replied the magician in a gentle tone. "I am your uncle, your father's brother, and you must obey me. If you do as I tell you, you will be richer than all the monarchs of the world. Now listen carefully to my instructions. You have just seen how I opened the earth by my magic. Below this marble slab there is a treasure house that none but yourself may enter. Only you can lift the stone and go down the stairs that lie beneath. Do as I tell you, and we will divide the hidden riches between us."

Aladdin was amazed at the magician's words. He forgot his tears and the smarting blow he had received.

"Tell me what to do, uncle," he cried, "and I will obey you."

The magician went up to him and kissed him. "Nephew," he said, "you are dearer to me than a son. To see you a fine rich man is my utmost wish. Come, take hold of that ring and lift it."

"But, uncle," Aladdin replied, "I am not strong enough to lift it alone. Come and help me."

"No, my boy," said the magician. "If I help you we will gain nothing and all our labors will be lost. Try by yourself and you will find you can lift it with the greatest ease. Just take hold of the ring, and as you raise it pronounce your name, and your father's and mother's."

Aladdin summoned up all his strength and did as the magician had told him. The slab moved easily under his hand; he set it aside, and down below he saw a vaulted cave with a stairway of a dozen steps leading to the entrance.

"Now be careful, Aladdin," the magician cried. "Do exactly as I tell you, and omit nothing. Go down into the cave, and at the bottom you will find a great hall divided into four rooms. In each room you will see four gold coffers and other precious things of gold and silver. Walk straight on and take care not to touch the coffers or the walls, even with the skirt of your gown; for if you do you will at once be changed into black stone. When you reach the fourth room you will find another door, which opens onto a beautiful garden shaded with fruit trees. Pronounce the names you spoke over the slab and make your way through it. After walking some fifty yards you will come to a staircase of about thirty steps, leading up to a terrace. On the terrace you will find a lamp. Take down the lamp, pour out the oil in it, and put it away in the breast of your robe. Do not worry about your clothes, for the oil is no ordinary oil. On your way back you may pause among the trees and pluck off whatever fruit you fancy."

When he had finished speaking, the magician drew a ring from his finger and put it on one of Aladdin's.

"This ring, my boy," he said, "will deliver you from all dangers, so long as you do what I have told you. Be bold and resolute, and fear nothing. You are now a man, and not a child any more. In a few moments you will be the richest man alive."

Aladdin jumped down into the cave and found the four rooms with the four gold coffers in each. Bearing in mind the magician's instructions, he cautiously made his way through them and came out into the garden. From there he climbed up the staircase to the terrace, took down the lamp, poured out the oil, and put the lamp into the breast of his robe. Then he returned to the garden and stopped for the first time to admire the trees and the singing birds that perched upon the branches. The trees were laden with fruit of every shape and hue: white, red, green, yellow, and other colors. Now, Aladdin was too young to realize that these were pearls and diamonds, emeralds and rubies, and jewels such as no king ever possessed. He took them for colored glass of little value, and yet was so delighted with their brilliance that he gathered a great quantity of them and stuffed them into his pockets and the folds of his belt and gown. When he had loaded himself with as much as he could carry, he hurried back through the four rooms without touching the gold coffers and quickly climbed the staircase at the cavern's mouth. But because of his heavy load he could not climb the last step, which was higher than the others.

"Uncle," he shouted, "give me your hand and help me up."

"My dear boy," the magician replied, "you will do better first to give me the lamp. It is in your way."

The magician, whose only concern was to get hold of the lamp, persisted in his demand. Aladdin, on the other hand, had so burdened himself that he could not get at it, and was therefore unable to give it to him. Provoked by the obstinate refusal of the boy, who, he thought, wanted the lamp for himself, the magician flew into a terrible rage. He ran to the blazing fire, threw more incense upon it, and howled a magic charm. At once the marble slab moved into its place and the earth closed over the cave, leaving Aladdin underground.

Now, as I told you before, the old man was really a stranger and no uncle of Aladdin's. He was an evil magician from the darkest part of Morocco, an African skilled in the renowned black arts of his native land. From his earliest days he had given himself up to sorcery and witchcraft, so that after forty years' continuous study he discovered that near one of the remotest cities of China there was a vast treasure, the like of which no king had ever amassed. He had also learned that the treasure included an enchanted lamp that could make him richer and more powerful than any monarch in the world, and that it could be brought out only by a boy of humble birth called Aladdin, a native of that city. Convinced of his discovery, he set out for China and, after a long and arduous journey, sought out Aladdin and reached the place where the treasure was buried. But all his efforts having failed, he imprisoned the boy underground, so that neither he nor the lamp should ever come up out of the earth. Then the magician abandoned his quest and journeyed back to Africa with a heavy heart. So much for him.

As for Aladdin, when the earth closed over him, he realized he had been deceived, and that the magician was no uncle of his. Giving up all hope of escape, he went down weeping to the bottom of the stairs and groped his way in the dark to the garden; but the door, which had been opened by enchantment, was now shut by the same means. He returned to the entrance of the cave in despair and threw himself on the steps. There he sat for three long days without food or drink, and almost abandoned all hope of living. He wept and sobbed, wrung his hands, and prayed for God's help with all his heart. While he was wringing his hands together he happened to rub the ring that the magician had given him as a protection.

At once a great black jinnee appeared before him.

"I am here, master, I am here," the jinnee cried. "Your slave is ready to serve you. Ask what you will and it shall be done. For I am the slave of him who wears my master's ring."

The sight of this monstrous figure struck terror into Aladdin's heart. But, as he recalled the magician's words, his hopes revived and he summoned up all his courage.

"Slave of the ring," he cried, "I order you to carry me up to the earth's surface."

The words were scarcely out of his mouth when the earth was rent asunder and he found himself above ground on the very spot where the marble slab had been. It was some time before his eyes could bear the light after being so long in total darkness; but at length he looked about him and was amazed to see no sign of the cave or entrance. He would not have recognized the place but for the black cinders left by the magician's fire. In the distance he saw the city shimmering amid its gardens and hastened joyfully toward it, greatly relieved at his escape. He reached home worn out with hunger and fatigue, and dropped down fainting before his mother, who, for her part, had been grieving bitterly. The poor woman did all she could to restore her son; she sprinkled water over his face and gave him fragrant herbs to smell. As soon as he came to, he asked for something to eat.

"Mother, I am very hungry," he said. "I have had nothing to eat or drink these three days."

His mother brought him all the food that she could find in the house, and when he had eaten and recovered his strength a little he said, "You must know, Mother, that the man whom we supposed to be my uncle is a magician, a wicked imposter, a cruel fiend. He made me those promises only to destroy me. To think how we were deceived by his fine words! Listen, Mother, to what he did. . . ."

And with that, Aladdin proceeded to tell his mother of his adventure with the magician from beginning to end.

When she had heard his story, Aladdin's mother shook her head.

"I might have known from the very start that the old wretch was a liar and a fraud. Praise be to God, who has delivered you from his hands."

She went on comforting him in this way until Aladdin, who had not slept a wink for three days, was overcome by sleep. He did not wake till nearly noon the following day, and as soon as he opened his eyes he asked for food.

"Alas, my boy," his mother sighed, "I have not a crust of bread to give you; yesterday you ate all the food I had. But be patient a little. I have some cotton here that I have spun. I will go and sell it to buy you something to eat."

"Leave your cotton for the time, Mother," Aladdin answered, "and give me the lamp I brought. I will sell it in the

market, for it is sure to fetch a better price than your spinning."

Aladdin's mother brought him the lamp and, noticing
that it was dirty, said, "If we clean and polish it, it might
fetch a little more."

She mixed a little sand in water and began to clean the
lamp. But no sooner had she rubbed the surface than a tall
and fearsome jinnee appeared before her.

"What is your wish, mistress?" said the jinnee. "I am
your slave and the slave of him who holds the lamp. I and
the other slaves of the lamp will do your bidding."

The poor woman, who was not used to such apparitions,
was so terrified that she could not answer; her tongue became knotted in her mouth and she fell fainting to the
ground. Now, Aladdin had seen the jinnee of the ring in the
cave, and when he heard this jinnee speaking to his mother
he ran quickly to her aid and snatched the lamp out of her
hands.

"Slave of the lamp," he said, "I am hungry. Bring me
some good things to eat."

The jinnee vanished, and in a twinkling reappeared, carrying upon his head a priceless tray of solid silver that held
twelve dishes of the choicest meats, together with a pair of
silver goblets, two flasks of clear old wine, and bread as
white as snow. All these he set down before Aladdin and
disappeared again.

Seeing that his mother still lay unconscious on the floor,
Aladdin sprinkled rose water over her face and gave her
fragrant scents to smell.

"Get up, Mother," he said, when she came to. "Let us
sit down and eat."

Seeing the massive silver tray and the food upon it, she
asked in amazement, "Who may this generous benefactor be
who has discovered our poverty and hunger? We are surely

grateful to him for his kindness. Is it the Sultan himself who has heard of our wretched plight and sent us this tray?"

"Mother," Aladdin replied, "this is no time to ask questions. Get up and let us eat. We are starving."

They sat at the tray and fell to heartily. Aladdin's mother had never in all her life tasted such delicate food, which was worthy of a king's table. Nor did they know whether the tray was valuable or not, for they had never seen such things before. They ate until they were satisfied; yet enough was left over for supper and the next day. Then they got up, washed their hands, and sat chatting.

"Now, my child," said Aladdin's mother, "tell me what you did with the jinnee."

Aladdin told his mother what had passed between him and the jinnee from the time she fainted.

"I have heard," said the astonished woman, "that these creatures do appear to men, but I never saw any before this. He must be the same jinnee who rescued you in the cavern."

"No, Mother," Aladdin answered. "That was a different jinnee. The jinnee that appeared to you was the jinnee of the lamp."

"How is that, my child?" she asked.

"This jinnee was of a different shape," replied Aladdin. "The other was the slave of the ring; the one you saw belonged to the lamp that you were holding."

"My child," she cried, "I beg you to throw away both the lamp and the ring. I am terrified of those beings, and could not bear to see them again. Besides, it is unlawful for us to have any dealings with them."

"I would gladly obey you in anything, Mother," Aladdin replied, "but I cannot afford to lose the lamp or the ring. You have yourself seen how useful the lamp was to us when we were hungry. And remember: when I went down into the cave, that imposter of a magician did not ask me for gold and silver, although the four rooms of the treasure house were full of them. He told me to fetch him the lamp and nothing else; for he must have known its great value. That is why we must keep this lamp and take good care of it, for in having it we will never again be poor or hungry. Also, we must never show it to anyone. As for the ring—I could not bear to lose that, either. But for its jinnee, I would have died under the earth, inside the treasure house. Who knows what troubles and dangers the future holds for me? This ring will surely save my life. Still, I will hide the lamp away if you like, so that you need never set eyes on it again."

"Very well, my boy," said his mother, finding his arguments reasonable enough. "Do as you please. For my part, I will have nothing to do with them, nor do I wish ever to see that fearsome sight again."

For two days they went on eating the food the jinnee had brought them; and when it was finished, Aladdin took one of the dishes from the magic tray and went to sell it in the market. There he was approached by a crafty old silversmith. Aladdin, who did not know that it was solid silver, offered him the plate; and when the silversmith saw it, he drew the boy aside so that no one else should see it. He examined the dish with care and found that it was made of the purest silver, but did not know whether Aladdin was aware of its true value.

"How much do you want for it, sir?" asked the silversmith.

"*You* should know how much it is worth," Aladdin answered. Hearing the boy's businesslike reply, the silversmith was at a loss. He was at first tempted to offer him very little, but feared that Aladdin might know its value. Then he was inclined to give him a substantial sum. At last he took out one piece of gold from his pocket and offered it to him.

When Aladdin saw the piece of gold he took it and ran off in great joy, so that the old man, realizing that the boy had no idea of its value, bitterly regretted that he had not given him less.

Aladdin hurried away to the baker's and bought some bread; then he ran home and gave the bread and the change to his mother. "Mother," he said, "go and buy what we need."

His mother went down to the market and bought all the food they needed; and the two ate until they had had enough. Whenever the money ran out, Aladdin would go to the market and sell another dish to the silversmith, and thus the old rogue bought all the plates for very little. Even then he would have wished to give him less; but having rashly paid him one piece of gold on the first occasion, he feared that the boy would go and sell elsewhere. When the twelve dishes were all gone, Aladdin decided to sell the silver tray. As this was large and heavy, he fetched the old merchant to the house and showed it to him. The silversmith, seeing its tremendous size, gave him ten pieces. And with this money Aladdin and his mother were able to provide for their needs several days longer.

When the gold was finished Aladdin took out the lamp and rubbed it, and the jinnee appeared before him. "Master," he said, "ask what you will. I am your slave and the slave of him who holds the lamp."

"I order you," said Aladdin, "to bring me a tray of food like the one you brought before. I am hungry."

The jinnee vanished, and in the twinkling of an eye returned with a tray exactly like the first one, holding twelve splendid dishes full of delicate meats, two flasks of wine, and a fine, clean loaf. Having been warned beforehand, Aladdin's mother had left the house so that she would not see the jinnee; but when she returned and saw the tray with the silver dishes, and smelled the rich aroma, she marveled greatly and rejoiced.

"Look, Mother!" Aladdin cried. "You told me to throw the lamp away. Now see how valuable it is."

"You are right, my son," she replied. "Still, I do not want ever to see that jinnee again."

She sat down with her son and the two ate and drank together. What was left over they stored for the following day. When this was finished, Aladdin took one of the dishes under his robe and went off to search for the silversmith. It chanced, however, that while he was walking through the market he passed by the shop of an honest goldsmith, well known for his integrity and fair dealing. The old sheikh stopped Aladdin and greeted him.

"What brings you here, my son?" he asked. "I have often seen you pass this way and do business with a certain silversmith. I have watched you give him some articles, and perhaps you have something with you now that you intend to sell to him. You do not seem to realize, my child, that this man is a scoundrel and a cheat. What an easy prey he must have found you! If you have something to sell, show it to me and I will pay you the proper price for it: not a copper less."

Aladdin showed him the plate, and the goldsmith took it and weighed it in his scales.

"Have you been selling him plates like this one?" asked the old man.

"Yes," Aladdin replied.

"How much have you been getting for them?"

"One piece of gold for each," Aladdin answered.

"What a rascal," exclaimed the goldsmith, "to rob honest folk in this way! You must know, my boy, that this man has swindled you and made a real fool of you. This dish is made of the purest silver and is worth no less than seventy pieces. If you are willing to accept this price, take it."

The goldsmith counted out seventy pieces, and Aladdin took the gold and thanked the old man for his kindness. In due course he sold him the other dishes, at the same honest price. The youth and his mother grew very rich, yet they continued to live modestly, avoiding extravagance and foolish waste.

Aladdin had now given up his idle ways and bad companions and passed all his time in the markets of the city, speaking with persons of distinction and merchants great and small. He also visited the bazaars of the goldsmiths and jewelers, where he would sit and watch the jewels being bought and sold. As the months passed by, he came to realize that the varied fruits he had brought back from the treasure house were not colored glass or crystal but gems beyond the wealth of kings. He examined all the jewels in the market, but found none to be compared with the smallest of his own. Thus he went on visiting jewelers' shops, so that he might become acquainted with the people and learn from them the affairs of trade. He asked them questions about buying and selling, taking and giving, and in time came to know what was cheap and what was costly.

It so chanced that one morning, while he was on his way to the jewelers' market, he heard a herald crying in the streets, "By command of our Royal Master, the Sultan! Let all people close their shops and retire at once behind the doors of their houses; for the Princess Badr-al-Budur, the Sultan's daughter, desires this day to visit the baths. If anyone disregards this order he shall be punished by instant death."

When he heard this proclamation, Aladdin was seized with a great desire to see the Sultan's daughter, for her loveliness was the talk of all the people. He began casting around for some way to look upon her, and at last decided that it was best to stand behind the door of the baths and see her face as she entered. Without losing a moment, he ran straight off to the baths and hid himself behind the great door where none could see him. Presently the Princess left the palace and, after riding through the streets and seeing the sights of the city, halted at the baths. She lifted her veil as she went in. Her face shone like the radiant sun.

"Truly," murmured Aladdin to himself, "she is a credit to her Maker! Praise be to him who created her and gave her such beauty." He fell in love with her immediately.

Many a time he had heard tell of Badr-al-Budur's beauty, but he had never imagined her to be so lovely. He returned home in a daze. His mother questioned him anxiously, but he said nothing; she brought him his dinner, but he refused to eat.

"What has come over you, my child?" she asked. "Are you ill? Have you any pain? Tell me, my son, I beg you."

"Let me alone, Mother," he replied.

She went on pressing him to eat, and at last he ate a little. Then he threw himself upon his bed, where he lay thinking about the Princess all night and throughout the following day. His mother grew anxious about him and said, "If you are in pain, my child, tell me and I will call the doctor. There is now an Arab doctor in our city; he was sent for by the Sultan. People everywhere are talking of his great skill. Shall I go and fetch him for you?"

"I am not ill," Aladdin replied. "It is only this, Mother. Yesterday I saw the Princess Badr-al-Budur when she was going into the baths. I saw her face, for when she entered she lifted her veil. As I looked on her exquisite features, my heart quivered with love for her. I will have no rest until I have won her in marriage from her father the Sultan."

Hearing this, his mother thought he had gone mad.

"Heaven protect you, my child!" she exclaimed. "You must be out of your mind. Come, return to your senses."

"I am not mad, Mother," Aladdin replied. "Whatever you say, I will never change my mind. I cannot rest until I win the fair Badr-al-Budur, the treasure of my heart."

"Do not say such things," his mother implored. "If the neighbors hear you they will think you are insane. Why, who would demand such a thing of the Sultan? And even if you do decide to ask for her hand, who will have the audacity to present your suit?"

"Who else should present my suit for me when I have you, Mother?" he answered. "Whom can I trust more than you? I want you yourself to go and take my petition to the Sultan."

"Heaven preserve me from such folly!" she exclaimed. "Do you think I am mad, too? Consider who you are, my child. Your father was the poorest tailor in this city, and I, your mother, come from scarcely nobler folk. How then can you presume to demand the Sultan's daughter? Her father will marry her only to some illustrious prince no less powerful and noble than himself."

"I have thought about all this, Mother," replied Aladdin. "Nothing will turn me from my purpose. If you love me as your son, I beg you to do this kindness for me. Do not let me perish; for I will surely die if I fail to win my heart's beloved. Remember, Mother. I am your son."

"Yes, my son," she said. "You are my only child. My dearest wish is to see you married, and to rejoice in your happiness. If you want to marry, I will find you a wife who is your equal. But even then I will not know how to answer when they ask me if you have any trade or property. And if I cannot give an answer to humble people like ourselves, how can I presume to ask the Sultan for his only daughter? Just think of it, my child. Who is it that wants to marry her?

"Uncle," he shouted, "give me your hand and help me up." "My dear boy," the magician replied, "you will do better first to give me the lamp. It is in your way."

A tailor's son! Why, I know for sure that if I speak of such a thing we shall be utterly ruined; it may even put us in danger of our lives. Besides, how can I gain access to the Sultan? If they ask me questions, what answer can I give them? And supposing that I do gain admittance to the Sultan, what gift can I present him with? Yes, my son, I know that our Sultan is very kind, but he bestows his favors only on those who deserve them. Now tell me, child, what have you done for the Sultan or his kingdom to be worthy of such a favor?"

"What you say is quite true, Mother," Aladdin replied. "You ask me what present I have to offer the Sultan. Know then that I can offer him a gift the like of which no monarch has ever possessed. Those colored fruits that I brought with me from the treasure house, thinking them to be glass or crystal, are jewels of incalculable worth—not a king in the world has the least one of them. I have been going around with jewelers of late, and I know now that they are priceless gems. If you wish to judge them for yourself, bring me a large china dish and I will show you. I am convinced that with a present such as this your errand will be easy."

Half in doubt, the woman went and brought a large china dish. She set it before Aladdin, who took out the jewels from their hiding place and ranged them skillfully on the plate. As she looked upon them, her eyes were dazzled by their rich luster.

"Don't you see, Mother? Can there be a more magnificent present for the Sultan? I have no doubt that you will be well received and highly honored by him. Rise now, take the dish, and go to the Sultan's palace."

"Yes, my son," she answered. "I admit that your present is both precious and unique. But who in heaven's name could make so bold as to stand before the Sultan and demand his daughter? When he asks, 'What do you want?'

my courage will fail me and I will not know what to say. And suppose the Sultan were pleased to accept your present and asked me, as people do on such occasions, about your standing and your income, what would I tell him?"

"The Sultan will never ask you such a question after seeing these splendid jewels," Aladdin replied. "Do not trouble your mind with groundless fears, but go boldly about your errand and offer him these gems. And remember: I have a lamp that brings me whatever I want. If the Sultan asks you such a question, the lamp will provide me with the answer."

They went on chatting together for the rest of that evening. In the morning, Aladdin's mother made ready for her audience with a cheerful heart, now that she understood the properties of the lamp and all that it could do for them. After Aladdin had made her promise never to reveal the secret, she wrapped the dish of gems in a handsome shawl and set off for the Sultan's palace at an early hour, so that she might enter the audience hall before it was crowded. When she arrived, the hall was not yet full. After a short while the ministers and courtiers, the nabobs and princes and great ones of the palace came in; then the Sultan himself entered, and everyone stood up in respectful silence. The great Sultan sat down on his throne, and at his bidding all present took their seats, according to their rank.

The petitioners were now summoned before the throne and every case was judged upon its merits; but the greater part of them had to be dismissed for lack of time. Among these last was Aladdin's mother, for, though she had arrived before the others, no one spoke to her or offered to take her before the Sultan. When the audience was finished and the Sultan had retired, she returned home. Aladdin, who was waiting on the doorstep, saw her come back with the present in her hand, but said nothing and waited until she came in and told him what had happened.

"Be of good cheer, my son," she said at last. "I plucked up enough courage to enter the audience hall today, though, like many others, I could not speak to the Sultan. But have no fears: God willing, I will speak to him tomorrow."

Though vexed at the delay, Aladdin found comfort in his mother's words and consoled himself with hope and patience. Next morning the woman took the present and went again to the Sultan's palace, but found the audience chamber closed. The guards told her that the Sultan held an audience only three times a week, so she was obliged to return home. After that she went to the palace every day. When she found the hall open she would stand about helplessly and then, when the audience was finished, would make her way home; on the other days she would find the hall closed. This went on for a whole week. At the end of the final session the Sultan said to his vizier as they left the court, "For six or seven days I have seen a poor woman come to the palace with something under her cloak. What does she want?"

"Some trivial matter, I expect, Your Majesty," answered the vizier. "She probably has a complaint against her husband or one of her neighbors."

The Sultan, however, would not be put off by this reply. He ordered the vizier to bring the woman before him if she came once more.

"I hear and obey, Your Majesty," answered the vizier, lifting his hand to his brow.

Next morning, the Sultan saw Aladdin's mother standing wearily in the audience hall, as on the previous days.

"That is the woman about whom I spoke to you yesterday," he said to the vizier. "Bring her to me now, so that I can hear her petition and grant her request."

The vizier rose at once and led Aladdin's mother before the Sultan. She fell on her knees and, kissing the ground before him, wished him long life and everlasting glory.

"Woman," said the Sultan, "I have seen you come to the audience hall a number of times and stand there without a word. Make your request known to me that I may grant it."

Aladdin's mother again called down blessings upon the Sultan and, once more kissing the ground, said, "Before I speak of the extraordinary cause that compels me to appear before you, I beg Your Majesty to pardon and forgive the boldness of the plea I am about to make."

Being of a kind and generous nature, the Sultan ordered the audience chamber to be cleared so that she might be free to explain herself. When all but the vizier had been dismissed, he turned to Aladdin's mother and bade her speak out without fear.

"I have a son who is called Aladdin, Your Majesty," she began. "One day he heard the crier proclaim through the streets that Princess Badr-al-Budur was going to the baths. He was so anxious to see her face that he hid himself behind the door of the baths and saw her as she went in. He loved her from that instant, and has not known a moment's rest ever since. My son asked me to entreat Your Majesty to marry her to him; and, try as I might, I could not free his mind of this obsession. 'Mother,' he said to me, 'if I do not win the Princess in marriage I will die.' I beg you, great Sultan, to be indulgent and to forgive me and my son for the audacity of this request."

When she had finished speaking the Sultan laughed good-naturedly.

"Now tell me what you are carrying in that bundle," he said. Noticing that the Sultan was not angry, Aladdin's mother undid the shawl and presented him with the plate of jewels. At once the entire hall was lit up as if by chandeliers and colored torches. The dumbfounded Sultan gazed at the jewels and marveled at their brilliance, their size, and their beauty.

"Never in all my life have I seen the like of these jewels!" he exclaimed. "I do not think there is a single stone in my treasuries to be compared with them. What do you say, vizier? Have you ever seen such marvels?"

"Never, Your Majesty," agreed the vizier. "I doubt if the smallest of them is to be found among your treasures."

"Then do you not think," said the Sultan, "that the young man who sent them to me is worthier of my daughter's hand than any other?"

The vizier was greatly troubled to hear this, and did not know what to answer; for the Sultan had promised Badr-al-Budur to his own son.

"Great Sultan," he said in a whisper, "forgive me if I remind Your Majesty that you have promised the Princess to my son. I therefore beg you to allow him a delay of three months in which to find, with God's help, a present more valuable than this."

The Sultan knew well enough that neither the vizier nor the richest king in the world could find him a present equal to the treasure he had just received; but, as he did not wish to offend his minister, he granted him the delay he had requested.

"Go to your son," he said, turning to Aladdin's mother, "and tell him that my daughter shall be his. Only the marriage cannot take place for three months, as there are preparations to be made."

She thanked the Sultan and called down blessings upon him, then hurried home in a transport of joy. When Aladdin saw her return without the present, and noticed her happy smile, he felt sure she had brought him good news.

"I pray that the jewels have won the Sultan's heart," he exclaimed. "He received you graciously and listened to your request, I hope."

His mother told him how the Sultan had accepted the jewels and marveled at their size and beauty.

"He promised that the Princess should be yours," she went on. "But the vizier whispered something to him and after that he said the marriage could not take place for three months. My son, I fear that the vizier may use his cunning to change the Sultan's mind."

Ignoring this fear, Aladdin was overjoyed at the Sultan's promise and warmly thanked his mother for her labors.

"Surely now I am the richest and happiest of men!" he exclaimed.

For two months Aladdin patiently counted the days that separated him from the great occasion. Then, one evening, his mother went out to buy some oil and, as she walked down the street, she noticed that most of the shops were closed and that the city was adorned with lights. Windows were hung with flowers and candles, and the squares thronged with troops and mounted dignitaries carrying torches. Puzzled by all this, the old woman entered an oil shop that was open and, after buying what she needed, asked the reason for the commotion.

"Why, good woman!" replied the oil vendor. "You must surely be a stranger here, not to know that this is the bridal night of Princess Badr-al-Budur and the vizier's son. He will soon be coming out of the baths; those officers and soldiers will escort him to the palace, where the Sultan's daughter is waiting for him."

Aladdin's mother was very upset to hear this. She returned home with a heavy heart, not knowing how to break the alarming news to her son.

"My child," said she, as soon as she entered the house, "I have some bad news. I am afraid it will distress you."

"What is it, Mother?" Aladdin asked impatiently.

"The Sultan has broken his promise to you, my child," she answered. "This very night the vizier's son is to marry the Princess. Oh, how I feared that the vizier would change the Sultan's mind! I told you he whispered something to him after he had accepted your proposal."

"And how do you know," Aladdin asked, "that the vizier's son is to marry the Princess tonight?"

His mother described to him all that she had seen in the city: the lights and decorations, the soldiers and dignitaries waiting to escort the vizier's son on his bridal night. On hearing this, Aladdin was seized with a terrible rage; but he soon remembered the lamp and regained possession of himself.

"Upon your life, Mother," he said, "I do not think the vizier's son will be so happy tonight as he expects to be. Let us say no more about this. Get up and cook the dinner. Then I will go into my room and see what can be done. All will be well, I promise you."

After dinner, Aladdin shut himself in his own room and locked the door. He then brought out the lamp and rubbed it, and at once the jinnee appeared.

"Ask what you will," the jinnee said. "I am your slave, and the slave of him who holds the lamp: I and the other slaves of the lamp will do your bidding."

"Listen carefully," Aladdin said. "I asked the Sultan for his daughter and he promised that I should wed her after three months. He has now broken his promise and is marrying her to the vizier's son instead. The wedding takes place tonight. Now I command you, if you are indeed a trustworthy slave of the lamp, to take up the bride and bridegroom as soon as they have retired to sleep and bring them here in their bed. I will look after the rest myself."

This was no sooner said than done, and the jinnee carried in the royal bed and set it down before Aladdin.

"Now take away this wretch," Aladdin commanded, "and lock him in the cellar."

At once the jinnee carried away the vizier's son, laid him down in the cellar, and, breathing upon his body, left him paralyzed in every limb. Then he returned to Aladdin.

"Master, what else do you require?" he asked. "Speak, and it shall be done."

"Come again in the morning," Aladdin answered.

"I hear and obey," replied the jinnee; and so saying he vanished.

Aladdin could scarcely believe that all this had really happened, and that he was alone with the Princess whom he loved with a consuming passion.

"Adorable Princess," he said, "do not think that I have brought you here to harm you. Heaven forbid! I did this only to make sure that no one else would wed you, for your father, the Sultan, gave me his word that you would be my bride. Do not be alarmed; you will be safe here."

When the Princess suddenly found herself in that dark and humble dwelling, and heard Aladdin's words, she was so terrified that she uttered not a word. Presently Aladdin laid himself down beside her on the bed, placing an unsheathed sword between them. But because of her fright the Princess did not sleep a wink all night. Nor did the vizier's son, who lay motionless on the floor of the filthy cellar.

Next morning the jinnee returned, without Aladdin's rubbing the lamp.

"Master," he said, "command, and I will gladly do your bidding."

"Go," cried Aladdin. "Carry the bride and bridegroom back to the Sultan's palace."

In a twinkling the jinnee did as Aladdin told him. He laid the vizier's son beside the Princess and took them both to the royal palace, so swiftly that the terrified couple could not see who had thus transported them. Scarcely had the jinnee set them down and disappeared than the Sultan came in to visit his daughter. This greatly distressed the vizier's son, for he was just beginning to feel warmer after his cold night in the cellar. However, he jumped to his feet, and put on his clothes.

The Sultan kissed his daughter and bade her good morning. But the girl looked dejectedly at him and said nothing. He questioned her again and again, and still she made no answer. At last he left her room in anger, and, taking himself off to the Queen, gave her an account of his daughter's strange behavior.

"Do not be harsh with her," said the Queen, wishing to calm him. "In a short time she will return to her former ways and talk to people freely. I will go and speak to her myself."

The Queen immediately went off to visit her daughter. She approached Badr-al-Budur and, kissing her between the eyes, wished her good morning. But the Princess said nothing.

"Something very odd must have happened to her to upset her so," thought the Queen to herself. "What grief is this, my daughter?" she asked. "Tell me what has happened. Here I am, wishing you good morning, and you do not even return my greeting."

"Do not be angry with me, Mother," said the Princess, raising her head, "but pardon the disrespect I have shown you. Look what a miserable night I passed! Scarcely had we gone to bed, when someone came—we could not see who he was—and carried us away, bed and all, to a damp, dark, and dirty place."

Badr-al-Budur told her mother all that had passed during the night: how her husband had been taken away from her and replaced by another young man who lay beside her with a sword between them.

"Then, this morning," she continued, "the person who took us away returned and brought us back to this very room. As soon as he had set us down and gone, my father entered; but such was my terror at that moment that I had neither heart nor tongue to speak to him. If, for this reason, I have incurred his anger, I beg you to explain to him what has happened, so that he should not blame but pardon me for my offense."

"Dear child!" exclaimed the Queen. "Take care not to tell this story to anyone else. They will say the Sultan's daughter has gone mad. You were wise not to tell your father of all this. Say nothing about it to him, I warn you."

"But, Mother, I am not mad," the Princess replied. "I have told you nothing but the truth. If you do not believe me, ask my husband."

"Get up, child," said the Queen, "and drive this wild fantasy out of your head. Put on your clothes and go and watch the festivities that are being held all over the city in your honor. Listen to the drums and the singing; and look at the decorations, all celebrating your happy marriage."

The Queen called her attendants, who dressed the Princess and combed her hair. Then, returning to the Sultan, she told him that Badr-al-Budur had had dreams and nightmares, and begged him not to be angry with her.

Next she sent in secret for the vizier's son and questioned him. "Your Majesty, I know nothing of what you say," he answered; for he was afraid lest he should lose his bride. The Queen was now convinced that the Princess was suffering from a nightmare or some unfortunate illusion.

The festivities continued all day, with dancers and singers performing in the palace to the accompaniment of all kinds of music. The Queen, the vizier, and the vizier's son did their best to keep the merriment afoot, to cheer the bride, and to dispel her gloom. But for all their efforts she remained silent and thoughtful, brooding over the happenings of the previous night. True, the vizier's son had suffered even more than she. But he denied it all, dreading that he might lose the honor that had been given him; especially since everyone envied him his luck in marrying a girl so noble and so fair as the Princess.

Aladdin went out that day and watched the rejoicings in the city and the palace with laughter in his heart, particularly when he heard the people speak of the distinction that the vizier's son had gained, and how fortunate he was to have become the Sultan's son-in-law.

"Poor fools!" he thought to himself. "If only you knew what happened to him last night!"

In the evening he went into his room and rubbed the lamp. When the jinnee came he ordered him to bring the Sultan's daughter and her bridegroom, as on the previous night. The slave of the lamp vanished, and returned almost at once with the couple in the royal bed. Then he carried the vizier's son to the cellar, where he left him petrified with fear. Aladdin placed the sword between himself and the Princess and slept by her side. In the morning the jinnee brought back the husband and returned the bed to the palace. Aladdin was delighted with the progress of his plan.

When the Sultan woke up, his first thought was to go to his daughter to see if she would act as on the day before. He dressed at once and went off to Badr-al-Budur's room. On hearing the door open, the vizier's son hurriedly dressed himself, his ribs almost cracking with the cold, for the slave of the lamp had just brought them back to the palace. The Sultan went up to his daughter's bed, lifted the curtains, and, kissing her on the cheek, wished her good morning. He asked how she was, but instead of answering she frowned and stared sullenly at him; for she was now desperately bewildered and upset. Her silence once again provoked the Sultan, who immediately sensed that she was hiding something from him.

"What has come over you, my girl?" he cried, drawing his sword. "Tell me the truth, or I will cut off your head. Is this the respect you owe me? I speak to you, and you do not answer a single word."

The Princess was terrified to see her father brandishing his sword over her.

"Do not be angry with me, I beg you," she replied, lifting her head from the pillow. "When you have heard what I have suffered these last two nights, you will excuse and pity me; for I have always known you as a most loving father."

She then told the Sultan all that had happened.

"And now, Father," she added, "if you wish to confirm what I have said, ask my husband. He will tell you everything. I do not know what they did to him when they took him away, or where they put him."

Moved by his daughter's words, the Sultan sheathed his sword and kissed her tenderly.

"My child," he said, "why did you not tell me of all this, so that I could have protected you from those terrors last night? But have no fear; get up, and dismiss these unpleasant thoughts. Tonight I will post guards around your room, and you shall be safe from all dangers."

He returned to his room and at once sent for the vizier.

"What do you think of this business?" he cried, as soon

as the vizier presented himself. "Perhaps your son has told you what happened to him and my daughter?"

"Your Majesty, I have not seen my son these two days," the vizier answered.

The Sultan told him the Princess' story.

"Now go to your son," he added, "and find out the whole truth from him. My daughter may be so frightened that she does not really know what has happened; though, for my part, I am inclined to believe her."

The vizier called his son and asked him if what the Sultan had said was true or not.

"Heaven forbid that the Princess should tell a lie," the young man answered. "All that she says is true. These last two nights have been a nightmare for us both. What happened to me was even worse. I was locked up all night in a dark, frightful cellar, where I almost perished with cold."

And he told him the story in all its details.

"I now beg you, Father," he concluded, "to speak to the Sultan and ask him to release me from this marriage. I know it is a great honor to be the Sultan's son-in-law, especially as I am so deeply in love with the Princess. But I cannot endure again what I went through these last two nights."

The vizier was profoundly shocked to hear this, for his fondest wish had been to marry his son to the Sultan's daughter and thus make a prince of him.

"Be patient a little, my son," he said. "Let us see what happens tonight. We will post guards around your chamber. Do not so rashly cast away this great honor; no one else has attained it."

The vizier left his son and, returning to the Sultan, informed him that the Princess' story was true.

"Then here and now," rejoined the Sultan, "I declare

the marriage null and void." And he gave orders that the rejoicings should cease and the marriage be dissolved.

The people of the city were amazed at the sudden change, especially when they saw the vizier and his son come out of the palace with forlorn and angry looks. They began to ask what had happened and why the marriage had been broken off. But nobody knew the secret except Aladdin, who was full of glee at the strange proceedings.

Now, the Sultan had forgotten the promise he had given Aladdin's mother. When the three months elapsed, Aladdin sent her to demand fulfillment. She went off to the palace, and as soon as she entered the audience hall the Sultan recognized her.

"Here comes the woman who presented me with the jewels," said the Sultan, and after she had kissed the ground and wished him everlasting glory he asked her what she wanted.

"Your Majesty," she said, "the three months after which you promised to wed your daughter, the Princess, to my son, Aladdin, are up."

The Sultan was at a loss what to answer, for it was plain that the woman was among the humblest of his subjects. Yet the present she had brought him was indeed beyond price.

"What do you suggest now?" he asked the vizier in a whisper. "It is perfectly true that I made her such a promise. But they are such humble folk!"

The vizier, stung with envy, thought to himself, "How can such a wretch marry the Princess, and my son be robbed of the honor?"

"Your Majesty," he replied, "that is no difficult thing. We must rebuff this stranger; for it scarcely befits your station to give away your daughter to an unknown upstart."

"But how can we get rid of him?" rejoined the Sultan.

"I gave him my pledge, and a sultan's pledge must never be broken."

"I suggest," said the vizier, "that you demand of him forty dishes of pure gold filled with jewels like the ones he has already sent you; the dishes to be carried in by forty slave girls, attended by forty slaves."

"Well spoken, vizier!" replied the Sultan. "That is something he can never do; in this way we shall once and for all be rid of him."

The Sultan then turned to Aladdin's mother.

"Go to your son," he said, "and tell him that I stand by my promise. The marriage will take place when he has sent a fitting present for my daughter. I will require of him forty dishes of pure gold filled with the same kind of jewels as those you brought me, together with forty slave girls to carry them, and forty slaves. If your son can provide this gift, my daughter shall be his."

Aladdin's mother left the royal presence in silence, and set out for home crestfallen. "Where will my poor boy get all those plates and jewels?" she asked herself. "Even if he returns to the treasure house and strips the magic trees of their jewels—not that I really believe that he can do this, but suppose he does—where in heaven's name are the forty girls and forty slaves to come from?"

Deep in these reflections, the old woman trudged on until she reached her house, where Aladdin was waiting.

"My child," she said, as soon as she entered, "did I not tell you to give up all thought of the Princess? Did I not warn you that such a thing was impossible for people like us?"

"Tell me what happened," Aladdin demanded.

"The Sultan received me very kindly," she replied, "and I believe he was well disposed toward you. But your enemy is that odious vizier. When I had spoken to the Sultan and reminded him of his promise, he consulted his vizier, who whispered to him in secret. After that the Sultan gave me his answer."

And she told Aladdin of the present that the Sultan had demanded.

"My child," she added, "the Sultan expects your answer now. But I think there is no answer we can give him."

"So that is what you think, Mother," Aladdin replied, laughing. "You think it is impossible. Rise up now and get us something to eat; then you will see the answer for yourself. Like you, the Sultan thought that his demand was beyond my power. In fact it is a trifle. Go, I say, and get the dinner ready. The rest you can leave to me."

His mother went off to the market to buy the food she needed. Meanwhile, Aladdin entered his room, took the lamp, and rubbed it; and at once the jinnee appeared.

"Master," he said, "ask what you will."

"The Sultan is now willing to give me his daughter," Aladdin said. "But I must send him forty dishes of pure gold, each ten pounds in weight, filled to the brim with jewels like those in the garden of the treasure house. The dishes must be carried by forty girls, with forty slaves to attend them. Go and bring me these without delay."

"I hear and obey," the jinnee replied.

The slave of the lamp vanished, and after a while returned with forty girls, each attended by a handsome slave; on their heads the girls bore dishes of pure gold full of priceless gems. The jinnee led them before his master and asked if there was any other service he could render.

"Nothing at present," Aladdin answered.

The jinnee disappeared again. In time Aladdin's mother returned from the market and was much amazed to see the house crowded with so many slaves.

"Could all this be the work of the lamp?" she exclaimed. "Heaven preserve it for my boy!"

Before she had time to take off her veil, Aladdin said, "Mother, there is not one moment to be lost. Take the Sultan the present he has asked for. Go to him now, so that he may realize I can give him all he wants and more besides."

Aladdin opened the door and the girls and slaves marched out in pairs. When the passers-by saw this wondrous spectacle they stopped and marveled at the beauty of the girls, who were dressed in robes woven of gold and studded with jewels. They gazed at the dishes, too, and saw that they outshone the sun in their sparkling brilliance. Each dish was covered with a kerchief embroidered in gold and sewn with precious pearls.

Aladdin's mother led the long procession, and as it passed from street to street the people crowded around, agog with wonder and exclamations. At last the procession came to the palace and wound its way into the courtyard. The commanders and chamberlains marveled greatly at the sight, for never in all their lives had they seen anything like it. They were astounded by the magnificent robes the girls were wearing, and the dishes upon their heads, which glowed with such fiery radiance that they could scarcely open their eyes to look at them.

The courtiers went and informed the Sultan, who at once ordered the procession to be brought in. Aladdin's mother led them into his presence, and they all solemnly saluted the Sultan and called down blessings upon him. Then they set down their plates, lifted the covers, and stood upright with their arms crossed over their breasts. The Sultan was filled with wonderment at the rare elegance of the girls, whose beauty beggared description. He was dumbfounded when he saw the golden dishes brimful with dazzling gems, and was even more bewildered that all this could have happened in such a short time.

"What do you say now?" said the Sultan in a whisper, turning to the vizier. "What shall be said of a man who can produce such riches in so short a time? Does he not deserve to be the Sultan's son-in-law, and take the Sultan's daughter for his bride?"

Now, the vizier was even more amazed than the Sultan at this prodigious wealth; but envy got the better of him. "Your Majesty," he cunningly replied, "not all the treasures of the world are equal to the Princess' fingernail. Surely you overrate this gift in comparison with your daughter." But the Sultan ignored the vizier's remark.

"Go to your son," he said to Aladdin's mother, "and tell him that I stand by my promise: my daughter shall be his bride. Tell him to come to the palace, so that I may meet him. He shall be received with the utmost honor and consideration. The wedding shall begin this very night; only, as I told you, let him come here without delay."

Scarcely believing her ears, Aladdin's mother ran home swiftly as the wind to give the news to her son. The Sultan dismissed his court and ordered the slave girls to be brought in with the dishes to the Princess' room. The Princess marveled at the size of the jewels and the beauty of the slave girls, and was delighted to know that all this had been sent to her by her new husband. Her father, too, rejoiced to see her so happy and no longer cast down with gloom.

"Are you pleased with this present, my daughter?" he asked. "I am sure that this young man will prove a better husband than the vizier's son. I hope you will be happy with him."

So much for the Sultan. As for Aladdin, when he saw his mother enter the house beaming with joy, he knew that her mission had been successful.

"Rejoice, my boy," she cried. "You have gained your wish. The Sultan has accepted your present, and the Princess is to be your bride. Tonight the wedding festivities will begin. The Sultan is proclaiming you before the whole world as his son-in-law, and desires that you should call on him without delay."

Aladdin kissed his mother's hand and thanked her with all his heart. Then he returned to his room, took up the lamp, and rubbed it. At once the jinnee appeared.

"I am here," he said. "Ask what you will."

"Slave of the lamp," said Aladdin, "I order you to take me to a bath more magnificent than any in the world; also to bring me a splendid regal suit such as no king has ever worn."

"I hear and obey," the jinnee replied.

So saying, he took Aladdin upon his shoulder and in a twinkling brought him to a bath such as neither king nor emperor ever saw. It was made of agate and alabaster, and adorned with wondrous paintings that dazzled the eye. No mortal troubled the peace of that white vault. The slave of the lamp led him into an inner hall, thickly studded with jewels and precious stones, and there he was received and washed by a jinnee in human shape. After his bath, Aladdin was led back into the outer vault, where, instead of his former clothes, he found a magnificent regal suit. Cool drinks were brought to him, and coffee flavored with amber; and when he had refreshed himself, there came into the hall a train of slaves who perfumed him and dressed him in his sumptuous robes.

Aladdin, as you know, was the son of a poor tailor; yet anyone who saw him now would have taken him for some illustrious prince. As soon as he was dressed, the jinnee appeared again and carried him home.

"Master," said the jinnee, "is there anything else that you require?"

"Yes," Aladdin replied. "I want you to bring me a retinue of four dozen slaves, two dozen to ride before me and two dozen to ride behind me, complete with livery, horses, and weapons. Both slaves and horses must be arrayed in the finest and the best. After that, bring me a thoroughbred steed worthy of an emperor's stable, with trappings all of gold studded with rich jewels. You must also bring me forty-eight thousand gold pieces, a thousand with each slave. Do not delay; all these must be ready before I go to the Sultan. Lastly, be careful to select twelve girls of incomparable beauty, dressed in the most exquisite clothes, to accompany my mother to the royal palace; and let each girl bring with her a robe that would do credit to a queen."

"I hear and obey," the jinnee replied.

He vanished, and in the twinkling of an eye returned with everything Aladdin had asked for. In his hand he held the bridle of a horse unrivaled among all the Arabian steeds for beauty, with trappings of the finest cloth of gold. Aladdin at once called his mother and gave her charge of the twelve girls; he also gave her a robe to put on when she went with her attendants to the royal palace. Then he sent one of the slaves to see whether the Sultan was ready to receive him. The slave departed, and in a flash returned.

"Master," he said, "the Sultan is waiting for you."

Aladdin mounted his horse, while his attendants mounted before and behind him. As they rode they scattered handfuls of gold among the crowd. And so handsome and radiant did Aladdin look that he would have put to shame the greatest of princes.

All this was due to the power of the lamp; for whoever possessed it acquired beauty, wealth, and all knowledge. The people marveled at Aladdin's generosity; they were amazed at his good looks, his politeness, and his noble bearing. No one envied him; they all said he deserved his good luck.

Meanwhile the Sultan had assembled the great ones of his kingdom to inform them of the intended marriage. He told them to wait for Aladdin's arrival and to go out in a body to receive him. He also summoned the viziers and the chamberlains, the nabobs and the commanders of the army; and they all stood waiting for Aladdin at the gates of the palace. Presently Aladdin arrived and would have dismounted at the entrance; but one of the commanders, whom the Sultan had stationed there for the purpose, hastened to prevent him.

"Sir," he said, "it is His Majesty's wish that you should enter riding and dismount at the door of the audience hall."

The courtiers walked before him, and when he had reached the audience hall some came forward to hold his horse's stirrup, others to support him on either side, while yet others took him by the hand and helped him to dismount. The commanders and dignitaries ushered him into the hall, and as soon as he approached the throne and was about to kneel on the carpet the Sultan stepped forward, took him in his arms, and made him sit down on his right. Aladdin exchanged greetings with him and wished him long life and everlasting glory.

"Your Majesty," he said, "you have been graciously pleased to give me your daughter in marriage, although, being the humblest of your subjects, I am unworthy of so great an honor. Great Sultan, I lack the words to thank you for this signal favor. I beg Your Majesty to grant me a plot of land where I can build a palace worthy of Princess Badr-al-Budur."

The Sultan was greatly astonished when he saw Aladdin dressed in such splendor. He looked intently at him, and then at the tall and handsome slaves who stood around him.

He was even more amazed when Aladdin's mother made her entrance, radiant as a queen in her costly robes and surrounded by the twelve graceful girls, who were attending her with the utmost dignity and respect. He marveled, too, at Aladdin's eloquence and cultured speech; and so did all the others present in the audience hall except the vizier, who almost perished with envy. Having listened to Aladdin's words and observed his magnificence and modest bearing, the Sultan again took him in his arms.

"It is a great pity, my son," he said, "that we have not been brought together before this."

He ordered the musicians to start playing; then he took Aladdin by the hand and led him into the palace hall, where a wedding feast had been prepared. The Sultan sat down and made Aladdin sit on his right. The viziers, dignitaries, and noblemen also took their seats, each according to his rank. Music filled the air, and all the palace echoed with the sound of great rejoicing. The Sultan spoke to Aladdin and jested with him, while Aladdin replied with gallantry and wit, as though he had grown up in a royal palace and all his life kept company with kings. And the longer the Sultan talked to him, the more impressed he became with his accomplishments.

When they had finished eating, and the tables were removed, the Sultan ordered judges and witnesses to be brought in. They came, and duly wrote the marriage contract for Aladdin and the Princess. Then Aladdin got up and begged leave to go; but the Sultan prevented him.

"Where are you going, my son?" he cried. "All the wedding guests are here and the feast is not yet finished."

"Your Majesty," Aladdin replied, "I wish to build the Princess a palace befitting her high station. I cannot take her as my wife until I have done that. I hope that the palace will be ready in the shortest possible time. Eager as I am to be with the Princess, my duty prompts me to do this first, in proof of the great love I bear her."

"Take whatever land you like, my son," the Sultan said. "It is for you to choose. But to my mind it would be best to build it here, on the great square in front of my palace."

"I could wish for nothing better," Aladdin replied, "than to be so near Your Majesty."

With that he took leave of the Sultan and, mounting his horse, returned home amid the joyful shouts of the people.

There he went into his room and rubbed the lamp.

"Master, ask what you will," said the jinnee, as he appeared before him.

"I have an important task to set you," Aladdin replied. "I wish you to build me, with the least possible delay, a palace in front of the Sultan's; a marvel of a building, the like of which no king has ever seen. Let it be furnished royally and fitted with every comfort."

"I hear and obey," the jinnee answered.

He disappeared and, just before daybreak, returned to Aladdin, saying, "Master, the task is accomplished. Rise and look upon your palace."

Aladdin got up, and in the twinkling of an eye the slave of the lamp carried him away to the palace. When Aladdin saw it he was dumbfounded with wonder; it was all built of jasper and marble mosaics. The jinnee conducted him into a treasury heaped with all manner of gold and silver and precious stones beyond count or value. He then led him into the dining hall, where he saw plates and ewers, cups and spoons and basins, all of gold and silver. He next took him to the kitchen, and there he saw the cooks with their pots and utensils, also of gold and silver. From there he led him into another room, which he found stacked with coffers containing rich and wondrous garments, Chinese and Indian silks embroidered with gold, and thick brocades.

After that he ushered him into several other rooms, full of treasures beyond description, and finally took him into the stables, where he saw thoroughbred horses whose like no king ever possessed. In an adjoining storeroom lay costly saddles and bridles wrought with pearls and rich jewels. All this had been accomplished in one night.

Aladdin was bewildered and amazed at these marvels, which were beyond the dream of kings. The palace was thronged with slaves and serving girls of exquisite beauty. But the most wondrous thing of all was the dome of the building, which was pierced with four and twenty windows encrusted with emeralds, rubies, and other precious stones. At Aladdin's request, one of the windows had not been properly finished, for he wished to challenge the Sultan to complete it. Aladdin was overjoyed at the splendor of all he saw.

"There is only one thing lacking, which I forgot to mention," he said, turning to the slave of the lamp.

"Ask," the jinnee replied, "and it shall be done."

"I require a carpet of rich brocade, woven with thread of gold," said Aladdin. "It must be stretched from this palace to the Sultan's so that the Princess may walk upon it without her feet touching the ground."

The jinnee vanished, and almost at once returned.

"Master, your request is granted," he said.

He took Aladdin and showed it to him: a wonder of a carpet, stretching from his palace to the Sultan's. Then the jinnee carried him home.

When the Sultan woke that morning, he opened the window of his bedroom and looked out. In front of his palace he saw a building. He rubbed his eyes, opened them wide, and looked again. The building was still there, a towering edifice of astonishing beauty, with a carpet stretched from its threshold to the doorstep of his own palace. The

Without losing a moment, he ran straight off to the baths and hid himself behind the great door where none could see him.

doorkeepers and everyone else who saw it were no less astounded. At that moment the vizier entered the Sultan's apartment, and he too was utterly amazed to see the new palace and the carpet.

"Heavens!" they cried together. "No king on earth could ever build the like of that palace!"

"Now are you convinced that Aladdin deserves to be my daughter's husband?" said the Sultan, turning to his minister.

"Your Majesty," the vizier answered, "nothing short of magic could have produced that edifice. Not the richest man alive could build such a palace in one night."

"I marvel at you," the Sultan cried. "You seem to think nothing but ill of Aladdin. Clearly you are jealous of him. You were present yourself when I gave him this land to erect a palace for my daughter. The man who could present a gift of such jewels can surely build a palace in one night."

Realizing that the Sultan loved Aladdin too well to be aroused against him, the vizier held his peace and said no more.

As for Aladdin, when he felt that the time was ripe to present himself at the royal palace, he rubbed the lamp and said to the jinnee, "I must now go to the Sultan's court; today is the wedding banquet. I want you to bring me ten thousand pieces of gold."

The jinnee vanished and, in a twinkling returned with ten thousand gold pieces. Aladdin mounted his horse, and his slaves rode before and behind him. All along the way he scattered gold among the people, who now made him their idol on account of his generosity. As soon as he reached the palace, the courtiers and officers of the guard hurried to inform the Sultan of his arrival. The Sultan went out to receive him; he took him by the hand, led him into the hall, and seated him on his right. The entire city was decorated, and in the palace performers sang and made music.

Orders were now given by the Sultan for the banquet to begin. He sat at a table with Aladdin and all the courtiers, and they ate and drank until they were satisfied. Nor was the merriment confined to the royal palace; all the people of the kingdom, great and small alike, rejoiced on this happy occasion. Viceroys and governors had come from the remotest provinces to see the wedding and the nuptial celebrations.

Deep in his heart, the Sultan marveled at Aladdin's mother, how she had come to him in tattered clothes, while her son was master of such extraordinary riches. And when the guests saw Aladdin's palace, they were amazed that such a dwelling could have been built in one night.

When the banquet drew to an end, Aladdin rose and took leave of the Sultan. He mounted his horse and, escorted by his servants, rode over to his own palace to prepare himself for his meeting with the bride. As he rode he threw handfuls of gold to right and left amid the joyful blessings of the people, and on reaching his house alighted and took his seat in the audience hall. Cool drinks were brought to him, and after he had refreshed himself he ordered the servants and the slave girls, and everyone else in the palace, to make ready to receive his bride that evening.

In the cool of the afternoon, when the heat of the sun had abated, the Sultan ordered his captains and ministers to go down and take their places in the parade ground opposite his court. They all went down, including the Sultan; and Aladdin presently joined them, riding on a horse unequaled among the Arabian steeds for beauty. He galloped and sported around the square, excelling in his display of horsemanship. The Princess watched him from a window; she was captivated by his good looks and riding skill, and fell in love with him at sight. When all the cavaliers had finished their riding display, the Sultan returned to his palace and Aladdin to his.

In the evening the ministers and high officials called on Aladdin and took him in great procession to the royal baths. There he bathed and perfumed himself, then changed into even more magnificent clothes and rode home escorted by officers and soldiers. Four ministers walked about him with unsheathed swords, while all the townsfolk, natives and foreigners alike, marched ahead with candles and drums, pipes, and all manner of musical instruments. Reaching the palace, he dismounted and sat down with his attendants. The slaves brought cakes and sweetmeats and served drinks to countless men and women who had joined the procession. Then, at Aladdin's orders, the slaves went out to the palace gate and scattered gold among the people.

Meanwhile, on returning from the square, the Sultan had ordered his household to take the Princess to Aladdin's palace. The soldiers and courtiers immediately mounted; the servants and slave girls went out with lighted candles, and the Princess was brought in splendid procession to her husband's palace. Aladdin's mother walked by her side; in front marched the wives of ministers, noblemen, and courtiers, while in her train followed all the slave girls whom Aladdin had given her, each carrying a torch set into a golden candlestick encrusted with gems. They took her up to her room, accompanied by Aladdin's mother.

Presently Aladdin entered the chamber; he lifted the bridal veil, and his mother gazed in wonderment upon the Princess' loveliness and beauty. She also marveled at the bridal chamber, all wrought in gold and jewels, and at its golden chandelier, studded with emeralds and rubies. Nor was the Princess less astonished than Aladdin's mother at the magnificence of the palace.

A table was brought in and they feasted and made merry, while eighty slave girls, each holding a musical instrument, plucked the strings and played enchanting tunes. The Princess was so thrilled with the music that she stopped eating and listened with rapt attention. Aladdin plied her with wine, and the two rejoiced in each other's love.

In the morning Aladdin got up and dressed himself in a magnificent suit that his chief footman had prepared for him. Then he ordered the slaves to saddle his horses and rode with numerous escorts to the royal palace. The Sultan at once rose to receive him and, after embracing him as though he were his own son, seated him on his right. The Sultan and all the courtiers congratulated him and wished him joy. Breakfast was then served, and when they had finished eating, Aladdin turned to the Sultan and said, "Sir, would Your Majesty honor me with your presence at lunch today with the Princess? Let Your Majesty be accompanied by all your ministers and the nobles of your kingdom."

The Sultan gladly accepted. He ordered his courtiers to follow him and rode over with Aladdin to his palace. When he entered he marveled at the edifice, the stones of which were all of jasper and agate; he was dazed at the sight of such luxury, wealth, and splendor.

"What do you say now?" he exclaimed, turning to the vizier. "Have you ever seen anything like this in all your life? Has the greatest emperor in the world such wealth and gold and jewels as can be seen in this palace?"

"Your Majesty," the vizier replied, "this miracle is beyond the power of mortal kings. Not all the people of the world could build a palace like this; no masons are to be found who can do such work. As I told Your Majesty before, only magic would have brought it into being."

But the Sultan replied, "Enough, vizier. I know why you are telling me this."

The Sultan now came under the lofty dome of the palace, and his amazement knew no bounds when he saw that all the windows and lattices were made of emeralds, rubies, and other precious stones. He walked around and around, bewildered at the extravagant marvels, and presently caught sight of the window that Aladdin had deliberately left unfinished.

"Alas, poor window, you are unfinished!" observed the Sultan. And, turning to the vizier, he asked, "Do you know why that window and its lattices have not been properly completed?"

"Perhaps because Your Majesty hurried Aladdin over the wedding," the vizier replied. "He may not have had time enough to complete it."

Aladdin, who had meanwhile gone to inform his bride of her father's arrival, now returned, and the Sultan addressed the same question to him.

"Your Majesty," he replied, "the wedding took place at such short notice that the masons had no time to finish the work."

"Then I would like to finish it myself," said the Sultan.

"Heaven grant Your Majesty everlasting glory!" Aladdin cried. "May it stand as a memorial to you in your daughter's palace!"

The Sultan at once sent for jewelers and goldsmiths and ordered his lieutenants to give them all the gold and jewels they required out of his treasury. The jewelers and goldsmiths presented themselves before the Sultan, and he ordered them to finish the ornamentation.

While this was going forward, the Princess came out to meet her father. He noticed how happy she was, and took her into his arms and kissed her; then he went with her to her room, followed by all his courtiers. It was now lunchtime; one table had been prepared for the Sultan, the Prin-

cess, and Aladdin, and another for the vizier, the officers of
state, the high dignitaries, the chamberlains, the nabobs, and
the captains of the army. The Sultan sat between his daughter and his son-in-law, and as he ate he marveled at the
delicacy of the meats and the excellence of the dishes. Before him stood a troupe of eighty radiant girls, who plucked
the strings of their instruments and made such sweet music
as could not be heard even in the courts of kings and emperors.
Wine flowed freely; and when all had eaten and drunk, they
repaired to an adjoining chamber, where they were served
with fruits and sweetmeats.

Then the Sultan rose to inspect the jewelers' work, and
to see how it compared with the workmanship of the palace.
He went up to the unfinished window, but was disappointed
to find that there was a great difference, and that his
workers lacked the art to match the perfection of the whole.
The jewelers informed him that they had brought all the
gems they could find in his treasury, and that they needed
more. He ordered that the great imperial treasury be
opened and that they should be given all they required; if
that was not enough, they were to use the jewels that Aladdin had sent him. The jewelers did as the Sultan had
directed, but found that all those gems were not sufficient to
ornament one half of the lattice. The Sultan next commanded that all the precious stones that could be found in
the houses of the viziers and rich notables should be taken.
The jewelers took all of these and worked with them, but
still they needed more.

Next morning Aladdin went up to the jewelers and,
finding that they had not finished even half the lattice, told
them to undo their work and restore the gems to their
owners. The jewelers did so, and went to inform the Sultan
of Aladdin's instructions.

"What did he say to you?" the Sultan asked. "Why did

he not let you finish the window? Why did he destroy what you had done?"

"We do not know, Your Majesty," was their reply.

The Sultan called for his horse and rode at once to his son-in-law's palace.

Now, when Aladdin had dismissed the jewelers, he had entered his room and rubbed the lamp. The jinnee appeared before him, saying, "Ask what you will, your slave is at your service."

"I want you to complete the unfinished window," Aladdin commanded.

"It shall be as you wish," the jinnee replied.

He vanished, and after a short while returned.

"Master," he said, "the task is accomplished."

Aladdin climbed up to the dome of the palace and saw that all its windows were now complete. While he was examining them his footman came in to inform him that the Sultan had come. Aladdin went down to receive him.

"Why did you do that, my son?" cried the Sultan as soon as he saw him. "Why did you not let the jewelers complete the lattice, so that there would remain nothing amiss in your palace?"

"Great Sultan," Aladdin replied, "it was left unfinished at my request. I was not incapable of completing it myself; nor would I wish to receive Your Majesty in a palace where there was something missing. May it please Your Highness to come up and see if there is anything imperfect now."

The Sultan mounted the stairs and went into the dome of the palace. He looked right and left, and was astonished to see that all the latticework was now complete.

"What an extraordinary feat, my son!" he exclaimed. "In a single night you have finished a task that would have occupied the jewelers for months. Why, there cannot be anyone like you in the whole world!"

"Your Majesty," Aladdin replied, "your servant is unworthy of such praise."

"My son," the Sultan cried, "you deserve all praise, because you have done that which no jeweler on earth could ever do."

From that time on, Aladdin went out into the city every day, his slaves scattering gold before him as he rode. The hearts of all the people, old and young, were drawn to him on account of his good deeds, and his fame spread far and wide throughout the realm.

It also happened at that time that certain enemies marched against the Sultan, who gathered his armies and appointed Aladdin commander in chief. Aladdin led the troops to the battlefield, unsheathed his sword, and with extraordinary courage attacked the opposing forces. A mighty battle took place, in which the raiders were defeated and put to flight. Aladdin plundered their goods and belongings and returned in glorious triumph to the capital, which had been gaily decked to receive him. The Sultan came out to meet him; he congratulated him on his victory and took him into his arms amid the rejoicings of the people. He ordered the entire kingdom to be decorated in honor of the occasion. The soldiers and all the people now looked only to God in heaven and to Aladdin on earth. They loved him more than ever on account of his generosity and patriotism, his horsemanship and heroic courage. So much for Aladdin.

Now to return to the Moorish sorcerer. When he had left Aladdin to perish in the cave, he journeyed back to his own land and passed his days bemoaning the vain hardships he had endured to secure the lamp. It pained him to think how the long-sought morsel had flown out of his hand just when it had reached his mouth, and he cursed Aladdin in his rage.

"I am very glad," he would sometimes say to himself, "that the little wretch has perished under the ground. The lamp is still safe in the treasure house, and I may get it yet."

One day he cast his magic sand to ascertain Aladdin's death and the exact position of the lamp. He studied the resulting figures attentively, but he saw no lamp. Angrily he cast the sand a second time to confirm that the boy was dead, but he did not see him in the treasure house. His fury mounted when he learned that Aladdin was alive; he realized that he must have come up from the cave and gained possession of the lamp.

"I have suffered many hardships, and endured pains such as no other man could bear, on account of the lamp," he thought to himself. "Now this worthless boy has taken it. It is all too clear that if he has discovered its magic power, he must now be the wealthiest man on earth. I must seek to destroy him."

He cast the sand once more and scanned the figures. He found that Aladdin was master of great riches, and that he was married to a princess. Mad with envy, he set out for China. After a long journey he reached the capital where Aladdin lived, and put up at a travelers' inn. There he heard the people talk of nothing but the magnificence of Aladdin's palace. When he had rested a little, he changed his clothes and went out for a walk in the streets of the city. Wherever he passed he heard tell of nothing but the beauty of Aladdin and his manly grace, his generosity and rare virtues. The magician went up to a man who was praising Aladdin in these terms and said, "Tell me, my good friend, who is this man of whom you speak so highly?"

"Why, sir, you must be a stranger in these parts," came the reply. "But even if you are, have you never heard of Prince Aladdin? His palace is one of the wonders of the world. How is it that you have never heard of it?"

"I would very much like to see the palace," said the magician. "Would you be so kind as to direct me to it? I am indeed a stranger in this city."

"Why, gladly," the man replied and, walking before the magician, brought him to Aladdin's palace.

The magician looked at the building and realized that it was the work of the enchanted lamp.

"Ah," he thought to himself, "I must dig a pit for this vile tailor's son who could never earn an evening's meal before. If fate allows it, I will destroy him utterly, and send his mother back to her spinning wheel."

Eaten up with sorrow and envy, he returned to his lodging and took out his magic board. He cast the sand to find out where the lamp was hidden, and saw that it was in the palace and not on Aladdin's person.

"My task is easy now," he cried with joy. "I know a way of getting the lamp."

He went off to a coppersmith and said to him, "Make me a few copper lamps. I will pay you well if you finish them fast enough."

"I hear and obey," replied the coppersmith and set to work at once.

When they were finished, the magician paid him without haggling, took the lamps, and returned to his lodging. There he put them in a basket, and went about the streets and markets, crying, "Who will exchange an old lamp for a new one?"

When the people heard his cry, they laughed at him.

"No doubt the man is mad," they said to each other. "Who would go around offering to change old lamps for new?"

A great crowd followed him, and the street urchins ran after him from place to place, shouting and laughing. But the magician took no notice of them and proceeded on his way until he found himself in front of Aladdin's palace. Here he began to shout at the top of his voice, while the children chanted back, "Madman! Madman!" At last the Princess, who happened to be in the hall of the latticed dome, heard the noise in the street and ordered one of the maids to go and find out what it was all about.

The maid returned to the Princess and said, "Your Highness, outside the gate there is an old man crying, 'Who will exchange an old lamp for a new one?' Little boys are laughing at him."

The Princess laughed, too, at this strange offer. Now, Aladdin had left the lamp in his room and forgotten to lock it up. One of the girls, who had chanced to see it there, said, "Mistress, there is an old lamp in my master Aladdin's room. Let us take it down to the old man and see if he will really exchange it for a new one."

"Fetch it to me, then," said the Princess.

Badr-al-Budur knew nothing of the lamp or its magic powers, nor was she aware that it was this lamp that had brought Aladdin such vast wealth. She merely wished to see what sort of madness drove the magician to change old things for new.

The maid went up to Aladdin's room and returned with the lamp to her mistress, who then ordered a servant to go and exchange it for a new one. The servant gave the lamp to the Moor, took a new one in return, and carried it to the Princess. Badr-al-Budur examined it and, finding that it really was new, laughed at the old man's folly.

When the magician recognized the lamp he quickly hid it in the breast of his robe and flung his basket with all its contents to the crowd. He ran on and on until he came outside the city and reached the empty plains. Then he waited for the night and, when all was darkness, took out the lamp and rubbed it. At once the jinnee appeared before him.

"I am here, master," he said; "ask what you will."

"Slave of the lamp," the magician said, "I order you to lift up Aladdin's palace with all its contents and to transport it, and me as well, to my own country in Africa. You know my native city; there you shall set it down, among the gardens."

"I hear and obey," the jinnee replied. "Shut your eyes and open them and you shall find yourself in your own land with the palace."

At once the thing was done. In a flash the magician and Aladdin's palace, together with all that it contained, were carried off to Africa.

So much for the Moorish magician.

Now to return to the Sultan and Aladdin. When the Sultan got up next day he opened the window and looked out, as was his custom every day, in the direction of his daughter's palace. But he saw nothing there, only a vast, bare space as in the former days. He was greatly astonished and perplexed; he rubbed his eyes, opened them wide, and looked again. But he saw not a trace or vestige of the palace, and could not understand how or why it had vanished. He wrung his hands in despair and tears began to roll over his beard, for he did not know what had become of his daughter. At once he summoned the vizier; and when the vizier came in and saw the Sultan overcome with grief, he cried, "Heaven preserve Your Majesty from all evil! Why do I see you so distressed?"

"Is it possible that you do not know the reason?" the Sultan asked.

"By my honor, I know nothing," returned the vizier, "nothing at all."

"Then you have not looked in the direction of Aladdin's palace?" the Sultan cried.

"No," the vizier answered.

"Since you know nothing about the matter," groaned the Sultan, "pray have a good look from the window and see where Aladdin's palace is."

The vizier crossed over to the window and looked out toward Aladdin's palace. He saw nothing there, neither palace nor anything else. Confounded at the mystery, he returned to the Sultan.

"Well," said the Sultan, "do you know now the reason for my grief?"

"Great Sultan," the vizier answered, "I have told Your Majesty time and time again that the palace and the whole affair were magic from beginning to end."

"Where is Aladdin?" cried the Sultan, blazing with rage.

"Gone to the hunt," the vizier replied.

The Sultan instantly ordered a troop of officers and guards to go and bring Aladdin before him, manacled and bound with chains. The officers and guards rode off on their mission, and before long met Aladdin.

"Pardon us, master," they said. "We are commanded by the Sultan to take you to him in chains. We beg you to excuse us; we are acting under royal orders, which we cannot disobey."

Aladdin was dumbfounded at these words, for he could think of no possible reason.

"Good friend," he said at last to the officers, "do you know why the Sultan gave these orders? I know I am innocent; I have committed no crime against the Sultan or his realm."

"Master," they replied, "we know nothing at all."

"Then you must carry out your orders," said Aladdin,

dismounting. "Obedience to the Sultan is binding on all his loyal subjects."

The officers chained their captive and dragged him in fetters to the capital. When the citizens saw Aladdin treated in this way, they realized that he was going to be put to death. But since they all loved him, they crowded in the street and, arming themselves with clubs and weapons, pressed at his heels to find out what would happen to him.

The troops took Aladdin to the palace and informed the Sultan, who thereupon commanded the executioner to strike off his head. When the citizens learned of this order they locked up the gates of the palace and sent a warning to the Sultan, saying, "This very hour we will pull down your dwelling over your head and the heads of all who are in it, if Aladdin comes to the slightest harm."

The vizier went in and delivered the warning to the Sultan.

"Your Majesty," he said, "this order will be the end of us all. It would be far better to pardon Aladdin, or the consequences would be terrible indeed. Your subjects love Aladdin more than us."

Meanwhile the executioner made ready to do his work. He had just bandaged Aladdin's eyes and walked around him three times, waiting for the final order, when the Sultan saw his subjects storming the palace and climbing over the walls to destroy it. At once he ordered the executioner to stay his hand, and bade the crier go out among the people and proclaim that the Sultan had spared Aladdin's life.

Freed from his fetters, Aladdin went up to the Sultan.

"Your Majesty," he said, "since you have been graciously pleased to spare my life, I beg you to tell me what I have done to earn your displeasure."

"Traitor," the Sultan exclaimed, "do you dare pretend you know nothing of what has happened?" Then, turning to the vizier, he said, "Take him, and let him see from the window where his palace is!"

The vizier led Aladdin to a window, and he looked out toward his palace. He found the site desolate and empty, with not a trace of any building upon it. He returned, utterly bewildered, to the Sultan.

"What did you see?" the Sultan asked. "Where is your palace? And where is my daughter, my only child?"

"Great Sultan," Aladdin answered, "I know nothing of all this, nor do I know what has happened."

"Listen, Aladdin," the Sultan cried. "I have released you only that you may go and investigate this mystery and seek out my daughter for me. Do not return without her. If you fail to bring her back, I swear by my life that I will cut off your head."

"I hear and obey, Your Majesty," Aladdin replied. "Only grant me a delay of forty days. If I do not bring her to you by that time, cut off my head and do with me what you will."

"Very well," the Sultan said. "I grant you the delay. But do not think you can escape my reach; for I will bring you back even if you are above the clouds."

The people were glad to see Aladdin free. He came out of the palace pleased at his escape; but the disgrace of what had happened, and the triumphant glee of his enemies, caused him to hang his head. For two days he wandered sadly about the town, not knowing what he should do, while certain friends secretly brought him food and drink. Then he struck aimlessly into the desert and journeyed on until he came to a river. Thirsty and worn out, he knelt down upon the bank to wash and refresh himself. He took up the water in the hollow of his hands and began to rub between his fingers; and in so doing he rubbed the ring that the magician had given him. Thereupon a jinnee appeared, saying, "I am here. Your slave stands before you. Ask what you will."

Aladdin rejoiced at the sight of the jinnee.

"Slave of the ring," he cried, "bring me back my wife and my palace with all its contents."

"Master," the jinnee replied, "that is beyond my power, for it concerns only the slave of the lamp."

"Very well," Aladdin said. "Since you cannot do this, take me away and set me down beside my palace, wherever it may be."

"I hear and obey, master."

So saying, the jinnee carried him up, and in the twinkling of an eye set him down beside his palace in Morocco, in front of his wife's room. Night had fallen; and as he looked at his palace his cares and sorrows left him. He prayed, after he had given up all hope, to be united with his wife again. As he had had no sleep for four days on account of his anxiety and grief, he stretched himself out by the palace and slept under a tree; for, as I have told you, the palace stood among the gardens of Africa, outside a town.

Thus, despite the anxious thoughts that troubled him, he slept soundly under the tree until daybreak, when he awoke to the singing of birds. He got up and walked down to a nearby river that flowed into the town, washed his hands and face, and said his prayers. Then he returned and sat down under the window of the Princess' room.

The Princess, very distressed at being separated from her husband and father, neither ate nor drank, and passed her days and nights weeping. As luck would have it, however, on that morning, when one of the maids came in to dress the Princess, she opened the window to cheer her mistress with the delightful view and saw Aladdin, her master, sitting below.

"Mistress, mistress!" she exclaimed. "There is my master Aladdin, sitting below!"

The Princess rushed to the window, and husband and wife recognized each other in a transport of joy.

"Come up, quickly!" the Princess shouted. "Enter by the secret door. The magician is not here now."

Her maid ran down and opened a secret door, by which Aladdin went in to his wife's room. Laughing and crying, they fell into each other's arms.

"Before all else, Badr-al-Budur," said Aladdin, when they had both sat down, "tell me what became of that copper lamp that I left in my room when I went out hunting."

"Alas, my love!" sighed the Princess. "That lamp and nothing else was the cause of our ruin."

"Tell me everything."

Badr-al-Budur recounted to him all that had happened since the day she exchanged the old lamp for a new one.

"Next morning," she said, "we suddenly found ourselves in this country. And the man who cheated us told me that it was all done by his witchcraft and the power of the lamp; that he was a Moor from Africa and that we were now in his native city."

"What does the scoundrel intend to do with you?" asked Aladdin, when the Princess had finished speaking. "What does he say to you? What does he want of you?"

"He comes to me once every day," she replied, "and tries to win my heart. He wants me to forget you and to take *him* for my husband. He says that the Sultan has cut off your head, that you come of a poor family, and that you owe your wealth to him. He tries to endear himself to me, but gets nothing in return except silence and tears. He has never heard a kind word from me."

"Now tell me where he keeps the lamp."

"He always carries it with him," the Princess replied, "and never parts from it even for a moment. But he once drew it from his robe and showed it to me."

Aladdin was very glad to hear this.

"Listen to me, Badr-al-Budur," he said. "I will leave the palace now, and return in a disguise. Do not be alarmed when you see me. Post one of the maids at the secret door, so that she may let me in. I have hit upon a plan to destroy this foul magician."

Aladdin set off in the direction of the city, and presently met a peasant on the way.

"Good friend," he said, "take my clothes and give me yours."

The peasant refused; so Aladdin took hold of him, forced him to cast off his clothes, put them on himself, and gave him his own costly robes in return. Then he walked on to the city and made his way to the perfume sellers' market, where he bought a powerful drug.

Returning to the palace, he went in by the secret door to the Princess' room.

"Listen, now," he said to his wife. "I want you to put on your finest robes and jewels and to look your radiant self again. When the magician comes, give him a joyful welcome and receive him with a smiling face. Invite him to dine with you; pretend you have forgotten your husband and your father, and you are in love with him. Ask him for red wine, and drink his health with a show of merriment. When you have given him two or three glasses, drop this powder into his cup and fill it to the brim with wine. As soon as he has drunk it off, he will fall over on his back like a dead man."

"That will be difficult," the Princess replied. "Yet it must be done if we are to rid ourselves of the monster. To kill such a man is certainly a good deed."

Then Aladdin ate and drank with the Princess, and when he had satisfied his hunger he got up and quickly left the palace.

The Princess sent for her maid, who combed her hair, perfumed her, and dressed her in her finest garments. By and by, the Moor came in. He was delighted to see her so changed, and was agreeably surprised when she received him with a welcoming smile. She took him by the hand and seated him by her side.

"If you wish, sir," she said in a tender voice, "come to my room tonight and we will dine together. I have had my fill of grief; and were I to sit mourning for a thousand years, Aladdin would never come back from the grave. I have thought about what you told me yesterday, and do believe that my father may well have killed him in his sorrow at being parted from me. Therefore you must not be surprised to see me changed. Pray let us meet tonight, that we may have dinner and drink a little wine together. I would particularly like to taste your African wine; perhaps it is better than ours. I have here some wine from our own country, but would much prefer to try some of yours."

Taken in by the affectionate regard that the Princess displayed toward him, the magician concluded that she had given up all hope of Aladdin. Therefore he rejoiced and said, "My dear, I will gladly obey your every wish. I have in my house a cask of African wine, which I have stored deep under the earth these eight years. I will now go and fetch from it sufficient for our needs, and return to you without delay."

But to coax him more and more, the Princess replied, "Do not leave me alone, dearest. Send one of your servants for the wine, and sit here by my side, that I may cheer myself with your company."

"Dear mistress," the magician answered, "no one knows where the cask is hidden but myself. I will not be long."

So saying, he went out and after a little while returned with a flaskful of the wine.

"Dearest," said the Princess when he entered, "you have tired yourself on my account."

"Not at all, my love," the magician replied. "It is an honor for me to serve you."

The Princess sat beside him at the table, and the two ate together. She asked for a drink, and her maid filled her cup and then the Moor's. They drank cheerfully to each other's health, the Princess using all her art to win him with her words. The unsuspecting Moor supposed all this to be heartfelt and true; he did not know that this love of hers was but a snare to destroy him. When they had finished eating and the wine had vanquished his brain, the Princess said, "We have a custom in our country; I do not know if you observe it here."

"And what is this custom?" he asked.

"When dinner is over," she replied, "each one takes his companion's cup and drinks from it."

She thereupon took his cup and filled it with wine for herself; then she ordered the maid to give him her cup, in which the wine had already been mixed with the drug. The girl acted her part well, for all the maids and servants in the palace wished his death and were in league with their mistress to destroy him. So the girl gave him the cup, while the drunken Moor, flattered by this show of love, imagined himself to be Alexander the Great in all his glory.

"Dearest," the Princess said, swaying from side to side and placing her hand in his, "here I have your cup and you have mine. Thus shall we drink from one another's cup."

The Princess kissed his glass and drank; then she went over to him and kissed him on the cheek. The delighted Moor wanted to do the same; he raised the cup to his lips and gulped it down. At once he rolled over on his back like a dead man, and the cup fell from his hand. The Princess rejoiced, and the maids rushed out to the door of the palace to admit their master Aladdin.

Aladdin hastened to his wife's room and found her sitting at the table, with the Moor lying motionless before her. He took her joyfully into his arms and thanked her for all that she had done.

"Now go with your maids into the inner room," he said, "and leave me to myself awhile. I have some work to do."

When they were all gone, Aladdin locked the door behind them and, going over to the magician, thrust his hand into the breast of his robe and took out the lamp. Then he drew his sword and cut off the Moor's head. Aladdin rubbed the lamp, and at once the jinnee appeared.

"I am here, master, I am here," he said. "What would you have?"

"I order you," Aladdin said, "to lift up this palace and set it down where it stood before, in front of the Sultan's palace in China."

"I hear and obey, my master," the jinnee replied.

Aladdin went in and sat down with his wife. Meanwhile, the jinnee carried the palace and set it down on its former site, in front of the Sultan's palace. Aladdin ordered the maids to bring the table, and he and the Princess feasted and made merry to their hearts' content. Next morning he got up and awakened his wife. The maids came in and dressed the Princess, and Aladdin dressed himself also. The two looked forward eagerly to meeting the Sultan.

As for the Sultan, after setting Aladdin free, he continued to grieve over the loss of his daughter; he passed his days wailing like a woman for her, his one and only child. Every morning, as he left his bed, he would look out toward the spot where Aladdin's palace had been, and weep until his eyes were dry and his eyelids sore. Rising that day as usual, he opened the window and looked out and saw before him a building. He rubbed his eyes and stared intently at it, until he had no doubt that it was Aladdin's palace. He at once called for his horse and rode over to his son-in-law's dwelling.

When Aladdin saw him approaching he went down and met him in the middle of the square. Taking him by the hand, he led him up to the Princess' room. Badr-al-Budur was overjoyed at her father's arrival. The Sultan caught his daughter in his arms, and the two mingled their joyful tears together. Then he asked her how she was and what had happened to her.

"Father," she replied, "my spirits did not revive until yesterday, when I saw my husband. He rescued me from a vile Moorish magician. Had it not been for Aladdin I would never have escaped from him, nor would you have seen me again in all your life. I had been pining with grief, not only because I was taken away from you, but also because I was separated from my husband. I shall ever be bound to him in gratitude for delivering me from that wicked enchanter."

The Princess related to the Sultan all that happened.

"If you doubt our story, Your Majesty," added Aladdin, "come along and look at the magician's body."

The Sultan followed Aladdin into the apartment and saw the corpse. He ordered his men to take it out and burn it and scatter the ashes to the winds.

"Forgive me, my son," he said to Aladdin, "for the injustice I have done you. I may well be excused for what I did, for I thought I had lost my only daughter, who is dearer to me than all my kingdom. You know the great love parents bear their children; mine is greater still, for I have none besides Badr-al-Budur."

"Great Sultan," Aladdin replied, "you have done me no wrong, nor have I offended against Your Majesty. It was all the fault of that wicked magician."

The Sultan ordered the city to be decorated. The streets were gaily decked, and a month of celebrations was observed in all the kingdom, to mark the return of Badr-al-Budur and her husband.

Nevertheless, Aladdin was not yet entirely safe from danger, although the magician's body had been burned and its ashes scattered to the winds. The detestable fellow had a brother viler than himself, and as skilled in magic and divination. As the proverb has it, they were as like as the two halves of a split pea. Each dwelt in a different corner of the earth and filled it with his witchcraft, guile, and malice.

Now, it chanced that one day this magician wished to know what had become of his brother. He therefore cast the sand, marked out the figures, and scanned them carefully. He learned to his dismay that his brother was dead. He cast the sand a second time, to see how he had died and where. He discovered that he had died a hideous death in a palace in China at the hands of a youth called Aladdin. Thereupon he rose and made ready for a journey. He traveled over deserts and plains and mountains for many months until he arrived in China and entered the capital where Aladdin lived. There he put up at the foreigners' inn and, after resting a little,

went down to walk about the streets in search of some
means to avenge his brother's death. Presently he came to a
coffee shop in the market. It was a large place and many
people were gathered there, some playing backgammon and
others chess. He sat at one of the tables and heard those next
to him talk of a saintly woman called Fatimah who practiced her devotions in a cell outside the town and came to
the city only twice a month. She was renowned for her
healing powers.

"Now I have found what I was looking for," said the
magician to himself. "By means of this woman I will carry
out my design."

Then, turning to the people who were praising her virtues, he said to one of them, "Good sir, who is this holy
woman, and where does she live?"

"Why, man," his neighbor cried, "who has not heard
of Mistress Fatimah's miracles? It is evident you are a
stranger here, never to have heard of her piety, her long
fasts, and her religious exercises."

"You are right, sir, I am a stranger," said the magician.
"I arrived in your city only last night. Pray tell me about
the miracles of this good woman and where she lives. I have
been down on my luck lately, and wish to go to her and
seek her prayers, so that I may find comfort in them."

The man told him of the miracles of Holy Fatimah and
her saintliness. Then he took him by the hand and showed
him the way to her dwelling in a cave at the top of a little
mountain. The magician thanked the man for the trouble he
had taken, and then returned to his lodgings.

As chance would have it, the following day Fatimah
herself came down to the city. The magician left his lodgings in the morning and noticed the people crowding in the
street. He went up to inquire the cause of the hubbub, and
found the hermit standing in their midst. All the sick and

The passengers went ashore and set to work to light a fire. Some busied themselves with cooking and washing, some fell to eating and drinking and making merry, while others, like myself, set out to explore the island.

ailing thronged about her, asking for her blessings and her prayers. As soon as she touched them they were cured. The magician followed her about until she returned to her cave, and then waited for nightfall. When evening came he entered a wine shop, drank a glass of liquor, and made his way to Holy Fatimah's cell. He found her fast asleep, lying on her back on a piece of matting. He stole toward her without a sound, sat on her stomach, and woke her up. She opened her eyes and was terrified to see a stranger crouching over her.

"Listen!" he cried. "If you breathe one syllable or scream I will kill you. So get up and do as you are told." And he swore to her that if she did his bidding he would not harm her. Then he rose and helped her to her feet.

"First," he said, "take my clothes and give me yours." She gave him her clothes, together with her headdress, shawl, and veil.

"Now," said the magician, "you must stain me with some ointment to make my face the same color as yours."

The old woman went to a corner and fetched a jar of ointment; she took some in the palm of her hand and rubbed his face with it until its color became like hers. She also gave him her staff and taught him how to walk with it, and what to do when he went down to the city. Finally she placed her beads around his neck and handed him a mirror.

"Look," she said. "There is not the slightest difference now between us."

The magician looked into the mirror and saw that he was indeed her very image. Having gained his objective, he now broke his oath and slew the poor old woman. In the morning he made his way to the city and stood in front of Aladdin's palace. The people gathered around him, taking him for Holy Fatimah. He did all the things she used to do; he laid his hand on the sick and ailing and recited hymns and prayers for them. Hearing the noise, the Princess ordered one of the servants to find out what was going on. He went to look and presently returned.

"Mistress," he said, "it is Holy Fatimah, curing people by her touch. If it is your wish, I will call her in, so that you may receive her blessing."

"Go and bring her to me," said the Princess. "I have heard tell of her miracles and virtues and would much like to see her."

The servant brought in the magician, disguised in Fatimah's clothes. On coming to the Princess he offered up a long prayer for her continued health, and no one doubted that he was the saint herself. The Princess got up to receive him; she greeted him and made him sit down beside her. "Mistress Fatimah," she said, "I wish you to stay with me always, so that I may obtain your blessing and follow your example in the ways of piety and goodness."

This invitation was the very thing the magician wanted. But to complete his deception, he said, "I am a poor woman, my lady. I pass my days in a solitary cave. Hermits like myself are not fitted to live in a palace."

"Do not worry about that," the Princess replied. "I will give you a room of your own in my house, where you can worship undisturbed."

"I am in duty bound to obey you, my lady," said the magician. "Only I beg you to let me eat and drink and sit in my room by myself, with no one to intrude on me." He requested this for fear he should lift his veil while eating and expose his plot.

"Fear nothing, Mistress Fatimah," said the Princess. "It shall be as you wish. Get up now, and I will show you your room." She led the disguised magician to the place she had assigned for the holy woman's use.

"Mistress Fatimah," she said, "this room is yours alone. Here you will live in peace and quiet."

The magician thanked her for her kindness and called down blessings upon her. The Princess then showed him the jeweled dome with its four and twenty windows, and asked him what he thought of it.

"It is truly beautiful, my daughter," the magician replied. "There cannot be another place like it in the whole world. Yet I can see that it lacks one thing."

"And what may that be, Mistress Fatimah?" asked the Princess.

"The egg of a bird called the roc," said the magician. "If that were hung from the middle of the dome, this hall would be the wonder of the world."

"What is this bird," asked the Princess, "and where can its egg be found?"

"It is a huge bird, my lady," the villain replied. "Its strength and size are such that it can carry camels and elephants in its claws and fly with them. This bird is mostly found in the Mountain of Kaf. The builder who constructed this palace can bring you one of its eggs."

It was now lunchtime. The slave girls laid the table, and the Princess invited her guest to eat with her. The magician, however, declined. He retired to his own room, where he ate by himself.

In the evening, Aladdin came home. Finding his wife thoughtful and anxious, he asked her the cause in some alarm.

"It is nothing at all, dearest," she answered. "I always thought there was nothing missing or deficient in our palace. Yet . . . if only a roc's egg were hung from the jeweled dome of the hall, our palace would be unrivaled in the world."

"If that is all," Aladdin replied, "there is nothing

simpler. Cheer up, my sweet. Just name the thing you fancy and I will bring it to you upon the instant, even if it be hidden in the darkest caverns of the earth."

Leaving his wife, Aladdin went into his room, took out the lamp, and rubbed it; and at once the jinnee appeared before him, saying, "Ask what you will!"

"I wish you to bring me a roc's egg," said Aladdin, "and to hang it in the dome of the palace."

But the jinnee scowled on hearing these words.

"Ungrateful human," he roared. "Are you not content to have me and all the other slaves of the lamp at your beck and call? Must you also command me to bring you the sacred egg of our mistress and hang it in the dome of the palace for your amusement? By heaven, you and your wife deserve to be burned alive this instant. But as you are both ignorant of this offense and have no knowledge of its consequences, I forgive you. You are not to blame. The real offender is that wicked magician, the Moor's brother, who is now staying in your palace disguised as Holy Fatimah. He put on her clothes and killed her in her cave, then he came here to avenge his brother's death. It was he who prompted your wife to make this request."

And so saying, the jinnee vanished.

Aladdin was thunderstruck when he heard this, and all his limbs trembled with fear. But he soon recovered himself, thought of a plan, and went back to his wife, saying that his head ached; for he knew that the holy woman was renowned for her healing powers. The Princess sent at once for Fatimah, so that she might lay her hand on his head.

"Fatimah will soon cure you of your pain," she said, and told him that she had invited the saintly woman to stay with her in the palace.

Presently the magician came in; Aladdin rose to receive him and, pretending to know nothing of his intent, welcomed him as he might have welcomed the holy woman herself.

"Mistress Fatimah," he said, "I beg you to do me a kindness. I have long heard of your great skill in curing ailments. Now I have a violent pain in my head."

The magician could scarcely believe his ears, for he wished for nothing better. He came near and, laying one hand on Aladdin's head, stretched the other under his robe and drew out his dagger to kill him. But Aladdin was on his guard; he caught him by the wrist, wrenched the weapon from him, and thrust it into his heart.

"Oh, what a woeful crime!" exclaimed the terrified Princess. "Have you no fear of heaven to kill Fatimah, this virtuous and saintly woman, whose miracles are the wonder of our time?"

"Know then," Aladdin replied, "that the villain whom I have killed was not Fatimah but the man who murdered her. This is the brother of the Moorish magician who carried you off by his magic to Africa. He came to this country and thought of this trick. He murdered the old woman, disguised himself in her habit, and came here to avenge his brother's death on me. It was he who incited you to ask for a roc's egg, for that was a sure way to destroy me. If you doubt my words, come and see who it is that I have slain."

Aladdin lifted off the magician's veil, and the Princess saw a man in disguise. At once the truth dawned upon her.

"My love," she said, "this is the second time I have put you in danger of your life."

"Never mind, Badr-al-Budur," Aladdin replied, "I gladly accept whatever befalls me through you."

He took her into his arms and kissed her, and they loved each other more than ever.

At that moment the Sultan arrived. They told him all that had happened and showed him the magician's body.

The Sultan ordered that the corpse be burned and the ashes scattered to the winds, like his brother's.

Aladdin dwelt with the Princess in contentment and joy, and thereafter escaped all dangers. When the Sultan died, Aladdin inherited his throne and reigned justly over the kingdom. All his subjects loved him, and he lived happily with Badr-al-Budur until death overtook them.

The Donkey

Two rogues once saw a simple-looking fellow leading a donkey on the end of a long rope on a deserted road.

"Watch this," said one to the other. "I will take that beast and make a fool of its master. Come along and you will see."

He crept up behind the simple fellow without a sound, unfastened the rope from the donkey, and put it around his own neck. He then jogged along in the donkey's place, while his friend made off with the beast.

Suddenly the thief, with the donkey's rope around his neck, stopped in his tracks and would go no farther. The silly fellow, feeling the pull on the rope, looked over his shoulder, and was utterly amazed to find his donkey changed into a human being.

"Who in heaven's name are you?" he cried.

"Sir," the thief replied, "I am your donkey; but my story is quite extraordinary. It all happened one day when I came home very drunk—as I always did. My poor old mother scolded me terribly and begged me to mend my ways. But I took my stick and beat her. In her anger she called down Allah's curse upon me, and I was at once changed into the donkey that has served you faithfully all these years. My mother must have taken pity on me and prayed today to the Almighty to change me back into human shape."

"Good Heavens!" cried the simpleton, who believed every word of the rascal's story. "Please forgive all that I have done to you and all the hardships you put up with in my service."

He let the robber go and returned home, bewildered and upset.

"What has come over you, and where is your donkey?" asked his wife when she saw him.

He told her the strange story.

"Allah will be angry with us," the woman cried, wringing her hands, "for having used a human being so cruelly."

And she fell down on her knees, praying for forgiveness.

For several days afterward the simple fellow stayed idle at home. At last his wife told him to go and buy another donkey, so that he could do some useful work again. He went off to the market, and as he was taking a look at the animals on sale, he was astonished to see his own donkey among them. When he had identified the beast beyond all doubt, he whispered in its ear, "Well, you old scoundrel! Have you been drinking and beating your mother again? Upon my life, I will not buy you *this* time!"

Sindbad the Sailor and Sindbad the Porter

Once upon a time, in the reign of the Caliph Harun al-Rashid, there lived in Baghdad a poor man who earned his living by carrying loads upon his head. He was called Sindbad the Porter.

One day, as he was staggering under a heavy load in the heat of the summer sun, he passed a merchant's house that stood in a pleasant, shaded spot on the roadside. The ground around it was well swept and watered, and, seeing a broad wooden bench just outside the gates, Sindbad put down his load and sat there to rest and to wipe away the sweat that trickled down his forehead. A cool, fresh breeze blew through the doorway, and from within came the melodious strains of a lute and singing voices. They mingled with the songs of pigeons and thrushes, larks and turtledoves.

Filled with great joy, he went up to the open door and saw a courtyard with a beautiful garden, around which stood numerous slaves and servants, and such a crowd of attendants as can be found only in the courts of mighty kings. And all about the place hung the aroma of the choicest meats and wines.

Still marveling at the splendor of the palace, Sindbad

lifted up his burden and was about to go on his way when a handsome and well-dressed little page came to him and took him by the hand, saying, "Please come in; my master wishes to speak with you."

The porter refused very politely, but the boy pressed him to go in. So Sindbad left his load with the doorkeeper and followed the page into the house.

He was led into a magnificent hall, where a distinguished company of nobles was seated according to rank. Before the nobles were tables spread with the richest meats and wines and gaily decked with flowers and fruit. On one side of the hall sat beautiful slave girls who sang and made music; and on the other sat the host, a venerable old man with a long white beard. Bewildered by what he saw, the porter thought to himself, "This must be either a corner of paradise or the palace of some king."

He greeted them all politely, kissed the ground before them, and wished them joy, then stood in silence.

The master of the house welcomed him kindly and asked him to sit down. Then he ordered his slaves to set before him a choice of delicate foods and pressed him to eat. Sindbad pronounced a blessing on the food and fell to. When he had eaten his fill he washed his hands and thanked the old sheikh for his hospitality.

"You are welcome, my friend," said the host, "and may this day bring you joy. We would gladly know your name and calling."

"My name is Sindbad," he answered, "by trade a porter."

"How strange a chance!" said the old man, smiling. "My name, too, is Sindbad. They call me Sindbad the Sailor, and people marvel at my strange history. I will now tell you the story of my seven voyages, and of the hardships I suffered before I rose to my present state and became the lord of this mansion where we are now assembled."

The First Voyage
of Sindbad the Sailor

Know, my friends, that my father was the chief merchant of this city and one of its richest men. He died while I was still a child, leaving me great wealth and many estates and farmlands. As soon as I came to manhood and had control of my inheritance, I took to extravagant living. I wore the most expensive clothes, ate and drank lavishly, and went about with wasteful young men, thinking that this mode of life would last for ever.

It was not long before I woke up to my folly only to find that I had squandered my entire fortune. This made me stop and think, for I did not much like the idea of being poor. So I sold what remained of my lands and household goods and made up my mind to trade with the proceeds in foreign countries.

I bought a large quantity of merchandise and prepared for a long voyage. Then I joined a company of merchants and set sail in a river ship bound for the port of Basra. There we put to sea and voyaged many days and nights from isle to isle and from shore to shore, buying and selling and exchanging goods wherever the ship anchored. At last we came to a little island as beautiful as the garden of Eden.

Here the captain of our ship cast anchor and put out the landing planks.

The passengers went ashore and started to light a fire. Some busied themselves with cooking and washing, some fell to eating and drinking and making merry, while others, like myself, set out to explore the island. While we were thus occupied we suddenly heard the captain cry out to us from the ship, "All aboard, quickly! Abandon everything and run for your lives! The mercy of Allah be upon you, for this is no island but a gigantic whale floating on the bosom of the sea, on whose back the sands have settled and trees have grown since the world was young! When you lit the fire the whale felt the heat and moved. Hurry, I say, or soon it will plunge into the sea and you will all be lost!"

Hearing the captain's cries, the passengers made for the ship in panic-stricken flight, leaving behind their cooking pots and other belongings. Some reached the ship in safety, but others did not, for suddenly the island shook beneath our feet and dived with all that stood upon it to the bottom of the ocean.

Together with my luckless companions, I was swallowed up by the tide, but Providence came to my aid, casting in my way a large wooden trough that had been used by the ship's company for washing. I held fast to the trough and paddled away with my feet as the waves tossed and buffeted me on every side. Meanwhile the captain hoisted sail and set off with the other passengers. I followed the ship with my eyes until it vanished from sight, and resigned myself to certain death.

Darkness soon closed in upon the ocean. All that night and throughout the following day I drifted on, lashed by the wind and the waves, until the trough brought me to the steep shores of a densely wooded island, where trees hung over the sea.

I caught hold of one of the branches and used it to scramble ashore. Arriving on dry land, after fighting so long for my life, I found that I had lost the use of my legs, and my feet began to smart from the bites of fish.

Tired and aching all over, I sank into a deathlike sleep, and it was not until the next morning when the sun rose that I came to my senses. But my feet were so sore and swollen that I could move about only by crawling on my knees. By good fortune, the island had many fruit trees, which provided me with food, and springs of fresh water, so that after a few days my body was restored to strength and my spirits revived. I cut myself a stick from the branch of a tree, and with the help of it set out to explore the island and to admire the fine plants that grew there.

One day, while roaming over the beach in an unfamiliar part of the island, I caught sight of a strange object in the distance that appeared to be some wild beast or sea monster. Drawing near and looking at it more closely, I saw that it was a noble mare of uncommonly high stature, tied to a tree. On seeing me, the mare gave an ear-splitting neigh that made me take to my heels in terror. Presently there emerged from under the ground a man, who pursued me, shouting, "Who are you and where have you come from? What are you doing here?"

"Sir," I replied, "I am a luckless voyager, abandoned in the middle of the sea; but it was Allah's will that I should be rescued from the fury of the waves and cast upon this island."

The stranger took me by the hand and led me to an underground cave, where he placed some food before me and invited me to eat. He then asked about the fortunes of my voyage, and I related to him all that had befallen me.

"Now, what brings *you* here?" I asked my host.

"I am one of the many grooms of King Mahrajan," he

replied. "We have charge of all his horses, and every month we bring them to pasture in this meadow. This evening, when we have finished our work, I will take you to our King and show you our city. Allah be praised for this happy meeting; for had you not chanced to cross our path you would have surely died in the solitude of these wild parts."

I thanked him and called down blessings upon him. We went out of the cave into the open, and while we were talking, the other grooms, each leading a horse, approached us. My companion explained to them how I had come to be there, and after exchanging greetings we rode to the city of King Mahrajan.

As soon as the King was informed of my arrival he summoned me to his presence. He marveled at my story, saying, "By Allah, my son, your escape was a miracle."

I rose rapidly in the King's favor and soon became a trusted courtier. He vested me with robes of honor and appointed me Registrar of Shipping at the port of his kingdom. During my stay I saw many marvels and met travelers from different foreign lands. One day I entered the King's throne room and found him entertaining a company of Indians. I exchanged greetings with them and asked them about their country.

In the course of the conversation I learned that there were several castes in India. The noblest of them were skilled breeders of horses and cattle and were known for their piety and fair dealing.

Not far from the King's dominions there is a desert island where at night is heard a mysterious beating of drums and rattle of tambourines. It was there that I once saw a fish two hundred cubits in length, and another with a head resembling an owl's. This I saw with my own eyes, and many other things no less strange and wondrous.

Whenever I walked along the quay I talked with the sailors and travelers from far countries, asking whether any of them had heard tell of the city of Baghdad and how far off it lay, for I never lost hope that I would one day find my way back to my native land. But there was none who knew of that city, and as the days passed away my longing for home weighed heavily on my heart.

One day, however, as I stood on the wharf, leaning on my stick and gazing out to sea, a ship bearing a large company of merchants came sailing into the harbor. As soon as it was moored, the sails were furled and landing planks put out. The crew began to unload the cargo, and I stood by, entering up the merchandise in my register. When they had finished I asked the captain if all the goods had now been brought ashore.

"Sir," he replied, "in the ship's hold I still have a few bales that belonged to a merchant who was drowned at an early stage of our voyage. We will put them up for sale and take the money to his people in Baghdad, the City of Peace."

"What was the merchant's name?" I asked.

"Sindbad," he answered.

I looked more closely into his face and, recognizing him at once, uttered a joyful cry.

"Why, these goods are mine!" I exclaimed. "I am Sindbad, who was left to drown with many others when the great whale plunged into the sea. But the waves cast me onto the shore of this island. I tell you I am the true owner of these goods, which are my only possessions in the world."

The captain now recognized me. He marveled at my story and was overjoyed to see me alive. My goods were brought ashore, and I found the bales intact and sealed as I had left them. I selected some of the choicest and most precious articles as presents for King Mahrajan, and had them carried by the sailors to the royal palace, where I laid them at his feet. I told the King of the sudden arrival of my ship and the recovery of all my goods. He was astonished at this chance, and in return for my presents bestowed upon me priceless treasures.

I sold my wares at a substantial profit and re-equipped myself with the finest produce of that island. When all was ready for the homeward voyage, I presented myself at the King's court and thanked him for the many favors he had shown me, and he gave me leave to return to my land and people.

Then we set sail, and after voyaging for many days and nights arrived safely in Basra. I spent only a few days in that town and then, loaded with treasure, set out for Baghdad. I was overjoyed to be back in my native city and, hastening to my old street, entered my own house, where, by and by, my friends and kinsmen came to greet me.

I bought fine houses and rich farmlands, serving girls and African slaves, and became richer than I had ever been before. I kept open house for my old companions and, soon forgetting the hardships of my voyage, resumed my former mode of living.

That is the story of the first of my adventures. Tomorrow, if Allah wills, I will relate to you the tale of my second voyage.

The day was drawing to its close, and Sindbad the Sailor invited Sindbad the Porter to join the guests in the evening meal. When the feast was finished he gave him a hundred pieces of gold, saying, "You have delighted us with your company today."

The porter thanked him for his generous gift and departed, marveling at all he had heard.

Next morning he went again to the house of the old sheikh, who received him courteously and seated him by his side. Presently the other guests arrived, and when they had feasted and made merry, Sindbad the Sailor began:

The Second Voyage
of Sindbad the Sailor

For some time after my return from my first voyage I continued to lead a free and easy life, but I soon longed to travel again about the world and to visit distant cities and islands in quest of profit and adventure. So I bought a great quantity of goods, made preparations for a new voyage, and sailed down the river Tigris to Basra. There I joined a band of merchants and embarked in a fine vessel that set sail the same day.

Helped by a favorable wind, we voyaged for many days from port to port and from island to island; and wherever we cast anchor we sold and bartered our goods, and haggled with officials and merchants. At last our ship reached the shores of an uninhabited island, rich in fruit and flowers, and echoing with the singing of birds and the murmur of crystal streams.

Here passengers and crew went ashore, and we all set off to enjoy the delights of the island. I strolled through the green meadows, leaving my companions far behind, and sat down in a shady thicket to eat a simple meal by a spring. Lulled by the soft and fragrant breeze that blew around me, I lay upon the grass and presently fell asleep.

I cannot tell how long I slept, but when I woke I saw none of my companions and feared the ship had left. I ran in frantic haste toward the sea, and on reaching the shore saw the vessel, a white speck upon the vast blue ocean, dissolving into the far horizon.

Broken with terror and despair, I threw myself upon the sand, crying, "Now your end has come, Sindbad! The jar that drops a second time is sure to break!" I repented my folly in venturing again upon the perils of the sea, and wished with all my heart that I had stayed safe at home. I wandered about aimlessly for some time, and then climbed into a tall tree. From the top I gazed in all directions, but could see nothing except the sky, the trees, the birds, the sands, and the boundless ocean. As I scanned the interior of the island more closely, however, I gradually became aware of a white object looming in the distance. At once I climbed down the tree and made my way toward it. Drawing near, I found to my astonishment it was a white dome of extraordinary size. Walking all around it, I could see no door or entrance of any kind; and so smooth and slippery was its surface that any attempt to climb it would have been fruitless. I made a mark in the sand near its base, walked around it again, and found that its circumference measured more than fifty paces.

While I was doing this, the sun was suddenly hidden from my view as by a great cloud and the world grew dark around me. I lifted up my eyes toward the sky and was confounded to see a gigantic bird with enormous wings, which, as it flew through the air, screened the sun, hiding it from the island.

This strange sight instantly brought back to my mind a story I had heard in my youth from pilgrims and adventurers: how in a far island dwelt a bird of monstrous size called the roc, which fed its young on elephants; and at once I realized that the white dome was none other than a roc's egg. In a twinkling, the bird alighted upon the egg, covered it completely with its wings, and stretched out its legs behind it on the ground. And in this posture it went to sleep.

Rising swiftly, I unwound my turban from my head, then doubled it and twisted it into a rope with which I tied myself securely to one of the great talons of the monster.

"It may be," I said to myself, "that this bird will carry me away to a civilized land; wherever I am set down, it will surely be better than an uninhabited island."

I lay awake all night, fearing to close my eyes lest the bird should fly away with me while I slept. At daybreak the roc rose from the egg and, spreading its wings, took to the air with a terrible cry. I clung fast to its talon as it winged its flight through the void and soared higher and higher until it almost touched the sky. After some time it began to drop and, floating swiftly downward, came to earth on the brow of a steep hill.

In great fear I hastened to untie my turban before the roc became aware of my presence. Scarcely had I released myself when the monster darted off toward a great black object lying near, clutched it in its claws, and took wing again. As it rose in the air I saw that this was a serpent of immeasurable length; and with its prey the bird vanished from sight.

Now to find out where I was! I was looking out over an exceedingly deep and wide valley. On all sides there were rocky mountains whose towering summits no man could ever climb. I was stricken with fear and repented my rashness.

"If only I had stayed on that island!" I thought to myself. "There at least I lacked neither fruit nor water, while these barren rocks offer nothing to eat or drink. I have indeed come into worse misfortune."

On making my way down the hill I marveled to see that the ground was thickly covered with the rarest diamonds, so that the entire valley was bathed in a glorious light. But crawling among the glittering stones were deadly snakes and vipers, dread keepers of the fabulous treasure. Thicker and longer than giant palm trees, they could have swallowed whole elephants at one gulp. They were returning to their sunless dens, for by day they hid themselves from their enemies the rocs and the eagles, and moved about only at night.

Half crazed with terror, I roamed the valley all day searching for a shelter where I might pass the night. At dusk I crawled into a narrow-mouthed cave and blocked its entrance with a great stone. At daybreak I rolled back the stone and went out of my hiding place.

As I walked about I noticed a great piece of flesh come tumbling down into the valley from rock to rock. On examining it, I found it to be a whole sheep, skinned and drawn. I was deeply puzzled by the mystery, for there was not a soul in sight; but at that moment there flashed across my mind the memory of a story I had once heard from travelers who had visited the Diamond Mountains—how men obtained the diamonds from this remote and treacherous valley by a strange device. Before sunrise they would throw whole carcasses of sheep from the top of the mountains, so that the gems on which they fell cut through the soft flesh and became embedded in it. At midday rocs and mighty vultures would swoop down upon the mutton and carry it away in their talons toward their nests in the mountain heights. Shouting loudly, the merchants would then rush at the birds and force them to drop the meat and fly away, after which all that remained was for them to look through the carcasses and pick out the diamonds.

As I recalled this story, a plan of escape formed in my mind. I selected a great quantity of substantial stones and hid them about me; I filled my pockets with them and pressed them into the folds of my belt and garments. Then I unrolled my turban, stuffed it with more diamonds, twisted it into a rope as I had done before and, lying under the carcass, tied it firmly to my chest. I had not remained long in that position when I suddenly felt myself lifted from the ground by a huge vulture whose talons had tightly closed upon the meat. The bird climbed higher and higher and finally alighted upon a mountaintop. As soon as it began to tear at the flesh there arose from the nearby rocks a hue and cry, at which the bird took fright and flew away. At once I freed myself and sprang to my feet.

A man came running to the spot and stopped in alarm as he saw me. Without uttering a word, he cautiously bent over the carcass to examine it, looking at me suspiciously all the while, but, finding no diamonds, he wrung his hands and started back in fear.

"Who are you?" he cried. "And what are you doing here?"

"Do not be alarmed, sir," I replied. "I am no thief but an honest man, a merchant by profession. My story is very strange, and the adventure that has brought me to these mountains is more extraordinary than all the marvels men have seen or heard. But first, please accept some of these diamonds, which I myself gathered in the fearful valley below."

I took some splendid jewels from my pocket and offered them to him, saying, "These will bring you all the riches you can desire."

The merchant was overjoyed at the unexpected gift; he thanked me warmly and called down blessings upon me. While we were talking, several other merchants came up from the mountainside. They crowded around us and listened in amazement to my story. Then they led me to their tent. They gave me food and drink, and I slept soundly for many hours. Early next day, we set out from our tent and, journeying over a vast range of mountains, came at last to the seashore. After a short voyage we arrived at a pleasant, densely wooded island, covered with trees so huge that beneath only one of them a hundred men could shelter from the sun.

There I saw a gigantic beast called the karkadan, or rhinoceros, which grazes in the fields like a cow or buffalo. It is as big as a camel and has a single horn in the middle of its forehead. The rhinoceros attacks the elephant, impales it upon its horn, and carries it aloft from place to place until its victim dies. Before long, however, the elephant's fat melts in the heat of the sun and, dripping down into the rhinoceros' eyes, blinds it, so that the beast blunders helplessly along and finally drops dead. Then the roc swoops down upon both animals and carries them off to its nest in the high mountains. I also saw many strange breeds in that island.

I sold several of my diamonds for a large sum and exchanged more for a vast quantity of merchandise. Then we set sail and traded from port to port and from island to island, at last arriving safely in Basra. After a few days I set out for Baghdad, the City of Peace.

Loaded with precious goods and the finest of my diamonds, I hastened to my old street and entered my own house, rejoicing to see my friends and kinsfolk. I gave them gold and presents, and distributed a large sum among the poor of the city.

Soon I forgot the perils and hardships of my travels, and took again to extravagant living. I ate well, dressed well, and kept open house for innumerable gallants and merry companions.

From far and near, men came to hear me speak of my

Rising swiftly, I unwound my turban from my head, then doubled it and twisted it into a rope with which I securely tied myself to one of the great talons of the monster.

adventures and to learn from me the news of foreign lands. All were astounded at the dangers I had escaped and wished me joy of my return. Such was my second voyage.

Tomorrow, my friends, if Allah wills, I shall relate to you the extraordinary tale of my third voyage.

The famous mariner stopped speaking, and the guests marveled at his story.

When the evening feast was over, Sindbad the Sailor gave Sindbad the Porter a hundred pieces of gold, which he took with thanks and blessings, and departed, lost in wonderment at all he had heard.

Next day the porter rose and, after reciting his morning prayers, went to the house of his illustrious friend, who received him kindly and seated him by his side. And when all the guests were gathered, Sindbad the Sailor began:

The Third Voyage
of Sindbad the Sailor

Know, my friends, that for some years after my return to
Baghdad my life was happy and tranquil. But I grew weary
of my idleness and once again longed to roam the world in
search of fresh adventures. Forgetting all I had been
through, I resolved to set out on another voyage. I bought
some more goods, took them down the river Tigris, and set
sail from Basra with a band of honest merchants.

We called at many foreign ports and traded profitably
with our merchandise. One day, however, while we were
sailing in mid-ocean, we heard the captain of our ship, who
was on deck scanning the horizon, suddenly break into a
loud lament. He beat himself about the face, tore at his
beard, and rent his clothes.

"We are lost!" he cried, as we crowded around him.
"The treacherous wind has driven us off our course toward
that island which you see before you. It is the Isle of Zughb,
where dwell a race of dwarfs more akin to apes than men.
No voyager has ever escaped alive from their clutches!"

Scarcely had he uttered these words than a multitude of
apelike savages appeared on the beach and swam toward
the ship. In a few moments they were upon us, thick

as a swarm of locusts. Barely two feet in height, they were the ugliest of living creatures, with gleaming yellow eyes and bodies thickly covered with black fur. And so numerous were they that we did not dare to fight them or try to drive them away, lest they should set upon us and kill us to a man by force of numbers.

They scrambled up the masts, gnawed the cables with their teeth, and bit them to shreds. Then they seized the helm and steered the vessel to their island. When the ship had run ashore, the dwarfs carried us one by one to the beach and, promptly pushing off again, climbed on board and sailed away.

We set out to search for food and water and by good fortune came upon some fruit trees and a running stream. Here we refreshed ourselves, and then wandered about the island until at length we sighted among the trees a massive building, where we hoped to pass the night in safety. Drawing near, we found that it was a towering palace surrounded by a high wall, with a great ebony door, which stood open. We entered the spacious courtyard, but saw no one there. In one corner lay a great heap of bones, and on the far side were a broad bench, an open oven, pots and pans of enormous size, and many iron spits for roasting.

Exhausted and sick at heart, we lay down in the courtyard and went to sleep. At sunset we were awakened by a noise like thunder. The earth shook beneath our feet and we saw a colossal black giant approaching from the doorway. He was a fearsome sight—tall as a palm tree, with red eyes burning in his head like coals of fire; his mouth was a dark well, with lips that drooped, like a camel's, loosely over his chest, while his ears, like a pair of large round disks, hung back over his shoulders; his fangs were as long as the tusks of a boar, and his nails were like the claws of a lion.

The sight of this monster struck terror into our hearts,

We cowered motionless on the ground as we watched him stride across the yard and sit down on the bench. For a few moments he looked at us one by one in silence; then he got up, reached out toward me, lifted me up by the neck, and began feeling my body as a butcher would a lamb. Finding me little more than skin and bone, he flung me to the ground and, picking up each of my companions in turn, pinched and prodded them and set them down until at last he came to the captain.

Now, the captain was a well-built fellow, tall and broad-shouldered. The giant gripped him as a butcher grips a fatted ram, thrust an iron spit through him, and, lighting the fire in the oven, carefully turned him around and around before it until he was well cooked, and then ate him. After he had finished his meal, the ogre went to sleep on the bench and his snores were as loud as the grunts of a wild bull. When morning came, he rose and went out of the palace, leaving us half crazed with terror.

As soon as we were certain that the monster had gone, we began lamenting our evil fortune and wished we had been drowned in the sea or killed by the apes. We left the palace to search for some hiding place, but could find no shelter in any part of the island and had no choice but to return to the palace in the evening. Night came, and with it the black giant, announcing his approach with a noise like thunder. He snatched up one of the merchants and prepared his supper as on the night before; then, stretching himself out to sleep, he snored the night away.

Next morning, when the giant had gone, we discussed our desperate plight.

"By Allah," cried one of the merchants, "let us rather throw ourselves into the sea than remain alive to be roasted and eaten!"

"Listen, my friends," said another, "we must kill this

monster, for only by destroying him can we end his wickedness and save good men from his cruelty."

These words were received with general approval: so I
got up in turn and addressed the company.

"If we are all agreed to kill this monster," I said, "let us
first build a raft on which we can escape if our plot miscar-
ries. Maybe our raft will take us to some other island, where
we can board a ship bound for our country. If we are
drowned, we shall at least escape roasting and die a martyr's
death."

"By Allah," cried the others, "that is a wise plan."

So we set to work at once. We hauled several logs
from the great pile of wood stacked beside the oven, and
carried them out of the palace. Then we fastened them together into a raft, which we left ready on the seashore.

In the evening, the earth shook beneath us as the black
giant burst into the yard, barking and snarling like a mad
dog. Once more he seized upon the stoutest of my companions and prepared his meal. When he had eaten his fill, he
lay down on the bench, as was his custom, and went to
sleep.

Noiselessly we now rose, took two of the great iron
spits from the oven, and thrust them into the fire. As soon
as they were red-hot we carried them over to the snoring
monster and plunged their ends into his eyes. He gave a
deafening shriek that cast us back onto the ground many
yards away. Then he leaped up from the bench and groped
for us with outstretched hands, but, as he could not see where
we were, we managed to get out of the palace and made off
toward the beach. As soon as we reached the water we
launched our raft and jumped on board; but scarcely had we
rowed a few yards when we saw the blind savage running
toward us, guided by a female of his own kind. On reaching
the shore they stood howling at us for a while, and then

caught up massive boulders and hurled them at our raft with stupendous force. Missile followed missile until all but two of my companions were drowned; but we three who escaped soon managed to paddle beyond the range of the flying boulders.

Lashed by the waves, we drifted on in the open sea for a whole day and a whole night until we were cast upon the shore of another island. Half dead with hunger and exhaustion, we threw ourselves upon the sand and fell asleep.

On awaking next morning, we found ourselves encircled by a great serpent, which lay about us in a coil. Before we could move a limb the beast suddenly lifted its head, seized one of my companions, and swallowed him. Presently, however, the serpent glided away, leaving us two stricken with grief at the horrible fate of our comrade and amazed at our own narrow escape.

"By Allah," we cried, "we have fled from one form of death only to meet with another equally hideous. How shall we escape this serpent? There is no strength or help except in Allah!"

The warmth of the newborn day gave us fresh courage, and we struck inland to search for food and water. Before nightfall we climbed into a tall tree and perched ourselves as best we could upon the topmost branches. But as soon as darkness fell we heard a fearful hissing and a noise of heavy movement on the ground; and in a twinkling the serpent had seized my friend and carried him off. That was the end of the last of my companions.

At daybreak I climbed down from my hiding place. My first thought was to throw myself into the sea and thus end a life that had already endured more than its share of hardships and ordeals. But when I reached the shore my courage failed me, for life is very precious. I clung instinctively to the hope of a speedy rescue, and a plan to protect myself from the serpent began to form in my mind.

I collected some thick planks of wood and fastened them together into a coffin-shaped box, complete with lid. When evening came I shut myself in, shielded on all sides by strong boards. By and by the snake approached and circled around me, writhing and squirming. All night long its dreadful hissing sounded in my ears, but with the approach of morning it turned away and vanished into the undergrowth.

When the sun rose, I left my shelter and made for the shore. What should I now see but a ship sailing near the island!

At once I tore off a great branch from a tree and, yelling at the top of my voice, waved it frantically above my head. The crew must have seen my signal, for to my great joy the ship suddenly turned off its course and headed for the island.

When I came aboard, the captain gave me a clean robe to put on and offered me food and drink. Little by little I regained my strength, and after a few days of rest became my old self again. I rendered thanks to God for rescuing me from my ordeal, and soon my past sufferings were no more than half-forgotten dreams.

After a few days we cast anchor at a small island. On board our ship were some merchants, who now went ashore with their goods to trade with the people. While I was standing idly by, watching the busy scene, the captain came up and spoke to me.

"Listen, my friend," he said, "you say you are a penniless stranger who has lost everything at sea. I will make you an offer that will be greatly to your advantage. A few years ago I carried in my ship a merchant who, alas, was left behind on a desert island. No news has since been heard of him, and no one knows whether he is alive or dead. Take his goods and trade with them, and a share of the profit shall be yours. The remainder of the money I will take back to the merchant's family in Baghdad."

I thanked the captain with all my heart. He ordered the crew to unload the merchandise and called the ship's clerk to enter up the bales in his register.

"Whose property are they?" the clerk asked.

"The owner's name was Sindbad," the captain replied, "but from now on they will be in the charge of this passenger."

A cry of astonishment escaped my lips, and I at once recognized him as the captain of the ship in which I had sailed on my second voyage.

"Why!" I exclaimed. "I am Sindbad, that very merchant who many years ago was left behind on the Island of the Roc. I fell asleep there, and when I awoke I found that the ship had gone. The merchants who saw me on the Diamond Mountains and heard my adventure will bear witness that I am indeed Sindbad."

On hearing mention of the Diamond Mountains, one of the merchants, who by this time had gathered around us, came forward and peered into my face. Then he turned to his friends, crying, "By Allah, this is the man I once met on the Diamond Mountains, after he had been carried up from the valley by a mighty vulture! It was he who presented me with those rare diamonds."

The captain questioned me about the contents of my bales, and I readily gave him an exact description. I also reminded him of a certain incident that had happened during our voyage, and he now recognized me and, taking me in his arms, congratulated me warmly. My goods were brought ashore, and I sold them at a substantial profit. Then we set sail and after a few days came to the land of Sind, where we also traded profitably.

In those Indian waters I saw many marvels. There was a sea monster that resembled a cow and another with a head like a donkey. I also saw a bird that hatches from a sea shell and remains floating on the water all its life.

From Sind we set sail again, and after some weeks came to Basra. I stayed there for a few days and then journeyed upstream to Baghdad, where I was joyfully welcomed by my friends and kinsmen. I gave generously to the poor and to widows and orphans, for I had returned from this voyage richer than ever before.

Tomorrow, my friends, if Allah wills, I shall tell you the story of my fourth voyage, which you will find even more extraordinary than the tales I have already related.

When the evening feast was ended, Sindbad the Sailor gave Sindbad the Porter a hundred pieces of gold, and the company took leave of their host and went their way, marveling at the wonders they had heard.

Next morning the porter returned, and when the other guests had arrived, Sindbad the Sailor began:

The Fourth Voyage
of Sindbad the Sailor

The idle and extravagant life I led after returning to Baghdad did not make me forget the excitement of travel in distant lands. My longing to see the world, despite the dangers I had met, was as strong as ever. At last I yielded to the call of the sea and, making preparations for a long voyage, set sail with merchandise from Basra, in the company of some well-known merchants of that port.

Helped by a favorable wind, we sailed peacefully along, trading from port to port and from island to island. One day a violent tempest suddenly sprang up in mid-ocean, rolling gigantic waves as high as mountains against our ship. We all fell on our knees in prayer and lamentation. The gale tore the sails to ribbons and snapped the mast in two; then a tremendous wave crashed down upon us from above, breaking up the vessel and tossing us all into the raging sea.

I clung fast to a floating beam, together with some of my companions who had also managed to reach it. Now paddling with our hands and feet, now swept by wind and current, we were at length thrown, half dead with cold and weariness, upon the shore of an island.

We lay down on the sand and fell asleep. Next morning we rose and made our way inland, and after a few hours came to a high building among the trees. A number of wild-looking men came out of a door and, without a word, took hold of us and led us into the building. Seated upon a throne was their King.

He ordered us to sit down, and presently his servants set before us dishes of such meat as we had never seen in all our lives. My famished companions, not noticing that the people did not eat of it themselves, devoured the meat greedily; but my own stomach revolted at the sight of the food and, in spite of my hunger, I could not eat a single mouthful. As it turned out, that abstinence saved my life, for as soon as they had swallowed the meat my friends began to lose their intelligence and to act like beasts. After a few hours of continuous feeding they became little better than savages.

While they were still eating, the natives fetched a pot of ointment, which they rubbed into the bodies of my companions. This brought about an astonishing change in their appearance: their eyes sank into their heads and their stomachs became swollen; and as the swelling increased so did their hunger.

I was horrified at this spectacle. I discovered that these barbarous men were cannibals who fattened their victims before eating them.

Robbed entirely of their human faculties, my changed companions were put into the care of a herdsman, who led them out every day to feed in the meadows. The savages lost all interest in me, for I was reduced to a shadow by hunger and fear, and my skin was soon shriveled upon my bones. One day I slipped out of my prison house and made off across the island. Away on the distant grasslands I met the herdsman with his wretched flock. But instead of chasing me or ordering me to return, he appeared to take pity on my helpless condition, and pointed to the right, as if to say, "Go this way; fear nothing."

I ran on and on across the plains. When evening came I ate some roots and herbs and lay down on the grass to rest, but fear of the cannibals had robbed me of any wish to sleep, and at midnight I was up again and plodding painfully on. After journeying for seven days I came on the morning of the eighth toward the opposite side of the island.

I spotted human figures in the distance, and as I drew nearer found they were a party of peasants gathering pepper in a field. They crowded around me, speaking in my own language, and asked who I was and where I had come from. In reply I gave them the story of my misfortunes, and they were all amazed to hear it. They congratulated me on my escape, offered me food and water, and let me rest until evening. When their day's work was done they took me with them in a boat to their capital, which was on a neighboring island.

I was presented to their King, who received me kindly and listened with astonishment to my story. Their city, I found, was prosperous and densely populated, with many shops and markets. Many people, both rich and poor, owned fine horses, but I was surprised to see that these were ridden bareback.

During my next audience with the King I asked him why his subjects did not use a saddle and stirrups.

"Saddle?" he asked, somewhat puzzled. "What may that be? I have never seen such a thing in all my life."

"In that case, allow me to make one for you," I replied. "Then you may try it and find how comfortable and useful it can be."

The King was pleased at my offer, and at once I looked for a skillful carpenter and instructed him to make a wooden frame for a saddle of my own design. Then I taught a blacksmith to forge a bit and a pair of stirrups. I fitted the frame with a padding of wool and leather and added a girth and tassels. When all was ready, I chose the finest of the royal horses, saddled and bridled it, and led it before the King.

He was delighted with the appearance of the new equipment, and rewarded me with a fine gift and a large sum of money. His vizier saw the saddle and begged me to make one for him. I did so; and it was not long before every courtier and nobleman in the kingdom owned a handsome saddle.

My skill soon made me the richest man on the island. The King showered honors upon me and I became a trusted courtier.

One day, as we sat chatting together in his palace, he said, "You must know, Sindbad, that we have come to love you like a brother; we cannot bear the thought that you might someday leave our kingdom. Therefore we will ask a favor of you, which we hope you will not refuse."

"God forbid," I replied, "that I should refuse you anything, Your Majesty."

"We wish you to marry a beautiful girl who has been brought up in our court," he said. "She is intelligent and wealthy and will make you an excellent wife. I trust you will settle down happily with her in this city for the rest of your life. Do not refuse me this, I beg you."

I was deeply embarrassed and did not know what to say.

"Why do you not speak, my son?" he asked.

"Your Majesty," I faltered, "it is my duty to obey you."

The King sent at once for a judge and witnesses, and I

was married that day to a rich woman of noble birth. The King gave us a magnificent palace and set aside for us a retinue of slaves and servants.

We lived there happily and contentedly, although in my heart of hearts I always longed to return to my own homeland with my wife, for I loved her dearly. But alas, no man can control his fate.

One day the wife of one of my closest friends died, and I went to his house to offer my condolences. Finding him overcome with grief, I tried to comfort him.

"Allah may soon give you another wife as loving and as worthy as the one he has taken from you," I said. "May he lighten your sorrow and prolong your life!"

But he did not raise his eyes from the ground.

"Alas," he sighed. "How can you wish me a long life when I have only a few hours to live?"

"Courage, my friend," I said. "Why do you speak of death when, thank God, you are in perfect health, sound in mind and body?"

"In a few hours," he replied, "I will be buried with my dead wife. It is an ancient custom in this country. When a wife dies her husband is buried with her, and if he should die first his wife is buried with him. Both must leave this world together."

"By Allah," I cried in horror, "this is a most barbarous custom! How can men of sense allow such cruelty?"

While we were talking, his friends and relations, accompanied by a large crowd, came into the house and began to condole with him on the loss of his wife and his own impending death. Soon the funeral preparations were completed, and the corpse was laid upon a bier. A long procession of mourners, headed by the husband, formed outside the house and set out for the burial ground.

We all halted at the foot of a steep mound overlooking the sea. A stone was rolled away from the mouth of a deep pit, and into this pit the corpse was thrown. The band of mourners then laid hold of my friend and lowered him, by means of a long rope, into the pit, together with seven loaves of bread and a pitcher of water. The stone was rolled back and we all returned to the city.

I hastened with a heavy heart to the King's palace, and when I was admitted to his presence fell on my knees before him, crying, "My noble master, I have visited many far countries and lived among all types of men, but in all my life I have never seen or heard of anything so barbarous as your custom of burying the living with the dead. Are strangers, like myself, obliged to conform to this custom, Your Majesty?"

"Certainly they are," he replied. "They, too, must be buried with their dead wives. It is a time-honored custom that all must observe."

At his reply I hurried home, dreading lest my wife should have died while I was out of the house. Finding her in perfect health, I comforted myself as best I could with the thought that I might one day find a way of returning to my own country, or might even die before my wife.

But things turned out otherwise. Soon afterward my wife was taken ill and in a few days died.

The King and all his courtiers came to my house to comfort me. The body of my wife was perfumed and arrayed in fine robes and rich ornaments. And when all was ready for the burial I was led behind the bier, at the head of a long procession.

We came to the mound. The stone was lifted from the mouth of the pit and the body of my wife thrown in. The mourners gathered around me to say farewell, paying no attention to my cries. They tied me with a long rope and lowered me into the pit, with the customary loaves and a pitcher of water. Then they rolled back the stone and went their way.

When I touched the bottom of the pit I found myself in a vast cavern filled with bones. I threw myself upon the earth, crying, "You deserve this fate, Sindbad! Here you will pay the final penalty for your ambition and greed! Why did you marry on this island? If only you had died on the bare mountains or perished in the sea!"

But the love of life still glowed within me, and after some time I unfastened the loaves and pitcher of water, and ate and drank a little.

For several days I lived on my provisions, and when they were finished I prepared myself to die. I had become resigned to my fate, when one day I heard a sound of movement near by. Springing to my feet, I followed the noise closely until I could faintly see the form of some animal scurrying before me. As I ran in pursuit of the creature, stumbling here and there in the dark, I gradually made out at the far side of the cavern a speck of light that grew larger and brighter as I advanced toward it. When I reached the end of the cave the fleeing animal disappeared. To my great joy, I realized I had come upon a tunnel that the wild beasts had burrowed from the other side of the mound. I scrambled into this tunnel, crawling on all fours, and soon reached the opening. I was at the foot of a high cliff, with the blue sky and the yellow sand before me.

I fell upon my knees in prayer and thanked the Almighty for my escape. The warm and wholesome air breathed new life into my veins. I rejoiced to see again the loveliness of earth and sky.

Strengthened with hope and courage, I made my way

back along the tunnel and gathered up all the jewels, pearls, and precious ornaments that I could find in the cave. These I fastened into bales and carried to the seashore, where I remained scanning the horizon until nightfall. Next morning, as I was sitting beneath a rock, praying for a speedy rescue, I saw a sail far off upon the sea. Hoisting my turban on a stick, I waved it frantically about as I ran up and down the beach. The ship's crew saw my signal and at once sent a boat to fetch me.

"How did you find your way to this wild spot?" asked the captain in astonishment. "I have never seen a living man here in all my days."

"Sir," I replied, "I was shipwrecked off this shore many days ago. These bales are the remnants of my goods that I managed to save." I kept the truth from him lest there should be some on board who were citizens of that island.

From one of my packages I took out a rare pearl and offered it to him. "Please accept this," I said, "as a reward for saving my life."

But the captain politely refused the gift. "It is not our custom," he said, "to accept payment for a good deed. We have rescued many a voyager, fed him and clothed him, and finally set him ashore with a little present of our own besides. Allah alone is the giver of rewards."

I thanked him with all my heart and called down blessings upon him. Then the ship resumed its voyage. As we sailed from island to island and from sea to sea, I eagerly looked forward to seeing my native land again. At times, however, the thought of that terrible cavern would come back to me and make me shudder.

At last we arrived safely in Basra. I stayed there for a few days, then sailed up the river to Baghdad. Loaded with treasure, I hastened to my own house, where I was joyfully welcomed by my friends and relatives. I sold the precious stones for a fabulous sum and gave generously to widows and orphans.

That is the story of my fourth voyage. Tomorrow, if Allah wills, I shall give you an account of my fifth voyage.

After the evening feast, Sindbad the Sailor gave Sindbad the Porter a hundred pieces of gold. The company took leave of their host and went their way, marveling at all they had heard. Next morning the porter returned, and when all the other guests had assembled, Sindbad the Sailor began:

The Fifth Voyage
of Sindbad the Sailor

Know, my friends, that the merry and peaceful life I led after my return soon made me forget my sufferings in the Land of the Cannibals and in the Cavern of the Dead. I remembered only the pleasures of adventure and the considerable gains that my travels had earned me, and once again longed to sail new seas and explore new lands. So I equipped myself with goods suitable for selling in foreign countries, packed them up in bales, and took them to Basra.

One day I saw from the wharf a newly built ship with tall masts and fine sails that caught my fancy. I bought her outright and filled her with my merchandise. Then I hired an experienced captain and a well-trained crew, and accepted as passengers several other merchants who offered to pay their passages in advance.

Blessed with a favorable wind, we voyaged many days and nights, trading from sea to sea and from shore to shore, and came at length to a desert island. Here we caught sight of a solitary white dome, half buried in the sand. This I recognized at once as a roc's egg; and the passengers begged leave to land, so as to get a closer look at it.

As ill luck would have it, some of the merchants were

thoughtless enough to throw stones at the egg. When the shell was broken, they decided to have a feast, dragged out the young bird, and cut it up in pieces. They returned on board to tell me of their adventure.

I was filled with horror and cried, "We are lost! The parent birds will now pursue our ship and destroy us all!"

Scarcely had I finished speaking when the sun was suddenly hidden from our view as by a great cloud, and the world grew dark around us as the two rocs came flying home. On finding their egg broken and their young one destroyed, they uttered deafening cries, took to the air again, and soon vanished from sight.

"All aboard, quickly!" I shouted. "We must flee from this island at once."

The captain weighed anchor and with all speed we sailed toward the open sea. But before long the world grew dark again, and in the ominous twilight we could see the gigantic birds hovering overhead, each carrying in its talons an enormous rock. When they were directly above us, one of them dropped its load, which narrowly missed the ship and opened such a chasm in the ocean that for a moment we could see the sandy bottom. The waves rose mountain high, tossing us up and down. Presently the other bird dropped its rock and this time hit its mark. Those of us who were not crushed to death were hurled into the sea and swept away by the giant waves.

Through the grace of Allah I managed to cling to a floating piece of wreckage. Sitting astride this, I paddled with my feet and, aided by wind and current, at last reached the shore of an island.

I threw myself upon the sand and lay down for a while to recover my breath. Then I rose and wandered about the island, which was as beautiful as the Garden of Eden. The air was filled with the singing of birds, and wherever I turned, I saw trees loaded with luscious fruit or crystal brooks meandering among banks of flowers. I refreshed myself with the fruit and water and, when evening came, lay down upon the grass.

Early next morning I set off to explore the island. After a long stroll among the trees I came to a little stream. On the bank sat a gray-haired old man. His body was covered with a cloak of leaves.

Taking him for a shipwrecked voyager like myself, I greeted him in my own language; but he replied only with a mournful nod. When I asked him how he came to be there, instead of answering he begged me with signs to take him upon my shoulder and carry him across the brook. I readily bent down, lifted him upon my back, and waded through the stream. On reaching the opposite bank I stooped again for him to get off; but instead of alighting, the old wretch powerfully threw his legs, which I now saw were covered with a rough black skin like a buffalo's, around my neck and crossed them tightly over my chest. Seized with fear, I desperately tried to shake him off, but the monster pressed his thighs tighter and tighter around my throat until I could no longer breathe. The world darkened before my eyes and with a choking cry I dropped unconscious to the ground.

When I came to, I found the old monster still crouching upon my shoulders, although he had now sufficiently relaxed his hold to let me breathe. As soon as he saw that I had recovered my senses, he pushed one foot against my belly and, violently kicking my side with the other, forced me to get up and walk under some trees. Leisurely he plucked the fruits and ate them. Every time I halted against his will or failed to do his bidding he kicked me hard, so that I had no choice but to obey him. All day long he remained seated on my shoulders; I was no better than a beast of burden. At night he made me lie down, but never for one moment loosened his hold around my neck. Next morning he roused me with a kick and ordered me to carry him among the trees.

Day after day he stayed glued to my back, driving me pitilessly from glade to glade. I cursed the charitable instinct that had prompted me to help him, and longed for death to deliver me from my evil plight.

After many weeks of miserable slavery I chanced one day to come upon a field where gourds were growing in abundance. I picked up one large gourd, which was sun-dried and empty, cleaned it thoroughly, and squeezed into it the juice of several bunches of grapes; then, carefully stopping the hole that I had cut into its shell, I left the juice in the sun to ferment.

Returning with the old man a few days afterward, I found the gourd filled with the purest wine. The drink gave me new strength, and I began to feel so light and cheerful that I went tripping merrily among the trees, scarcely aware of my hateful burden.

Noticing the effect of the wine, my captor asked me to let him taste it. I did not dare refuse. He took the gourd from my hand, raised it to his lips, and gulped down the liquor to the dregs. Soon, overcome with the wine, he began to sway from side to side, and his legs gradually relaxed their hold around my neck. With one violent jerk of my shoulders I hurled him to the ground, where he lay motionless. Then I quickly picked up a great stone from among the trees and fell upon the fiend with all my strength. That was the end of my tormentor; may Allah have no mercy on him!

Overjoyed at my new freedom, I roamed the island for many weeks, eating of its fruit and drinking from its springs. One day, however, as I sat on the shore thinking about the ups and downs of my life and recalling memories of my native land, I saw, to my great joy, a sail heading toward the island. On reaching land the vessel anchored, and the passengers came ashore to fill their pitchers with water.

I ran in haste to meet them. They were greatly astonished to see me and gathered around, asking who I was and where I came from. I told them all that had befallen me since my arrival, and they replied, "It is a marvel that you have escaped alive, for the monster who crouched on your shoulders was none other than the Old Man of the Sea. Praise be to Allah for your deliverance!"

They took me to their ship. The captain received me kindly and listened with astonishment to my adventure. Then we set sail, and after many days and nights cast anchor in the harbor of a city perched on a high cliff, and known among travelers as the City of Apes on account of the multitude of monkeys that infested it by night.

I went ashore with one of the merchants from the ship and wandered about the town in search of some employment. Soon we fell in with a crowd of men who were on their way to the gates leading out of the city. They had sacks of pebbles on their shoulders. My friend the merchant gave me a large cotton bag and said, "Fill this with pebbles and follow these people into the forest. Do exactly as they do, and thus you will earn your livelihood."

I filled the sack with pebbles and joined the crowd. The merchant recommended me to them, saying, "Here is a shipwrecked stranger; teach him to earn his bread and Allah will reward you."

When we had marched a great distance from the city we came to a vast valley, covered with coconut trees so straight and tall that no man could ever climb them. As we drew nearer I saw among the trees innumerable monkeys. They fled at our approach and swiftly climbed up to the fruit-laden fronds.

My companions now set down their bags and began to pelt the monkeys with pebbles; and I did the same. The tormented animals retaliated by pelting us with coconuts, and these we gathered up and put into our sacks. When they were full we returned to the city and sold the nuts in the market place.

Thereafter I went every day to the forest with the coconut hunters and traded profitably with the fruit. When I had saved enough money for my homeward voyage, I said good-by to my friend the merchant and embarked in a vessel bound for Basra, taking with me a large cargo of coconuts and other produce.

In the course of our voyage we put in at many heathen islands, where I sold some of my coconuts at a substantial profit and exchanged others for cinnamon, pepper, and Chinese aloe. On reaching the Sea of Pearls, I engaged several divers who, in a short time, brought up a large quantity of priceless pearls.

After that we set sail again. Voyaging many days and nights, we arrived at last in Basra. I spent a few days in that town and then, loaded with treasure, set out for Baghdad.

I was glad to be back in my native city. Hastening to my old street, I entered my own house, where all my friends and kinsmen gathered to greet me. I gave them gold and many presents, and distributed a large sum in charity among widows and orphans.

That is the story of my fifth voyage. Tomorrow, my friends, if Allah wills, I shall tell you the tale of my sixth voyage.

The evening feast came to an end. Sindbad the Sailor gave Sindbad the Porter a hundred pieces of gold, and the company departed, marveling at all they had heard. Next morning the porter returned, and when the other guests had arrived, Sindbad the Sailor began:

The Sixth Voyage
of Sindbad the Sailor

One day I was sitting peacefully and comfortably at home, when a band of merchants who had returned from abroad called on me to give me news of foreign lands. At the sight of these travelers I remembered the joy of returning from a far journey to be united with friends and kinsmen after a long absence; and soon afterward I made ready for another voyage and left Basra with a rich cargo.

We sailed many days and nights, buying and selling wherever the ship anchored and exploring the unfamiliar places at which we called. One day, as we were sailing in mid-ocean, we heard a loud cry from the captain. He beat himself about the face, tore at his beard, and hurled his turban onto the deck. We gathered around him, asking what had gone wrong.

"Alas, we are lost!" he cried. "We have been driven off our course into an unknown ocean, where nothing can save us from final wreck but Allah's mercy. Let us pray to him!"

Then, while some passengers fell on their knees praying and others were bidding each other farewell, the captain climbed the mast to trim the sails. Scarcely had he reached the top than we were swept up in a violent squall, which dashed the ship against a craggy shore at the foot of a high cliff. The vessel split to pieces and we were all flung into the raging sea. Some were drowned, while others, like myself, managed to survive by clinging to the jutting rocks.

Scattered all along the shore were the remains of other wrecks, and the sands were strewn with countless bales from which rare merchandise and costly ornaments had broken loose. I wandered among these treasures for many hours and then, winding my way through the rocks, suddenly came upon a river that flowed from a gorge in the mountain. I followed its course with my eyes and was surprised to find that, instead of running into the sea, the river plunged into a vast rocky cavern and disappeared. The banks were covered with jewels, and I could see that the bed was studded with rubies, emeralds, and other precious stones. The entire river glowed with a fiery brilliance.

Meanwhile, the others who had escaped drowning lay in a sad plight on the shore, counting the days as they dragged by and waiting for the approach of death. One by one my companions died as they came to the end of their food, and we who survived buried them. Eventually I was left quite alone.

When I realized that death was near, I lay down on the cold earth and gave myself up to utter despair. "Why," I cried, "oh, why was I not content to be safe and happy in Baghdad? Had I not enough riches to last me twice a lifetime?"

Rousing myself at last, I wandered again to the river. As I watched it plunge into the cavern, I struck upon a plan.

"By Allah," I thought, "this river must have both a beginning and an end. If it enters the mountain on this side, it must somehow emerge into daylight again; and if I could follow its course, the current might in the end bring me to some inhabited land. If I am destined to survive this, Allah will guide me to safety; if I perish, it will not be worse than the miserable fate of starving to death that awaits me here."

Encouraged by these thoughts, I collected a few large branches, laid them on some planks from the wrecked vessels and bound them with some cables into a raft. This I loaded with sacks of rubies, pearls, and other stones; then, commending myself to Allah, I launched the raft upon the water and jumped aboard.

The fast current carried me along, and I soon found myself in the brooding darkness of the cavern. My raft began to bump violently against the jagged sides, while the passage grew smaller and smaller, until I was compelled to lie flat on my stomach for fear of striking my head. It was not long before I was wishing that I could return to the open shore. But the current became faster and faster as the river swept headlong down its channel, and I resigned myself to certain death. Overcome by terror and fatigue, I sank at last into a heavy sleep.

I cannot tell how long I slept, but when I woke I found I was lying on my raft close to the riverbank, under the open sky. The river was flowing gently through a stretch of pleasant meadowland, and on the bank stood Indians and Abyssinians.

As soon as these men saw that I was awake, they gathered about me, asking questions in a language I did not understand. Presently one of them came forward and greeted me in my own tongue.

"Who may you be," he asked, "and where have you come from? We were working in our field when we saw you drifting down the river. We secured your raft to the bank and, not wishing to wake you, left you here in safety. Now tell us, what accident cast you on this river that flows from under the mountain?"

I begged them first to give me some food, and promised

to answer all their questions after I had eaten. They brought me a variety of meats, and when I had regained my strength a little I gave an account of all that had happened to me since my shipwreck. My miraculous escape so astonished them that they insisted on taking me to their King, so that I might tell him of my adventure.

Carrying my raft with all its contents upon their shoulders, they led me to their city. The King received me courteously and listened in profound astonishment to my story. Opening my treasures in his presence, I laid at his feet a priceless choice of emeralds, pearls, and rubies. In return he conferred upon me the highest honors of the kingdom and invited me to stay at the palace as his guest.

I rose rapidly in the King's favor and soon became a trusted courtier. One day he asked me about my country and its far-famed Caliph. I praised the wisdom, piety, and goodness of Harun al-Rashid and spoke at length of his glorious deeds. The King was deeply impressed by my account.

"This monarch," he said, "must indeed be a great man. We desire to send a present worthy of him, and appoint you the bearer."

"I hear and obey," I replied. "I will gladly deliver your gift to the Commander of the Faithful, and will inform him that in Your Majesty he has a worthy ally and a trusted friend."

The King gave orders that a magnificent present be prepared, and a new ship was built for the voyage. When all was ready for departure, I presented myself at the royal palace, thanked the King for the favors he had shown me, and took leave of him and his courtiers.

Then I set sail, and after many days arrived safely in Basra. I hastened to Baghdad with the royal gift, and when I had been admitted to the Caliph's presence I kissed the ground before him and told him of my mission. Al-Rashid marveled at my adventure and gave orders that the story be written on parchment in letters of gold, so that it might be kept among the treasures of the kingdom.

Then I hurried to my old street and entered my own house, where I rejoiced to meet my people. I gave them gold and costly presents, and distributed alms among the poor of the city.

Such is the story of my sixth voyage. Tomorrow, if Allah wills, I shall recount to you the tale of my seventh and last voyage.

When the evening feast was ended, Sindbad the Sailor gave Sindbad the Porter a hundred pieces of gold, and the guests departed, marveling at all they had heard.

Next morning the porter returned, and when the other guests had assembled, Sindbad the Sailor began:

The Last Voyage
of Sindbad the Sailor

For many years after my return I lived happily in Baghdad, feasting with my favorite companions and squandering the riches that my travels had earned me. But though I was now past the prime of life, my spirit was still untamed and once more I longed to see the world and travel in the lands of men. I boarded a good ship in company with some eminent merchants, and set sail with a fair wind and a rich cargo.

We voyaged peacefully for many weeks, but one day, while we were sailing in the China Seas, a violent gale arose. The rain came down in torrents. Quickly we covered our bales with canvas to protect them, while the captain climbed up the mast and scanned the horizon in all directions. After a few moments he came down trembling with fear.

"Pray to Allah," he cried, "that he may deliver us from the peril into which we have fallen! Say your farewells, for the wind has driven us off our course into the world's farthermost seas!"

Opening one of his cabin chests, the captain took from it a small cotton bag filled with an ashlike powder. He sprinkled some water over the powder and inhaled it into his nostrils; then, opening a little book, he intoned some magic charms and turned to us, saying, "Know that we are now approaching the very edge of the world. Here the land teems with serpents of extraordinary size, and the sea is filled with giant whales that can swallow vessels whole. Farewell, my friends; and may Allah have mercy upon us!"

Scarcely had he finished speaking than the ship was tossed high in the air, then flung back into the sea. An ear-splitting cry, more terrible than thunder, boomed through the swelling ocean. Terror seized our hearts as we saw a gigantic whale, as big as a mountain, rush swiftly toward us, followed by another just as big, and a third greater than the two put together. This last monster leaped from the surging waves, opened its enormous mouth, and seized in its jaws the ship with all its contents. I ran quickly to the edge of the tilting deck and, casting off my clothes, jumped into the sea just before the whale swallowed the ship and vanished under the foam with its two companions.

With Allah's help, I clung to a piece of timber that had fallen from the lost vessel and, after struggling with the waves for two days and nights, was thrown upon an island covered with fruit trees and watered by many streams. I wandered aimlessly about the coast and soon came to a fast-flowing river. I hit upon the idea of building a raft and allowing myself to be carried downstream by the current, as I had done on my last voyage. "If I succeed in saving myself this time," I said, "all will be well with me and I solemnly vow never again to let the thought of voyaging enter my mind. If I fail, I shall at least find rest from the troubles and trials that my folly has earned me."

I made the raft by cutting branches from a tree and fastening them together with the stems of creeping plants. I loaded it with fruit and, putting my trust in Allah, pushed off down the river.

For three days and nights the current carried me along

so swiftly that I became weak and dazed, and eventually sank into unconsciousness. When I came to, I found myself heading toward a steep decline down which the waters of the river tumbled in a mighty cataract. I clung with all my strength to the branches of the raft and prayed silently for a merciful end. It was at the very brink of the waterfall that I suddenly felt the raft halted in its course and saw that I was caught in a net that a group of men had thrown from the bank. The raft was quickly hauled to land, and I was released from the net half dead with terror and fatigue.

As I lay on the mud, I gradually became aware of an old man bending over me. He greeted me kindly and wrapped me in warm garments, and when my strength had returned a little he helped me to my feet and led me slowly to the city baths. There I was washed with perfumed water, and then the old man took me to his own house, where I was given an excellent meal. After the feast, slaves washed my hands and wiped them on napkins of silk. In the evening my host conducted me to a beautiful room, ordered several of his slaves to wait upon me, and wished me good night.

The kind old man entertained me in this way for three days. When I was completely recovered he came to see me in my room and sat talking with me for an hour. Just before leaving my room, however, he turned and said, "If you wish to sell your goods, my friend, I will gladly go down with you to the market."

I was puzzled by this remark and did not know what to say. What goods was he talking about?

"Do not worry about them, my son," he went on. "If we receive a good offer, we will sell them; if not, I will keep them for you in my own storehouse until they fetch a better price."

Hiding my bewilderment, I replied, "I am willing to do whatever you suggest."

With this I got up and went with him to the market.

There I saw an excited crowd admiring an object on the ground with exclamations of the highest praise. Pushing my way among the merchants, I was astonished to find that the center of attention was none other than the raft on which I had sailed down the river. Presently the old man ordered a broker to begin the auction.

"Who will make the first bid for this precious sandalwood?" began the broker. "Come along, my friends. Have you ever in all your lives seen finer sandalwood than this?"

"A hundred pieces of gold!" one of the merchants cried.

"A thousand!" another shouted.

"Eleven hundred!" my host exclaimed.

"Agreed," I nodded.

Upon this, the old man ordered his slaves to carry the wood to his warehouse. When he got home he took me to his private chamber and paid me eleven hundred pieces of gold.

One day, as we sat talking, he suddenly asked, "My son, will you do me a great favor?"

"With all my heart," I replied, "if I have the power to do it."

"I am a very old man," he said, "and have no son of my own. Yet I have a young and beautiful daughter, who on my death will be mistress of my entire fortune. If you will have her for your wife, you will inherit my wealth and become chief of the merchants of this city."

I readily agreed to the proposal. A sumptuous feast was held, a judge and witnesses were called in, and I was married to the old man's daughter amid great rejoicings. When the wedding guests were gone I was conducted to the bridal room, where I was allowed to see my wife for the first time. I found her very beautiful.

We grew to love each other dearly and lived together in happiness and contentment. Not long afterward my wife's father died, and I inherited all his property. His slaves became my slaves and his goods my goods, and the merchants of the city appointed me their chief in his place.

One day I was surprised by a strange event that apparently took place annually. The men of that land, for a whole day each year, suffered a wondrous change in their bodies. They grew wings on their shoulders and flew high up in the air, leaving their wives and children behind. I was amazed at this occurrence, and begged one of my friends to let me cling to him when he next took his flight. He promised to grant my request, and when the long-awaited day arrived, I took a tight hold of my friend's waist and was at once carried up swiftly in the air. We climbed higher and higher into the void until I could hear the angels in their choirs singing under the vault of heaven. Moved with awe, I cried, "Glory and praise to Allah, Lord of the Creation!"

The words were scarcely out of my mouth when my flying companion dropped down through the air and alighted on the top of a desolate mountain. There, to my surprise, he threw me off his back and took to the air again, calling curses on my head.

As I sat thinking what I should do, I saw two youths approaching me. Their faces shone with an unearthly beauty, and each held a staff of red gold in his hand. I rose to my feet and wished them peace. They returned my greeting courteously.

"Who are you, and what brought you to this barren mountain?" I asked.

"We are worshipers of the true God," they replied. And so saying, one of the youths pointed to a path on the mountain, handed me his gold staff, and led the way with his companion.

Bewildered at these words, I set out in the direction he

indicated, leaning upon the staff as I walked. I had not gone far when I saw coming toward me the flier who had so roughly set me down upon the mountaintop. I went up to him and said gently, "Is this how friends behave toward friends?"

The winged man, who was no longer angry, replied, "Know that my fall was caused by your unfortunate mention of your god. The word has this effect upon us, and this is why we never utter it."

I assured him that I had meant no harm and promised to commit no such offense in future. Then I begged him to carry me home. He took me upon his shoulders and in a few moments set me down before my house.

My wife was overjoyed at my return, and when I told her of my adventure, she said, "We must no longer stay among these people. Know that they are the brothers of Satan and have no knowledge of the true God."

"How was it, then, that your father lived among them?" I asked.

"My father belonged to a different race," she replied. "He believed in none of their creeds and did not lead their life. As he is now dead, let us sell our property and leave this blasphemous land."

And so I made up my mind to return home. We sold our houses and estates, hired a vessel, and set sail with a rich cargo.

Aided by a favorable wind, we voyaged many days and nights and at last came to Basra and thence to Baghdad, the City of Peace. I carried to my stores the valuables I had brought with me and, taking my wife to my own house in my old street, rejoiced to meet my people. They told me that this voyage had kept me abroad for nearly twenty-seven years, and marveled exceedingly at my adventures.

I gave profound thanks to Allah for bringing me safely

home, and solemnly vowed never to travel again by sea or land. Such, dear guests, was the longest and last of my voyages.

When the evening feast was over, Sindbad the Sailor gave Sindbad the Porter a hundred pieces of gold, which he took with thanks and blessings. Then he went his way, marveling at all he had heard.

The porter remained a frequent visitor to the house of his famous friend, and the two lived in happiness and peace until the end of their lives.

The Tale of Khalifah the Fisherman

Once upon a time, in the reign of the Caliph Harun al-Rashid, there lived in the city of Baghdad a poor fisherman called Khalifah.

It so happened one morning that he took his net upon his back and went down to the river Tigris before the other fishermen arrived. When he reached the bank he rolled up his sleeves and tucked his robe into his belt; then he spread his net and cast it into the water. He cast his net ten times, but did not catch a single fish. In despair, he waded knee-deep into the river and threw his net as far as he could. He waited patiently for a long time, and then pulled hard on the cords. When at last he managed to haul the heavy net ashore, he was astonished to find in it a lame, one-eyed monkey. His astonishment quickly changed to frustration and anger. Tying the beast to a tree, he was on the point of lashing it with his whip when the monkey spoke in the voice of a human.

"Stay your hand, Khalifah," it pleaded. "Do not whip me. Cast your net again and you will soon have what you desire."

The fisherman once more spread his net and cast it into the water. After some time he felt the net grow heavy, but on bringing it to land, he was vexed to find in it another monkey, even more strange-looking than the first. Its eyelids were black and long, its hands were dyed with red, and it wore a tattered vest about the middle. Its front teeth, set wide apart, gleamed as it stared at the fisherman with an awkward grin.

"Praise be to Allah, who has changed the fishes of the river into monkeys!" exclaimed Khalifah. Then, running toward the first animal, he cried, "So this is the result of your advice! I began my day with the sight of your monstrous face and I shall doubtless end it in starvation and ruin."

He brandished his whip high above his head and was about to fall again upon the one-eyed monkey when it begged him for mercy.

"Spare me, Khalifah, in the name of Allah! it cried. "Go to my brother. He will give you good advice."

The bewildered fisherman flung away his whip and turned to the second monkey.

"If you mark my words and do as I tell you, Khalifah," said the second monkey, "you shall prosper."

"Well, what do you want me to do?" the fisherman asked.

"Leave me on this bank," came the reply, "and once more cast your net."

The fisherman spread his net again and cast it into the water. He waited patiently, and when he felt the net grow heavy, he gently drew it in, only to land yet another monkey, which had red hair and wore a blue vest about its middle.

"Surely this is a cursed day from first to last!" exclaimed the fisherman when he saw the third monkey. "There is surely not a single fish left in the river and we shall have nothing today but monkeys!"

Then, turning to the red-haired beast, he cried, "In heaven's name, what are you?"

"Do you not know who I am, Khalifah?" the monkey replied.

"Indeed I do not!" protested the fisherman.

"Know, then, that I am the monkey of Abu Ahmad, chief of the money-changers. To me he owes his good fortune and all his wealth. When I bless him in the morning he gains five pieces of gold, and when I say good night to him he gains five more."

"Mark that," the fisherman said, turning to the first beast. "*You* cannot boast of such blessings. Seeing your face this morning has brought me nothing but bad luck!"

"Leave my brother in peace, Khalifah," said the red-haired monkey, "and cast your net once more into the river. After that, come back and show me your catch. I will teach you how to use it to your best advantage."

"I hear and obey, King of all monkeys!" the fisherman answered.

Khalifah did as the monkey told him, and when he drew in his net he rejoiced to find a splendid fish with a large head, broad fins, and eyes that glittered like gold coins. Marveling at the quaintness of his prize, he took it and showed it to the red-haired animal.

"Now gather some fresh grass," said the monkey, "and spread it at the bottom of your basket; lay the fish upon it and cover it with more grass. Then carry the basket to Baghdad. Should anyone speak to you on your way, you must not answer, but go directly to the market of the money-changers. In the middle of it stands the shop of Abu Ahmad, their chief. You will find him sitting on a mattress with an embroidered cushion at his back, surrounded by his slaves and servants. In front of him you will see two boxes, one for gold and one for silver. Go up to him, set your basket before him, and say, 'Sir, I went down to the river Tigris this morning and in your name cast my net. I caught this fish.' He will ask, 'Have you shown it to any other man?' 'No,' you must answer.

"Then he will take the fish and offer you one piece of gold. You must refuse to sell it for that price. He will offer you two pieces, but you must still refuse. Whatever he offers, you must not accept, though it be the fish's weight in gold. He will ask, 'What, then, do you want?' And you will reply, 'I will exchange this fish for nothing more than a few simple words.' 'What are they?' he will ask, and you will answer, 'Stand up and say, *Bear witness, all who are present in this market, that I give Khalifah the fisherman my monkey in exchange for his monkey, and that I barter my fortune for his fortune.* That is the price of my fish: I demand no gold.'"

"If he agrees to this," went on the red-haired beast, "you will become my master; I will bless you every morning and every evening, and you will gain ten pieces of gold every day. As for Abu Ahmad, he will be plagued with the sight of my lame, one-eyed brother, and will suffer heavy losses. Bear in mind what I have told you, Khalifah, and you will prosper."

"I will obey you in every particular, royal monkey!" the fisherman replied. He untied the three animals, who leaped into the water and disappeared.

Khalifah washed the fish, placed it in his basket upon some fresh grass, and covered it over. Then he set out for the city, singing merrily.

As he made his way through the streets, many people greeted him and asked if he had any fish to sell. But he walked on without a word until he reached the market of the money-changers and stopped before Abu Ahmad's shop. The fisherman saw Abu Ahmad surrounded by numerous servants who waited upon him with such ceremony as can be found only in the courts of kings. He went up to the money-changer.

"Fisherman, what can we do for you?" Abu Ahmad asked.

"Chief of the money-changers," Khalifah replied, "this morning I went down to the Tigris, and in your name cast my net. I caught this fish."

"What a strange coincidence!" cried the delighted money-changer. "A holy man appeared to me in a dream last night, saying, 'You will receive a present from me tomorrow.' This must surely be the present. Only tell me, on your life, have you shown this fish to any other man?"

"No," the fisherman replied. "No one else has seen it."

The money-changer turned to one of his slaves and said, "Take this fish to my house and ask my daughter to have it dressed for dinner. Tell her to fry one half and to grill the other."

"I hear and obey," answered the slave, and departed with the fish to his master's house.

Abu Ahmad took a piece of gold from one of his coffers and offered it to the fisherman.

"Spend this on your family," he said.

Now, Khalifah, who had never before earned such money for a single day's labor, instinctively held out his hand and took the coin. But as he was about to leave the shop, he remembered the monkey's instructions.

"Take this and give me back my fish," he cried, throwing down the coin. "Would you make a fool of me?"

Thinking that the fisherman was jesting, Abu Ahmad smiled, then handed him three gold pieces; but Khalifah refused the gold.

"Since when have you known me to sell my fish for such a trifle?" he asked.

Abu Ahmad then gave him five pieces. "Take these," he said, "and do not be greedy."

The fisherman took the gold and left the shop, scarcely believing his eyes. "Glory be to God!" he thought. "The Caliph himself has not so much gold in his coffers as I have in my purse today!"

It was not until he reached the end of the market place that he recalled the monkey's advice. He hurried back to the money-changer and again threw down the coins before him.

"What has come over you, Khalifah?" asked Abu Ahmad. "Would you rather have the money in silver?"

"I want neither your gold nor your silver," the fisherman retorted. "Give me back my fish."

"I have given you five pieces of gold for a fish that is hardly worth ten coppers," exclaimed the money-changer angrily, "and yet you are not satisfied." Then, turning to his slaves, he cried, "Take hold of this rascal and thrash him soundly!"

The slaves immediately set upon the fisherman and beat him until their master called, "Enough!" But as soon as they let go of him, Khalifah rose to his feet as though he had felt no pain at all. "Sir," he said, "you should have known that I can take more blows than ten donkeys put together."

At this Abu Ahmad laughed.

"Enough of this fooling," he said. "How much do you want?"

"Only a few simple words," the fisherman replied. "I just want you to get up and say: 'Bear witness, all who are present in this market, that I give Khalifah the fisherman my monkey in exchange for his monkey, and that I barter my fortune for his fortune."

"Nothing could be easier than that," Abu Ahmad said and, rising to his feet, made the declaration. Then, turning to the fisherman, he asked, "is that all?"

"It is."

"Then I bid you good day."

Khalifah put the empty basket on his shoulder and hurried back to the river. As soon as he reached the bank he spread his net and cast it into the water. When he drew it in, he found it filled with fish of every kind. Presently a woman came up to him with a basket and bought a gold piece's worth of fish. Then a slave passed by and also bought a gold piece's worth. When the day was done, Khalifah had earned ten pieces of gold. And he continued to earn this sum day after day until he had a hundred pieces of gold.

Now, the fisherman lived in a hovel of a house at the end of the Lane of the Merchants. One night, as he lay in his lodging overcome with drink, he said to himself, "All your neighbors, Khalifah, think you are a penniless old fisherman. They have not seen your hundred pieces of gold. But they will soon hear of your wealth; and before long the Caliph himself will get to know of it. One day, when his treasury is empty, he will send for you and say, 'I need some money. I hear you have a hundred gold pieces. You must lend them to me.' 'Sire,' I will answer, 'your slave is a poor, humble fisherman. The man who told you that is a wicked liar.' The Caliph, of course, will not believe me. He will hand me over to the governor, who will strip me naked and whip me mercilessly. My best course, therefore, is to get my body used to the whip. I will get up now and prepare myself."

Khalifah took off all his clothes. He placed beside him an old leather cushion, took up his whip, and began lashing himself, aiming every other stroke at the cushion and yelling out, "A wicked lie! Oh, oh! I have no money!"

His cries and the sound of the whipping echoed in the stillness of the night and startled the neighbors out of their beds. They rushed out into the street, inquiring the cause of the disturbance. Thinking that thieves had broken into the fisherman's house, they hurried to his rescue. To their surprise, the door was locked and bolted.

"The thieves must have got in from the terrace next door," they said to each other. So they climbed up to the adjoining terrace and from there descended into the house. They found the naked fisherman whipping himself.

"What the devil has possessed you tonight, Khalifah?" his neighbors cried in amazement. And when he had told them the very secret he had been anxious to keep from them, they laughed at him and said, "Enough of this joke, you stupid man! May you have no joy in your treasure!"

When the fisherman woke up the next morning he was still worried about his gold. "If I leave my money at home," he said to himself, "I know it will be stolen. If I carry it in my belt, thieves will waylay me in some deserted place and cut my throat, and rob me of it. I must think of a better device."

Finally he decided to sew a pocket inside the breast of his robe, and to carry the gold there tied in a bundle. This done, he took up his net, his basket, and his stick and went down to the Tigris.

On reaching the river he stepped down the bank and cast his net into the water. But the net brought up nothing at all. Farther and farther he moved along the bank until he had traveled half a day's journey from the capital; but all to no purpose. At last he summoned up all his strength and hurled the net with such desperate force that the bundle of coins flew out of his pocket and plunged into the river.

Khalifah cast off his clothes and dived after the gold; but it was swept away by the current, and soon he had to abandon the search. Covered with mud and utterly exhausted, he walked back to the spot where he had left his clothes. But they were nowhere to be found.

For a few moments he looked at us one by one in silence; then he got up, reached out toward me, lifted me up by the neck, and began feeling my body as a butcher would a lamb.

In despair, he wrapped himself in his net and, like a raging camel, ran wildly up and down the bank.

So much for Khalifah the fisherman.

Now, it so chanced that the Caliph Harun al-Rashid (who is the other important figure in our tale) had at that time a friend among the jewelers of Baghdad called Sheikh Kirnas. He was known to all the merchants of the city as the Caliph's own broker; and his influence was such that nothing choice or rare, from jewels to slave girls, was put up for sale without being first shown to him.

One day, as Sheikh Kirnas was attending to his customers, the chief of the brokers brought into his shop a slave girl of astonishing beauty. Not only had she no equal in good looks, but she was also graced with many accomplishments. She could recite pretty verses, sing, and make music on all manner of instruments. Her name was Kut-al-Kulub. Sheikh Kirnas bought her right away for five thousand pieces of gold, and after he had dressed her in rich robes and adorned her with jewels worth a thousand more, he took her to his master the Caliph.

Al-Rashid was so delighted with her talents that next morning he sent for Sheikh Kirnas and gave him ten thousand pieces in payment for the girl. The Caliph loved his new favorite so deeply that for her sake he forsook his wife, the Lady Zubaidah, and all his other concubines. He stayed by her side for a whole month, leaving her only when he attended the public prayers.

It was not long, however, before the courtiers and officers of state became dissatisfied with their master's conduct. Unable to keep silent any longer, they complained to Jaafar, the Grand Vizier.

One day, while attending the Caliph at the mosque,

Jaafar discreetly hinted at his master's excessive attachment to the slave girl.

"By Allah, Jaafar," the Caliph replied, "my will is powerless in this matter, for my heart is caught in the snare of love, and try as I may, I cannot release it."

"Commander of the Faithful," said the vizier, "this girl is now a member of your household, a servant among your servants. Think of the pleasures of riding and hunting and other sports, for these may help you to forget her."

"You have spoken wisely, Jaafar," the Caliph replied. "Come, we will go hunting this very day."

As soon as the prayers were over, they mounted their steeds and rode out to the open country followed by the troops.

It was a hot day. When they had traveled a long way from the city, Al-Rashid, feeling thirsty, looked around to see if there was a sign of any encampment nearby. He observed an object far off on a mound. "Can you see what that is?" he asked Jaafar.

"It looks like a man," the vizier replied. "He is perhaps the keeper of an orchard or a cucumber garden. Maybe he can give us some water to drink. I will ride and fetch some."

But Al-Rashid ordered Jaafar to wait for the troops, who had lingered behind, and he himself galloped off more swiftly than the desert wind or the waterfall that thunders down the rocks. On reaching the hillside he found a man swathed in a fishing net, with hair disheveled and dusty, and bloodshot eyes blazing like torches.

Al-Rashid politely greeted the strange-looking figure, and Khalifah (for the man was no other than our fisherman) muttered a few angry words in reply.

"Have you a drink of water to give me?" the Caliph asked.

"Are you blind or stupid?" broke out the fisherman. "Can you not see that the river Tigris flows behind this hillock?"

Al-Rashid walked around the hillock and found that the river did indeed run behind it; so he drank and watered his horse. Then he returned to Khalifah.

"What are you doing here?" he asked. "What is your trade?"

"This question is even sillier than the last!" cried Khalifah. "Do you not see my net about my shoulders?"

"So you are a fisherman," said the Caliph. "But where have you left your cloak, your gown, and your belt?"

Now these were the very things that had been stolen from the fisherman. Therefore, when he heard them named, he did not doubt that the thief stood before him. At once he darted forward, swift as a flash of lightning, and caught the Caliph's horse by the bridle.

"Give me back my clothes," he shouted, "and stop this foolish joke!"

"By Allah, my friend," the Caliph replied, "I have never seen your clothes, nor can I understand what you are shouting about."

Now, Al-Rashid had a small mouth and round, plump cheeks, so that Khalifah took him for a piper or a flute player.

"Give me back my clothes, you scraper of beggarly tunes," he threatened, "or I will cudgel your bones with this stick."

When he saw the fisherman brandishing his heavy stick, the Caliph thought to himself, "By Allah, one stroke from this cudgel will be the end of me."

So, to humor Khalifah, he took off his splendid satin cloak and handed it to him.

"Here," he said, "take this in place of the things you lost."

"My clothes were worth ten times as much," muttered the fisherman as he turned the cloak about with obvious contempt.

Al-Rashid prevailed upon him to try it on. Finding it too long, Khalifah took the knife that was attached to the handle of his basket and cut off the lower part of the cloak, so that it hung just above his knees.

"Tell me, good piper," he said, "how much money does your playing bring you in a month?"

"Ten pieces of silver," the Caliph replied.

"By Allah, you make me feel sorry for you," the fisherman said. "Why, I make ten gold pieces a day. If you are willing to enter my service, I will teach you my trade and make you my partner. In this way you will earn a good round sum every day. And if your present master does not like it, this stick of mine will protect you."

"I accept your offer," the Caliph replied.

"Then get off your horse and follow me," the fisherman said. "We will begin work this instant."

Al-Rashid dismounted and tethered his horse to a nearby tree. Then he rolled up his sleeves and tucked his robe into his belt.

"Hold the net thus," said the fisherman; "spread it over you arm thus, and cast it into the water—thus."

Al-Rashid summoned up all his strength and did as the fisherman told him. When, after a few moments, he tried to draw the net in, it was so heavy that the fisherman had to come to his aid.

"Dog!" shouted Khalifah, as the two tugged together at the cords, "if you tear or damage my net I will take your horse from you and beat you black and blue. Do you hear?"

When at last they managed to haul the net ashore, they saw that it was filled with fish of every kind and color.

"Useless old piper though you are," said Khalifah, "you

may yet become an excellent fisherman. Off with you now to the market, and fetch me two large baskets. I will stay here and watch over the fish till you return. Then we will load the catch on your horse's back and take it to the fish market. Your job will be to hold the scales and receive the money. Go, waste no time!"

"I hear and obey," replied the Caliph and, mounting his horse, galloped away, scarcely able to contain his laughter.

When Al-Rashid rejoined Jaafar and the troops, the vizier, who had been anxiously waiting for him, said, "You no doubt came upon some pleasant garden on the way where you rested all this time."

At this the Caliph burst out laughing, and he proceeded to tell the company of his adventure with the fisherman. "My master is now waiting for me," he went on. "We are going to the market, to sell the fish and share the profit."

"Then let me provide you with some customers," said the vizier, laughing. But a mischievous fancy took hold of the Caliph's mind.

"By the honor of my ancestors," he cried, "whoever brings me a fish from my master Khalifah shall receive one gold piece from me."

And so a crier proclaimed the Caliph's wish among the guards and they all made for the river, in the direction of the hillock. The fisherman, still waiting for Al-Rashid (and the baskets), was astounded to see the guards swoop upon him like vultures, each grabbing as many fish as his hands could hold.

"There must surely be something very odd about these fish!" thought the terrified Khalifah. "O Allah, send the piper quickly to my aid!" And to protect himself from the raiders, he jumped right into the water with a fish in each hand.

The guards wrapped up the spoil in their large, gold-embroidered handkerchiefs and rode back to their master at full gallop. As soon as they were gone, however, the Caliph's chief footman arrived.

"Come here, fisherman," he said, when he saw Khalifah holding up the fish.

"Away with you, villain!" Khalifah shouted.

But the footman came nearer. "Give me your fish," he said persuasively. "I will pay you for them."

The fisherman still refused, and the footman lifted his lance and aimed it at him.

"Dog, do not throw!" Khalifah cried. "I would rather give you all than lose my life."

So saying, he scornfully threw the fish at the footman, who picked them up and wrapped them in his handkerchief. Then the footman thrust his hand into his pocket in order to pay the fisherman. But, as chance would have it, there was no money there.

"I am afraid you have no luck today," he said, "for I have not a copper about me. If you will come to the Caliph's palace tomorrow and ask for Sandal, the chief footman, you will receive a hearty welcome and a generous reward."

With this the footman leaped upon his horse and galloped away.

"This is indeed a joyless day!" groaned the fisherman. In despair he threw his net upon his shoulder and set out for the market.

As he walked through the streets of Baghdad, passers-by were puzzled to see a fisherman wearing a valuable satin cloak. Presently he entered the market place and passed by the shop of the Caliph's own tailor. The tailor recognized the garment, for he had made it himself. He called out to Khalifah.

"Where did you get that cloak?" he asked.

"What is it to you?" returned the fisherman angrily. "Yet, if you must know, it was given me by an apprentice of mine. The rascal had stolen my clothes; I took pity on him and, rather than have his hand cut off for theft, I accepted this thing in exchange."

The tailor was much amused to hear this and realized that the fisherman was the victim of the Caliph's latest prank.

Meanwhile, at the palace a plot was being hatched against the Caliph's favorite, Kut-al-Kulub. For when the Lady Zubaidah, his Queen, learned of her husband's new attachment, she became so jealous that she refused to eat or drink, and busily schemed to avenge herself on the slave girl. Hearing that Al-Rashid had gone hunting, she held a feast in her room and sent for Kut-al-Kulub to entertain the guests with her singing. The unsuspecting girl took up her instruments and was conducted to the Queen's chamber.

When her eyes fell on Kut-al-Kulub, the Lady Zubaidah could not help admiring the girl's exquisite beauty. She concealed her scheming thoughts and with a welcoming smile ordered her to sit down. The girl sang to the accompaniment of the lute and the tambourine. So sweetly did she sing that her audience was charmed into a magic trance, the birds paused in their flight, and the entire palace seemed to echo with a thousand voices.

"Al-Rashid is hardly to blame for loving her," thought the Lady Zubaidah, as the girl ended her song and gracefully bowed to the ground before her.

The servants set before Kut-al-Kulub a dish of sweetmeats into which the Queen had mixed a powerful drug. Scarcely had the girl swallowed a mouthful than her head fell backward and she sank to the ground unconscious. The Lady Zubaidah ordered her maids to carry the girl to her private room. Then, by her order, an announcement was made that Kut-al-Kulub had met with an accident and died. She also ordered a mock burial to take place in the grounds of the palace. The Queen threatened her servants with instant death if they revealed the secret.

When the Caliph returned from the hunt and news of his favorite's death was broken to him, the world darkened before his eyes and he was stricken with grief. He wept bitterly for Kut-al-Kulub and stayed by her supposed tomb for a long time.

Her plot having succeeded, the Lady Zubaidah ordered a trusted slave to lock the unconscious girl into a chest and carry it to the market. He was told to sell the chest immediately without revealing its contents.

Now to return to the fisherman. Early the next morning, Khalifah said to himself, "I can do nothing better today than go to the Caliph's palace and ask his footman for the money he owes me."

So off he went to Al-Rashid's court. As soon as he entered he saw Sandal, the Caliph's footman, in the doorway with a crowd of slaves waiting upon him. On the fisherman's approach, one of the slaves rose to bar his way and would have turned him back had not the footman recognized Khalifah. He greeted him with a laugh and, remembering the debt, put his hand into his pocket to take out his purse. At that moment, however, a shout was heard announcing the approach of Jaafar, the vizier. Sandal sprang to his feet, hurried off to the vizier, and fell into a long conversation with him.

Khalifah tried again and again to draw the footman's attention to him, but all to no avail. At last the vizier took notice of him and asked, "Who is that odd fellow?"

"That," Sandal replied, "is the selfsame fisherman whose fish we seized yesterday on the Caliph's orders." And he went on to explain the reason for Khalifah's visit.

When he had heard Sandal's account, the vizier smiled. "This fisherman," he said, "is the Caliph's instructor and business partner. He has indeed come at a time when we need him most. Today our master's heart is heavy with grief over the death of his loved one, and perhaps nothing will amuse him more than this fisherman's quaint humor. I will announce him to the Caliph."

Jaafar hurried to the Caliph's room. He found him bowed down with sorrow over the loss of Kut-al-Kulub. The vizier wished him peace and, bowing low before him, said, "On my way to you just now, Commander of the Faithful, I met at the door your teacher and partner, Khalifah, the fisherman. He is full of complaints against you. 'Glory to Allah,' I heard him say. 'Is this how masters should be treated? I sent him to fetch a couple of baskets and he never came back.'

"Now I pray you, Commander of the Faithful," Jaafar went on, "if you still have a mind to be his partner, let him know it; but if you wish to end your joint labors, tell him that he must seek another man."

The Caliph smiled at Jaafar's words, and his sorrow seemed to be lightened.

"Is this true, Jaafar?" he asked. "Upon my soul, this fisherman must be rewarded."

Then he added, with a mischievous twinkle in his eye, "If it is Allah's will that this man should prosper through me, it shall be done; and if it is his will that he should be punished through me, it shall be done also."

So saying, Al-Rashid took out a large sheet of paper and cut it into numerous pieces.

"Write down on twenty of these papers," he said to the vizier, "sums of money from one piece of gold to a thousand; and on twenty more all the offices of state from the smallest clerkship to the Caliphate itself. Also twenty kinds of punishment from the lightest beating to a terrible death."

"I hear and obey," Jaafar replied, and he did as his master told him.

"I swear by my holy ancestors," said Al-Rashid, "that Khalifah the fisherman shall have the choice of one of these papers, and that I will accordingly reward him. Go and bring him before me."

"There is no strength or help except in Allah," said Jaafar to himself as he left the Caliph's room. "Who knows what lies in store for this poor fellow?"

When he found the fisherman he took him by the hand and, followed by a crowd of slaves, conducted him through seven long corridors until they stood at the door of the Caliph's room.

"Be careful," said the vizier to the terrified fisherman. "You are about to be admitted to the presence of the Commander of the Faithful, Defender of the Faith."

With this he led him in; and Khalifah, who was so overawed by the magnificence of his surroundings that he could not understand the vizier's words, suddenly saw the Caliph seated on a couch with all the officers of his court standing around him. The fisherman recognized his former apprentice.

"It is good to see you again, my piper!" he cried. "But was it right to go away and leave me by the river all alone with the fish, and never return? Know, then, that thanks to your absence I was attacked by a band of mounted rogues, who carried off the entire catch. Had you returned promptly with the baskets we would have made a handsome profit. And what is worse, the ruffians have now put me under arrest. But tell me, who has imprisoned *you* in this dungeon?"

Al-Rashid smiled and held out the slips to the fisherman.

"Come closer, Khalifah," he said, "and draw me one of these papers."

"Only yesterday you were a fisherman," Khalifah remarked. "Now I see that you have turned fortuneteller. Have you not heard the proverb 'A rolling stone gathers no moss'?"

"Enough of this chatter," said Jaafar sternly. "Come, do as you are told: draw one of these papers."

The fisherman picked out one paper and handed it to the Caliph.

"Good piper," he said, "read me my fortune and keep nothing from me."

Al-Rashid passed the paper to his vizier and ordered him to read it aloud. Such was Khalifah's luck, however, that his choice was a hundred blows of the stick. Accordingly he was thrown down on the floor and given a hundred strokes.

"Commander of the Faithful," Jaafar said, "this unfortunate man has come to drink from the river of your charity and goodness. Do not send him away thirsty."

The vizier persuaded the Caliph to let the fisherman draw once more. The second paper decreed that Khalifah should be given nothing at all. Jaafar, however, prevailed upon the Caliph to let the fisherman draw a third. Khalifah drew again, and the vizier unfolded the paper and announced, "One gold piece."

"What!" cried the angry fisherman. "One piece for a hundred strokes? May Allah justly repay you for your wickedness!"

The Caliph laughed, and Jaafar took the fisherman by the hand and led him away from his master's presence. As Khalifah was leaving the palace, Sandal called out to him.

"Come, my friend," he said, "give me my share of the Caliph's reward."

"You want your share, rascal, do you?" broke out the fisherman. "All I earned was a hundred strokes and one piece of gold. You would indeed be welcome to one half of my beating; as for the miserable coin, why, you can have that, too!"

He flung the coin at him and rushed off angrily. Moved with pity, Sandal ordered some slaves to run after him and bring him back. Sandal took out a red purse and emptied a hundred gold coins into Khalifah's hands.

"Here," he said, "take this in payment of my debt, and go home in peace."

Khalifah rejoiced. He put the gold into his pocket, together with the coin that Al-Rashid had given him, and went out of the palace.

Now, it so happened that as he was walking home, lost in happy fancies, he came across a large crowd in the market place. Pushing his way among the merchants, he found that the center of attention was a large chest on which a young slave was sitting. Beside the chest stood an old man, who was calling out, "Gentlemen, merchants, worthy citizens! Who will bid first for this chest of unknown treasure from the harem of the Lady Zubaidah, wife of the Commander of the Faithful?"

"By Allah," said one of the merchants, "I will bid twenty pieces of gold."

"Fifty," another cried.

"A hundred," shouted a third.

"Who will give more?" inquired the auctioneer.

Breathless with excitement, Khalifah the fisherman shouted, "Let it be mine for a hundred and one pieces!"

"The chest is yours," the auctioneer replied. "Hand in your gold, and may Allah bless the bargain!"

Khalifah paid the slave, lifted the heavy chest with difficulty onto his shoulders, and carried it home. As he staggered along, he wondered what the precious contents might be. Presently he reached his dwelling, and after he had managed to get the chest through the door, he set to work to open it. But the chest was securely locked.

"What the devil possessed me to buy a box that cannot even be opened!" he cried.

Then he decided to break the chest to pieces, but it stoutly resisted all his blows and kicks. Utterly exhausted by the effort, he stretched himself out on the chest and fell asleep.

About an hour later he was awakened by a sound of movement underneath him. Out of his mind with terror, he leaped to his feet, crying, "This chest must be haunted by demons! Praise be to Allah, who prevented me from opening it! Had I freed them in the dark they would surely have put me to a miserable death!"

His terror increased as the noise became more distinct. He searched in vain for a lamp, and finally rushed out into the street yelling at the top of his voice, "Help! Help, good neighbors!"

Roused from their sleep, his neighbors peered from their doors and windows.

"What has happened?" they shouted.

"Devils!" the fisherman cried. "My house is haunted by devils! Give me a lamp and a hammer, in the name of Allah!"

The neighbors laughed. One gave him a lamp and another a hammer. His confidence restored, he returned home determined to break open the chest. In the light of the lamp he battered the locks with the hammer and lifted the lid. What was this?—a girl as lovely as the moon. Her eyes were half open, as if she had just wakened from a heavy sleep. Khalifah marveled at her beauty.

"In Allah's name, who are you?" he whispered, kneeling down before her.

When she heard his words the girl regained her senses.

"Who are *you?* Where am I?" she asked, looking intently into his face.

"I am Khalifah, the fisherman, and you are in my house," he answered.

"Am I not in the palace of the Caliph Harun al-Rashid?" asked the girl.

"Are you out of your mind?" the fishermen exclaimed. "Let me tell you at once that you belong to no one but me; it was only this morning that I bought you for a hundred and one pieces of gold. Allah be praised for this lucky bargain!"

The girl was hungry. "Give me something to eat," she said.

"Alas," the fisherman replied. "There is nothing to eat or drink in this house. I myself have hardly tasted anything these two days."

"Have you any money?" she asked.

"God preserve this chest!" he answered bitterly. "This bargain has taken every coin I had."

"Then go to your neighbors," she said, "and bring me something to eat, for I am famished."

The fisherman rushed into the street again. "Good neighbors," he cried, "who will give a hungry man something to eat?"

This he repeated several times at the top of his voice, until the unfortunate neighbors, awakened once more by his cries, opened their windows and threw down food to him; one gave him half a loaf of bread, another a piece of cheese, a third a cucumber. Returning home, he set the food before Kut-al-Kulub and invited her to eat.

"Bring me a drink of water," she now said. "I am very thirsty."

So Khalifah took his empty pitcher and ran again into the street, begging the neighbors for some water. They replied with angry curses; but unable to stand his cries any longer, they carried water to him in buckets, jugs, and ewers. He filled his pitcher and took it to the slave girl.

When she had eaten and drunk, the fisherman asked her how she came to be locked inside the chest. She told him all that had happened at the Caliph's palace. "This will make your fortune," she added, "for when Al-Rashid hears of my rescue, I know he will reward you."

"But is not this Al-Rashid the foolish piper whom I taught how to fish?" Khalifah cried. "Never in all my life have I met such a miserly rascal!"

"My friend," said the girl, "you must stop this senseless talk and make yourself worthy of the new station that awaits you. Above all, you must bear yourself respectfully and courteously in the presence of the Commander of the Faithful."

Such was the influence of Kut-al-Kulub's words on Khalifah that a new world seemed to unfold before him. The dark veil of ignorance was lifted from his eyes and he became a wiser man.

Early the next morning Kut-al-Kulub asked Khalifah to bring her pen, ink, and paper. She wrote to Sheikh Kirnas, the Caliph's jeweler, telling him where she was and all that had happened. Then she sent the fisherman off with the letter.

Straight to the jeweler's he went and, on entering, bowed to the ground before the merchant and wished him peace. But, taking Khalifah for a beggar, the merchant ordered a slave to give him a copper and show him out. Khalifah refused the coin, saying, "I beg no charity. Read this, I pray you."

As soon as he finished reading the girl's letter, Sheikh Kirnas raised it to his lips; then he got up and gave the fisherman a courteous welcome.

"Where do you live, my friend?" he asked.

Khalifah took him to his house, where he found the lovely Kut-al-Kulub waiting. The jeweler ordered two of his servants to accompany Khalifah to a money-changer's shop, where the fisherman was rewarded with a thousand pieces of gold. When he returned, Khalifah found the jeweler mounted on a magnificent mule with all his servants gathered around him. Nearby stood another splendid mule, richly saddled and bridled, which Sheikh Kirnas invited Khalifah to ride. The fisherman, who had never been on a mule's back in all his life, at first refused, but having finally been persuaded by the merchant, he decided to risk a trial and resolutely leaped upon the animal's back—facing the wrong way and grasping its tail instead of the bridle. The mule reared, and Khalifah was thrown off to the ground to the cheers and shouts of the onlookers.

Sheikh Kirnas left the fisherman behind and rode off to the Caliph's palace. Al-Rashid was overjoyed to hear the news of his favorite's rescue and ordered the merchant to bring her immediately to his court.

The girl kissed the ground before the Caliph, and he rose and welcomed her with all his heart. Kut-al-Kulub told him the story of her adventure. Her rescuer was a fisherman called Khalifah, she said, who was now waiting at the door of the palace.

Al-Rashid sent for the fisherman, who, on entering, kissed the ground before him and humbly wished the Caliph joy.

The Caliph marveled at the fisherman's humility and politeness. He bestowed on him a generous reward: fifty thousand pieces of gold, a magnificent robe of honor, a noble mare, and slaves from the Sudan.

His audience with the Caliph over, the fisherman again kissed the ground before him and left the court a proud, rich man. As Khalifah passed through the gates of the palace, Sandal went up to him and congratulated him on his new fortune. The fisherman produced from his pocket a purse containing a thousand gold coins and offered it to the footman. But Sandal refused the gold and marveled at the man's generosity and kindness of heart.

Then Khalifah mounted the mare that Al-Rashid had given him, and, with the help of two slaves holding the bridle, rode majestically through the streets of the city until he reached his house. As he dismounted, his neighbors flocked around him inquiring about his sudden prosperity. He told them all that had happened, and they marveled at his story.

Khalifah became a frequent visitor at the court of Al-Rashid, who continued to lavish on him high dignities and favors. He bought a magnificent house and had it furnished with rare and costly objects. Then he married a beautiful, well-born maiden, and lived happily with her for the rest of his life.

The Tale of Maaruf the Cobbler

Once upon a time, there lived in the city of Cairo a poor and honest cobbler who earned his living by patching old shoes.

He was married to an ugly woman called Fatimah, nicknamed by her neighbors the "Shrew" because of her quarrelsome disposition and her scolding tongue. She treated her husband cruelly, cursing him a thousand times a day and making his life a burden and a torment. Maaruf feared her malice and dreaded her fiery temper. He was a quiet, sensitive man and was ever anxious to avoid a scene.

One day his wife came to him and said, "See that you bring me a butter cake tonight, and let it be dripping with honey."

"May Allah send me good business today," the cobbler replied, "and you shall gladly have one. At present I have not a single copper, but the bounty of Allah is great."

"Talk not to me of Allah's bounty!" rejoined the shrew. "If you do not bring back a butter cake, dripping with honey, I will make your day blacker than the night!"

"Allah is merciful!" sighed Maaruf.

He left the house and went to open his shop, saying,

"O Lord, grant me this day the means to buy a honey cake for my wife, that I may save myself from her fury!"

As ill luck would have it, no customer entered his shop all day and he did not earn enough even for a loaf of bread. In the evening he locked the shop and walked along the street. He came to a pastry cook's, and as he gazed sadly at the confections in the window, his eyes filled with tears. Noticing his dejected look, the pastry cook called out to him, "Why so sad, Maaruf? Come in, and tell me your trouble."

When the cook heard the cause of the cobbler's unhappiness, he laughed and said, "No harm shall come to you, my friend. How much butter cake do you wish to have?"

"Five ounces," muttered Maaruf.

"Gladly," said the cook. "You can pay me some other time."

He cut a large slice, and added, "I fear I have no honey, only sugar-cane syrup. I assure you it is just as good."

He poured syrup and melted butter over the cake until it was worthy of a king's table. Then he handed the cake to the cobbler, together with a cheese and a loaf of bread for his supper. Maaruf could scarcely find words to thank the good man. He called down blessings upon him, and went home.

As soon as his wife saw him she demanded, "Have you brought me the butter cake?" Maaruf placed it before her.

In a loud, menacing voice she cried, "Did I not tell you it must be made with honey? You have brought me a syrup cake to spite me! Did you think I would not know the difference?"

Maaruf humbly stammered his explanation. "Good wife, I did not buy this cake," he said. "It was given me on credit by a kind hearted pastry cook."

"These excuses will not help you!" shrieked the furious woman. "There, take your miserable syrup dish!"

And she flung the cake in her husband's face and ordered him to go and fetch her another made with honey.
Then she dealt him a savage blow that knocked out one of
his teeth.

Losing all patience, Maaraf lifted his hand and gave the
woman a mild slap on the head. At this she flew into a desperate rage, gripped his beard with both her hands, and, raising her voice to its loudest pitch, shrieked, "Help, good people! Help! My husband is murdering me!"

The neighbors heard her cries and came rushing into
the house. After a struggle they managed to free the
cobbler's beard from her clutches, but when they saw his
injury and heard the cause of the dispute they rebuked her
and tried to reason with her.

"We are all content to eat syrup cake, and indeed find it
as good as the other kind," they said. "What has your poor
husband done that you should torment him so?"

Unable to bear with his wife any more, the long-suffer-
ing cobbler made up his mind to run away. He left the
house, and trudged dolefully toward the city gates. It was a
bleak winter evening, and as he came out of the town and
found himself among the garbage heaps, the rain began to
fall in torrents, drenching him to the skin. On and on he ran,
and at nightfall came to a ruined hovel where he took shelter
from the storm. He sat on the ground and wept bitterly.

"How shall I save myself from this fiend?" he cried.
"O Allah, help me to fly to some far-off land, where I shall
never see her again!"

While he was saying this the wall of the hovel suddenly
opened and a tall and fearsome jinnee appeared before him.

"Son of Adam," roared the jinnee, "what calamity can
have befallen you that you disturb my slumbers with your
wailing? I am the jinnee of this ruin and have dwelt here

these hundred years; yet never have I seen the like of this behavior."

But he was not as evil as he looked. Moved with pity, he said, "Tell me what you desire, and I will do your bidding."

Maaruf told him his unhappy story.

"Mount on my back," said the jinnee, "and I will take you to a land where your wife will never find you."

So the cobbler climbed onto the back of the jinnee, who flew with him between earth and sky all night, and at daybreak set him down on the top of a mountain.

"Son of Adam," said the jinnee, "go down this mountain and you will come to the gates of Ikhtiyan-al-Khatan. In that city you will find refuge from your wife."

And so saying, he vanished. Amazed and bewildered, Maaruf remained until sunrise on the spot where the jinnee left him. Then he climbed down the mountain and at length came to the walls of a city. He entered the gates and walked through the streets. The townsfolk stared at him with wondering eyes and gathered about him, marveling at his strange costume. Presently a man stepped forward and asked where he had come from.

"From Cairo," Maaraf replied.

"When did you leave Cairo?" the man asked.

"Last night," he answered, "just after dark."

At these words his questioner laughed incredulously and turned to the bystanders. "Listen to this madman! He tells us he left Cairo only last night!"

The crowd greeted this remark with laughter and pressed around Maaruf. "Have you lost your senses?" some asked. "How can it be that you left Cairo only last night? Do you not know that Cairo is at least a year's journey from here?"

Maaruf swore that he was speaking the truth and, to prove his story, took from his pocket a loaf of Cairo bread and held it up to them to see. All were astonished to see the loaf, which was of a kind unknown in their country and was still soft and fresh. A few believed the stranger, while others ridiculed him. As this was going on, a well-dressed merchant, followed by two slaves, came riding by. He stopped near the crowd and rebuked them sternly.

"Are you not ashamed to make fun of this man?" he said.

Then, turning to Maaruf, he spoke to him kindly and invited him to his house.

There his host dressed Maaruf in a merchant's robe worth a thousand pieces of gold, seated him in a splendid hall, and entertained him to an excellent meal. When they had finished eating, the merchant said to the cobbler, "Tell me, brother, what land you have come from. By your dress, you would seem to be an Egyptian."

"You are right, master," replied Maaruf. "I am an Egyptian, and Cairo is the city of my birth."

"What is your trade?" the merchant asked.

"I am a cobbler: I patch old shoes."

"Whereabouts in Cairo do you live?"

"In Red Lane," Maaruf replied.

"What folk do you know there?"

Maaruf named several of his neighbors in that street.

"Do you know Sheikh Ahmad the perfume seller?" asked the merchant eagerly.

"Do I know him?" Maaruf laughed. "Why, he is my next-door neighbor!"

"How is he keeping?"

"Allah be thanked, he is in the best of health," the cobbler replied.

"How many sons has he now?"

"He has three sons: Mustapha, Mohammed, and Ali."

"What do they do for a living?" inquired the host.

"The eldest, Mustapha," replied Maaruf, "is a school-master. Mohammed, the second, is a perfume seller and has set up a shop of his own next to his father's. As for Ali, he was the playmate of my childhood—and a couple of mischievous little rogues we certainly were. Together we would enter the mosques and steal the prayer books; then we would sell them in the market and buy sweets with the money. One day someone caught us red-handed and complained to our parents. Sheikh Ahmad gave his son a thrashing and poor little Ali ran away from home. No news has been heard of him these twenty years."

Here the merchant threw his arms around the cobbler's neck and wept for joy.

"Praise be to Allah!" he cried. "O Maaruf, I am that very Ali, the son of Sheikh Ahmad the perfume seller."

Then Ali asked his friend what had brought him to Ikhtiyan-al-Khatan, and the cobbler recounted all that happened to him since his disastrous marriage. He explained how he had chosen to flee the city rather than remain at the mercy of his wife, how he met the jinnee in the ruined hovel, and how he was carried overnight to that city.

Maaruf now asked his friend how he had risen to such prosperity.

"After I left Cairo," said Ali, "I wandered for many years from place to place and at last arrived, alone and friendless, in this city. I found the people honest and kindhearted, hospitable to strangers and always ready to help the poor. I told them—God forgive me!—that I was a rich merchant, the owner of a great caravan that would shortly arrive in their city. They gave me a splendid mansion for my use and lent me a thousand pieces of gold. With this money I bought a quantity of goods and sold them the next day at a profit of fifty pieces. I bought more goods, and, to make myself better known, sought the acquaintance of the richest

While they were still eating, the natives fetched a pot of ointment, which they rubbed into the bodies of my companions.

merchants in the town and entertained them lavishly in my house. I continued to buy and sell until I had amassed a large fortune.

"Now, my friend, if you tell the people of this city that you are a poor cobbler, that you have run away from a nagging wife, and that you left Cairo only yesterday, no one will believe you and you will become the laughingstock of the whole town. If you tell them you were carried here by a jinnee, you will frighten everyone away and they will think, 'The man is possessed of an evil spirit.' No, my friend, this will not do."

"Then what am I to do?" asked the perplexed Maaruf.

"Tomorrow morning," said Ali, "you will mount my finest mule and ride to the market with one of my slaves walking behind you all the way. There you will find me sitting among the richest merchants of the city. When I see you I will rise and greet you. I will kiss your hand and receive you with the utmost respect. After you have taken your seat among the other merchants, I shall ask you about many kinds of merchandise, saying, 'Have you such-and-such a cloth?' And you must answer, 'Plenty! Plenty!' When they ask me who you are, I will say you are a merchant of great wealth, and praise your generosity. If a beggar holds out his hand to you, you must give him gold. In this way you will earn the respect of the merchants. They will seek to know you and to trade with you, and before long you will indeed become a merchant of great wealth."

Seeing no other way out of his predicament, Maaruf reluctantly agreed to his friend's plan. Next morning, Ali clothed him magnificently, gave him a thousand gold pieces, and mounted him upon his best mule. At the appointed time the cobbler rode to the market, where he found his friend sitting among the merchants. As soon as Ali saw him approaching he bowed low and threw himself at his feet. He kissed his hand, and helped him from his mule. "May your day be blessed, great Maaruf!" he said.

When the newcomer had gravely taken his seat, the wondering merchants come to Ali one by one and asked in a low voice, "Who may this sheikh be?"

"He is one of the chief merchants of Egypt," Ali replied. "His wealth and the wealth of his father and forefathers are of proverbial fame. He possesses shops and storehouses in all corners of the earth, and his agents and partners are the pillars of commerce in every city of the East. Indeed, the wealthiest merchant in our town is but a poor peddler when compared with him."

Hearing this praise, the merchants thronged around Maaruf, vying with each other to welcome him. The chief of the merchants himself came to greet him and questioned him eagerly about the goods he had brought.

"Doubtless, sir," he said, "you have many bales of yellow silk?"

"Plenty! Plenty!" answered Maaruf, without a moment's hesitation.

"And blood-red damask?" asked another.

"Plenty! Plenty!" the cobbler replied.

To all their questions he made the same answer, and when one of the merchants begged him to show them a few samples, Maaruf replied, "Certainly, as soon as my caravan arrives."

He explained to the company that he was expecting a caravan of a thousand mules within the next few days.

Now while the merchants were chatting and marveling at the extraordinary richness of the caravan they would soon be seeing, a beggar came forward and held out his hand to each in turn. One or two gave him a silver piece, some a copper, but most of them turned him away.

Maaruf calmly drew out a handful of gold and gave it to the beggar.

The merchants raised their eyebrows and thought to themselves, "By Allah! this man must be richer than a king!"

Then a poor woman approached him, and to her also he gave a handful of gold. Scarcely believing her eyes, the woman hurried away to tell the other beggars, and they all came flocking around Maaruf with outstretched hands. The cobbler gave each a handful of gold, until the thousand pieces were finished.

"By Allah," he said, "to think there are so many beggars in this city! Had I known, I would have come prepared, for it is not my way to refuse money. What shall I do now if a beggar comes to me before my caravan arrives? If only I had, say, a thousand pieces of gold!"

"Do not let that trouble you," said the chief of the merchants.

He sent at once for a thousand gold pieces and handed the money to Maaruf. The cobbler continued to hand out gold to every beggar who passed by. When the muezzin's call summoned the faithful to afternoon prayers, he went with the merchants to the mosque, and what remained of the thousand pieces he threw over the heads of the worshipers.

As soon as the prayers were over he borrowed another thousand and there also he scattered among the poor. By nightfall Maaruf had obtained five thousand gold pieces from the merchants and given them all away, while his friend Ali, horrified at this extravagance, watched the proceedings helplessly. And to all his creditors the cobbler said, "When my caravan arrives, if you want gold, you shall have gold; and if you want goods, you shall have goods, for I have vast quantities of them."

That night Ali entertained the merchants at his house.

Maaruf spoke of nothing but jewels and rich silks, and whenever they asked him if he had this or that merchandise in his caravan, he replied, "Plenty! Plenty!"

Next morning he again, went to the market, talked to the merchants about his caravan, and borrowed more money to give away. By the end of twenty days he had taken sixty thousand pieces of gold on credit. And still no caravan arrived—no, not so much as a one-eyed mule.

At last the merchants, growing impatient at the caravan's delay, began to clamor for their money. They voiced their fears to their friend Ali, who, himself outraged at the cobbler's recklessness, took him aside and spoke to him.

"Have you taken leave of your senses, man?" he exclaimed. "I told you to toast the bread, not burn it! The merchants are demanding their money and say you owe them sixty thousand pieces of gold. You have squandered all this money among the beggars; how will you ever pay it back, idle as you are, with no work to do or goods to trade with?"

"Never mind," Maaruf replied. "What are sixty thousand pieces of gold? When my caravan arrives, if they want gold, they shall have gold; and if they want goods, they shall have goods, for I have vast quantities of them."

"Now glory be to Allah!" exclaimed his friend. "What goods are you talking about?"

"Why, the goods in my caravan," Maaruf replied. "I have countless bales of merchandise."

"Dog!" Ali exclaimed. "Are you telling *me* that story? Why, I will expose you to the whole world!"

"Away with you!" the cobbler answered. "Did you suppose I was a poor man? Know, then, I have priceless riches on the way. As soon as my caravan arrives, the merchants will be paid twofold."

At this Ali grew very angry.

"Scoundrel, I will teach you!" he cried.

"Do your worst!" the cobbler answered. "They must wait until my caravan arrives; and then they will have their money back and more."

In despair Ali left Maaruf and went away.

"If I now abuse him after commending him so highly," he said to himself, "I shall look like a twofold liar."

When the merchants returned, inquiring the outcome of his meeting with Maaruf, the harassed Ali said, "My friends, I had not the heart to speak to him about his debts, for I myself have lent him a thousand pieces. Speak to him yourselves. If he fails to pay you, denounce him to the King as an impostor and a thief."

The merchants went in a body to the King and told him all that had passed between them and Maaruf.

"Your Majesty," they said, "we do not know what to make of this merchant, whose generosity exceeds all bounds. He has borrowed from us sixty thousand pieces of gold, and scattered them in handfuls among the poor. Were he a poor man, he would never be so foolish as to give away so much; and if he is indeed a man of wealth, why has his vaunted caravan not yet arrived?"

Now, the King was an avaricious old miser. When he heard the merchants' account of Maaruf's extravagance, greed took possession of his soul and he said to his vizier, "This man must surely be a merchant of extraordinary wealth, or he would never have been so generous. His caravan is certain to arrive. Now, I will not allow these wolves of the market place to grab all the treasures for themselves, for they are already too rich. I must seek his friendship, so that when his caravan arrives I, too, will have a share. Why, I might even give him my daughter in marriage and join his wealth to mine!"

But the vizier replied, "The man is an impostor, Your

Majesty. Beware of avarice; avarice brings ruin and re-pentance."

"I will put him to the test," said the King, "and we will soon discover if he is a trickster. I will show him a costly pearl and ask his opinion of it. If he can tell its worth, we will know that he is a rich man accustomed to things of value. If he cannot, we will know that he is a liar and a fraud, and I will put him to a terrible death."

Maaruf was sent for, and when he had been admitted to the King's presence and had exchanged greetings with him, the King asked, "Is it true that you owe the merchants sixty thousand pieces of gold?"

Yes, it was true, Maaruf answered. "Why, then, do you not pay them their money?" asked the King.

"The day my caravan arrives," came the reply, "they will be paid twofold. If they want gold, they shall have gold; if they want silver, they shall have silver; and if they prefer goods, they shall have goods, for I have vast quantities of them."

Then, to test Maaruf, the King handed him a rare pearl worth a thousand gold pieces.

"Have you such pearls in your caravan?" he asked.

Maaruf examined the pearl for a moment and, throwing it disdainfully to the floor, crushed it under his heel.

"What is the meaning of this?" cried the King indignantly.

"This pearl," replied the cobbler with a laugh, "is scarcely worth a thousand pieces of gold. I have vast quantities of much larger pearls in my caravan."

At this the King's avarice knew no bounds. He sent for the merchants, told them that their fears were groundless, and assured them that the caravan would soon arrive. Then he summoned his minister.

"See that the merchant Maaruf is received with all

magnificence at the palace," he said. "Speak to him about my daughter, the Princess. Perhaps he will consent to marry her, and so we will gain possession of all his wealth."

"Your Majesty," the vizier replied, "I do not like the manner of this foreigner. His presence bodes evil for the court. I beg you to wait until we have visible proof of his caravan."

Now, the vizier himself had once sought the Princess' hand in marriage and his suit had been rejected. So when the King heard this warning, he flew into a rage.

"Villain," he cried, "you slander this merchant only because you wish to marry the Princess yourself. You would have her left on my hands until she is old and unacceptable. Could she ever find a more suitable husband than this accomplished, wealthy, and generous young man? Not only will he make her a perfect husband, but he will make us all rich into the bargain!"

Afraid of the King's anger, the vizier kept his own counsel and went off to see Maaruf.

"His Majesty the King desires you to marry his daughter, the Princess," he said. "What answer shall I give him?"

"I am honored by the King's proposal," replied Maaruf with an air of unconcern. "But do you not think it would be better to wait until my caravan arrives? The wedding present for such a bride as the Princess would be a greater expense than I can at present afford. I must give my wife at least five thousand purses of gold. Among the poor of the city I will have to distribute a thousand purses on the bridal night; to those who walk in the wedding procession I must give a thousand more; and I will need another thousand to entertain the troops. On the next morning I must present a hundred precious diamonds to the Princess, and as many jewels to the slave girls of the palace. All this is an expense that cannot be met before my caravan arrives."

When the vizier returned, the King was so overwhelmed by Maaruf's reply that he invited him at once to a
private audience.

"Honored and distinguished merchant," said the King
as soon as the cobbler entered, "let us celebrate this happy
union at once! I myself will meet the expenses of the marriage. My treasury is full; I give you leave to take from it all
that you require. You can send in the Princess' present when
your caravan arrives. By Allah, I will take no refusal!"

Without a moment's delay the King sent for the Imam
of the Royal Mosque, who drew up a marriage contract for
Maaruf and the Princess.

The city was gaily decorated on the King's orders.
Drums and trumpets sounded in the streets, and Maaruf the
cobbler sat enthroned in the great hall of the palace. A
troupe of singers, dancers, wrestlers, clowns, and acrobats
capered around the court to entertain the guests, while the
royal treasurer brought Maaruf bag after bag of gold to scatter among the merry throng. He had no rest that day, for
no sooner did he come to Maaruf staggering under the
weight of a hundred thousand coins than he was sent back
for another load.

The vizier watched this with rage in his heart, while
Ali the merchant, aghast at the proceedings, approached
Maaruf and whispered in his ear, "May Allah have no mercy
upon you! It is not enough that you have frittered away the
wealth of all the merchants? Must you also drain the royal
treasury?"

"What's that to you?" replied Maaruf. "Be sure that
when my great caravan arrives, I will repay the King a
thousandfold."

The extravagant rejoicings lasted forty days, and then
came the wedding day. The King, accompanied by his
ministers and the officers of his army, walked in the bridal

procession. Maaruf threw handfuls of gold to the crowds who lined the way.

Next morning he dressed himself in a princely robe and entered the King's council chamber, where he sat down by the side of his father-in-law to receive the good wishes of the ministers and the chief officers of the realm. He sent for the treasurer and ordered him to give robes of honor to all who were present; then he called for sacks of gold and gave handfuls to every member of the royal retinue from the highest courtier to the humblest kitchen boy.

For twenty days Maaruf continued to dissipate the King's treasure. There was still no news of the caravan, and at last came the day when the treasurer found all the coffers empty. He went to tell the King.

"Your Majesty," he said, "the treasure chests are empty and the great caravan of your son-in-law has not yet come to fill them."

Alarmed at these words, the King turned to his vizier.

"By Allah," he said, "it is true that there is still no sign of the caravan. What shall we do?"

"Allah prolong your life, my master!" replied the vizier with an evil smile. "Did I not warn you against the tricks of this impostor? I swear he has no caravan—no, not so much as a one-eyed donkey! He has married your daughter without a present and defrauded you of all your treasure. How long will Your Majesty put up with this rogue?"

"If only we could learn the truth about him!" sighed the King in great perplexity.

"Your Majesty," said the vizier, "no one is better able to find out a man's secrets than his wife. I beg you to call your daughter here and permit me to question her from behind a curtain."

"It shall be done!" the King replied. "On my life, if it

be proved that he has deceived me, he shall die the cruelest of deaths!"

A curtain was drawn across the hall, and the Princess was summoned by the King, who bade her sit behind it and speak with the vizier.

"What do you wish to know?" she asked.

"Honored lady," began the vizier, "the chests of the treasury are empty, thanks to the extravagance of Prince Maaruf, but the wondrous caravan, about which we have heard so much, has not yet come. Therefore the King has given me leave to ask what you know of this stranger and whether you have reason to suspect him."

"Night after night," replied the Princess, "he has promised me pearls and jewels and countless other treasures. But of these I have as yet seen nothing."

"Your Highness," said the vizier, "question him tonight, so that we may know the answer to this riddle. Beg him to tell you the truth, and promise to keep his secret."

"I hear and obey," the Princess replied. "I will speak to Maaruf tonight and tell you what he says."

In the evening the Princess threw her arms around her husband, saying, "Light of my eyes, flower of my heart, your love has kindled in me such fires that I would gladly die for you. Tell me the truth about your caravan and hide nothing from me. How long will you fool my father with such lies? For I fear that he will find you out at last and make you pay dearly for this deception. Tell me everything, my love, and I will think of a way to help you."

"Sweet Princess," replied Maaruf, "I will tell you all. I am no wealthy merchant, no master of caravans. In my own land I was a cobbler plagued with a vicious wife called . . ."

And he told the Princess the tale of his misfortuncs, from his marriage to his flight to Ikhtiyan-al-Khatan.

When she heard the cobbler's story, the Princess burst into a fit of laughter.

"Truly, Maaruf, you are an extraordinary rogue!" she said. "But what are we to do? What will my father say when he learns the truth? The vizier has already sown suspicions in his mind. He will surely kill you and I shall die of grief." She handed him a hundred pieces of gold and said, "Take these and leave the palace now. Ride away to some far country, and then send a courier to let me know your news."

"I am at your mercy, mistress," the cobbler replied.

He said good-by to the Princess and, disguising himself in the livery of a slave, mounted the fastest horse in the King's stables, and rode out into the night.

Next morning, the King sat in the council chamber with the vizier by his side and summoned the Princess to his presence. She came and took her seat behind the curtain as before.

"Tell us, my daughter, what have you learned about Prince Maaruf?"

"May Allah silence all slanderous tongues!" exclaimed the Princess.

"How so?" asked the King.

"Last night," she went on, "soon after Maaruf came to my room, the chief of the guards brought in a letter from ten richly dressed slaves who begged to see their master Maaruf. I took the letter and read aloud, 'From the five hundred slaves of the caravan to their master the merchant Maaruf. We would have you know that soon after you left us we were attacked by an army of two thousand mounted bedouin. We battled against them for thirty days and thirty nights. The caravan lost fifty of its slaves, a hundred mules, and two hundred loads of merchandise. This is the cause of our delay.'

"Yet the Prince was hardly perturbed at this bad news; he did not even ask details from the waiting messengers. 'What are two hundred bales and a hundred mules?' he said to me. 'At worst the loss cannot be more than seventy thousand pieces of gold. Think no more about it, my dear. One thing alone distresses me, that I shall have to leave you for a few days in order to hasten the arrival of the caravan.'

"He got up with a carefree laugh, embraced me tenderly, and said good-by. When he had gone I looked through the window of my room and saw him chatting with ten handsome slaves dressed in uniforms of rare magnificence.

"Presently he mounted his horse and rode away with them to bring the caravan home. Allah be praised that I did not question my husband in the manner you asked," added the Princess bitterly. "I would have lost his love and he would have ceased to trust me. It would have been the fault of your hateful vizier, whose only object is to revile my husband and discredit him in your eyes."

The King rejoiced at these words and exclaimed, "May Allah increase your husband's wealth and prolong his life, my daughter!" Then, turning to the vizier, he rebuked him angrily and told him henceforth to hold his tongue.

So much for the King, the vizier, and the Princess.

As for Maaruf, sadly he rode far into the desert until he came at midday to the outskirts of a little village. By this time he was tired and very hungry. Seeing an old plowman driving two oxen in a field, he went up him and greeted him. "Peace be with you," he said.

The peasant returned his greeting and, noticing the stranger's garb, inquired, "Doubtless, my master, you are one of the King's servants?"

When Maaruf replied that he was, the plowman welcomed him. "Dismount and by my guest," he said.

The cobbler thanked the poor peasant and politely declined his invitation. But the kind old man would take no refusal.

"Pray dismount," he insisted, "and grant me the honor of entertaining you. I will go now to the village and bring food for you and hay for your horse."

"Since the village is near, my friend," protested Maaruf, "I can easily ride there myself and buy food in the market."

But the peasant smiled and shook his head. "I am afraid you will find no market in a poor hamlet such as ours," he replied. "I beg you, in Allah's name, to rest here with your horse while I quickly run to the village."

Not wishing to offend the peasant, Maaruf dismounted and sat down on the grass, while his host hurried away.

As he waited for the peasant's return, Maaruf thought, "I am keeping this poor man from his work. I will make up for his lost time by working at the plow myself."

He went up to the oxen and drove the plow along the furrow. The beasts had not gone far, however, when the plowshare struck against an object in the ground and came to a sudden halt. Maaruf goaded the oxen on, but though they strained powerfully against the yoke, the plow remained rooted in the ground. Clearing away the soil, Maaruf found that the share had caught in a great ring of gold set in a marble slab the size of a large millstone. He moved the slab aside and saw below it a flight of stairs. Going down the stairs, he found himself in a square vault as large as a city's baths, with four separate halls. The first was filled with gold from floor to ceiling; the second, with pearls, emeralds, and coral; the third, with rubies and turquoises; and the fourth, with diamonds and other precious stones. At the far side of the vault stood a coffer of clearest crystal, and upon it a golden casket no larger than a lemon.

The cobbler marveled and rejoiced at this discovery.

He went up to the little casket and, lifting the lid, found in it a gold signet ring finely engraved with strange inscriptions that resembled the legs of creeping insects. He slipped the ring upon his finger and, in doing so, rubbed the seal.

At once a mighty jinnee appeared before him, saying, "I am here, master, I am here! Speak and I will obey. What is your wish? Would you have me build a capital, or lay a town in ruins? Would you have me slay a king, or dig a river bed? I am your slave, by order of the Sovereign of the World, Creator of the day and night! What is your wish?"

Maaruf was amazed at the apparition.

"Who are you?" he cried.

"I am the slave of the ring," the jinnee answered. "Faithfully I serve my master, and my master is he who rubs the ring. Nothing is beyond my power; for I am lord over seventy-two tribes of jinn, each two and seventy thousand strong. Each jinnee rules over a thousand giants, each giant over a thousand goblins, each goblin over a thousand demons, and each demon over a thousand imps. All these owe me absolute allegiance; and yet, for all my power, I have no choice but to obey my master. Ask what you will, and it shall be done. Be it on land or sea, by day or night, should you need me you have but to rub the ring, and I will be at hand to carry out your orders. Of one thing only I must warn you: if you rub the ring twice, I will be consumed in the fire of the powerful words engraved on the seal, and you will lose me for ever."

"Slave of the ring," said Maaruf, "can you tell me what this place is and who imprisoned you in this ring?"

"The vault in which you stand, my master," replied the jinnee, "is the ancient treasure house of Shaddad Ibn Aad, King of Iram. While he lived I was his servant and dwelt in this ring. Just before his death he locked it away in this treasure house, and it was your good fortune to find it."

"Slave of the ring," said the cobbler, "can you carry all this treasure to the open?"

"That is very easy," the jinnee replied.

"Then do so without delay," said Maaruf, "and leave nothing in this vault."

Scarcely had he uttered these words when the floor opened and there appeared before him several handsome boys with baskets upon their heads. These they quickly filled with gold and jewels and carried them above ground. In a few moments the four halls were emptied of their treasure.

"Who are these boys?" Maaruf asked.

"They are my own sons," the jinnee replied. "A light task such as this does not require the mustering of a mighty band. What else do you wish, my master?"

"I require a caravan of mules loaded with chests," replied the cobbler, "to carry these marvels to Ikhtiyan-al-Khatan."

The jinnee uttered a loud cry, and there appeared seven hundred richly saddled mules laden with chests and baskets, and a hundred slaves magnificently clad. In a twinkling the chests and baskets were filled with treasure and placed upon the mules, and the caravan stood in splendid array, guarded by mounted slaves.

"And now, slave of the ring," said Maaruf, "I require a few hundred loads of precious stuffs."

"Would you have Syrian damask or Persian velvet, Indian brocade or Roman silk or Egyptian gabardine?"

"A hundred loads of each!" cried Maaruf.

"I hear and obey," replied the jinnee. "I will at once dispatch my spirits to these distant lands. Tomorrow morning you shall have all that you require."

Then Maaruf ordered the slave of the ring to set up a pavilion and serve him food and wine. The jinnee provided his master with a silk pavilion and a sumptuous meal and departed on his mission.

As Maaruf was about to sit down to his feast, the old peasant returned from the village, carrying a large bowl of lentils for his guest and a sack of hay for the horse. When he saw the great caravan drawn up in the field, and Maaruf reclining in the tent, attended by innumerable slaves, he thought that his guest must be none other than the King.

"I will hurry back," he said to himself, "and kill my two chickens and roast them in butter for him." He was on the point of turning back when Maaruf saw him and ordered his slaves to bring him into the pavilion.

The slaves led the plowman to the tent, with his bowl of lentils and his sack of hay. Maaruf rose to receive him and gave him a courteous welcome.

"What is it you are carrying, brother?" he asked.

"Master," the peasant replied. "I was bringing you your dinner and some hay for your horse. Pardon my scant courtesy, I beg you. Had I known you were the King, I would have killed my two chickens and roasted them for you."

"Do not be alarmed, my friend," replied Maaruf. "I am not the King, but his son-in-law. A certain misunderstanding arose between us and I left the palace. I will return tomorrow morning with these messengers and these presents."

Then Maaruf thanked the peasant for his generosity and made him sit down by his side. "By Allah," he said, "I will eat nothing but the food of your hospitality."

He ordered the slaves to serve the peasant with the delicate meats and ate the lentils himself. When the meal was finished he filled the empty bowl with gold and gave it to the peasant.

"Take this to your family," he said, "and if you come to see me at the palace you will have a hearty welcome and a generous reward."

The old plowman took the gold and returned to the village, scarcely believing his good fortune.

When darkness fell, the slaves of the caravan brought into the tent a troupe of beautiful girls, who danced and made music. At daybreak Maaruf saw a great cloud of dust in the distance, and soon a long procession of mules drew near. They were laden with innumerable bales of merchandise, and at their head rode the jinnee, in the guise of a caravan leader, alongside a four-pillared litter of pure gold inlaid with diamonds. When the caravan arrived at the tent, the jinnee dismounted and kissed the ground before Maaruf.

"The task is accomplished, my master," he said. "Pray put on the garment that I have brought especially for you; you will find it worthy of a king. Then mount this litter."

"One thing more remains to be done," said Maaruf. "Before I set forth with the caravan, I wish you to hurry to Ikhtiyan-al-Khatan and announce my coming to the King."

"I hear and obey," the jinnee replied.

He transformed himself into the semblance of a courier and set off toward the city, arriving at the palace just as the vizier was saying to the King, "Be no longer deceived, Your Majesty, by the lies of this impostor. Do not be taken in by your daughter's story; for I swear by your precious life that Maaruf fled the city, not to speed the arrival of his caravan, but to save his skin."

As the vizier finished speaking, the courier entered the royal presence and kissed the ground before the King.

"Your Majesty," he said, "I bring you greetings from the illustrious Prince, your son-in-law, who is now approaching the city with his noble caravan."

With this the courier again kissed the ground before the King and hurried out of the palace. The King rejoiced. "Traitor," he said to the vizier, "may Allah blacken your face. How long will you revile my son-in-law and call him thief and liar?"

The dumbfounded vizier hung his head.

The city was decorated, and a procession marched out to meet the caravan. The King went to his daughter's room and told her the joyful news. The Princess was astounded to hear her father speak of the caravan and thought, "Can this be another of Maaruf's tricks? Or was he testing my love with an invented tale of poverty?"

But even more astonished than the Princess was her husband's friend, Ali the merchant. When he saw the great commotion in the city and learned the news of Maaruf's expected arrival at the head of a splendid caravan, he thought, "What new roguery is this? Can it be possible that this patcher of old slippers is really coming with a caravan? Or is it some fresh trick he has contrived with the aid of the Princess?"

Before long, the procession that had gone out to meet the caravan returned to the city. Maaruf, arrayed in a magnificent robe, rode triumphantly by the King's side in the golden litter, and as the long, winding caravan made its way through the streets, the merchants flocked near their prodigal debtor and kissed the ground before him. Ali the merchant managed to push his way through the throng and whispered to Maaruf, "How on earth has this come about, you sheikh of mad swindlers? And yet, by Allah, you deserve your good fortune!"

The procession halted at the royal palace. In the great council chamber, Maaruf sat beside the King. He ordered his slaves to fill the royal coffers with gold and jewels, and to unpack the bales of precious merchandise. Then he picked out the finest stuffs and said to the attendants, "Carry these silks to the Princess so that she may distribute them among her women; also take her this chest of jewels, which she may share among the slaves and serving girls."

After that he proceeded to deal out presents to the officers of the King's army, to the courtiers and their wives, to the merchants who were his creditors, and to the poor of the city; and while the treasures were being distributed, the King writhed upon his throne in an agony of greed and envy. As Maaruf threw handfuls of pearls and emeralds to right and left, the King whispered to him, "Enough, my son! There will be nothing left for us!" But Maaruf answered, "My caravan is inexhaustible."

It was not long before the vizier came and told the King that the treasury was full and could hold no more. The King cried, "Fill another hall!"

Then Maaruf hastened to his wife, who received him in a transport of joy and kissed his hand.

"Was it to mock me," she said, "or to test my love that you pretended to be a poor cobbler fleeing from a nagging wife? Whichever it was, I thank Allah I did not fail you."

Maaruf embraced her and gave her a gown splendidly embroidered in gold, a necklace threaded with forty pearls, and a pair of anklets fashioned by the art of mighty sorcerers. The Princess cried out for joy as she saw these marvels, and said, "I will keep them for festivals and state occasions only."

"Not so, my love," replied Maaruf. "I will give you ornaments like these each day."

Then he summoned the slave girls of the harem and gave each of them an embroidered robe adorned with ornaments of gold. Arrayed in this splendor, they were like black-eyed maidens of paradise, while the Princess shone in their midst like the moon among the stars.

At nightfall the King said to the vizier, "What have

you to say now? Does not the wealth of my son-in-law surpass all wonders?"

"Indeed, Your Majesty," the vizier replied, "the Prince's lavishness is that of no ordinary merchant; for where can a merchant find such pearls and jewels as your son-in-law has thrown away? Kings and princes have no treasures like these. There must surely be some strange reason for his conduct. I suggest, my master, that you make Prince Maaruf drunk if you wish to discover the source of his riches. When he is overcome with wine, let us ply him with questions until he tells us everything. Indeed, I already fear the consequences of this extraordinary wealth; for it is more than likely that in time he will win over the troops with his favors and drive you from your kingdom."

"You have spoken wisely, my vizier," said the King. "Tomorrow we must find out the whole truth."

Next morning, while the King was sitting in his council chamber, the grooms of the royal stables rushed in, begging leave to speak with him.

"Your Majesty," they cried, "the entire caravan of Prince Maaruf is gone! All the slaves, the horses, and the mules disappeared during the night, and nowhere can we find a trace of them."

Greatly troubled at this news, the King hastened to Maaruf's chamber and told him what had happened. But Maaruf laughed.

"Calm yourself, Your Majesty," he said. "The loss of these trifles is nothing to me. For what is a caravan of mules?"

"By Allah," thought the King in amazement, "what manner of man is this, to whom wealth counts for nothing? There must surely be a reason for all this!"

When evening came, the King sat with Maaruf and the vizier in a pavilion in the garden of the palace. Wine flowed freely; and when Maaruf was so flushed with drink that he could not tell his left hand from his right, the vizier said to him, "Your Highness, you have never told us the adventures of your life. Pray let us hear how you became so rich and rose to such prominence in business affairs."

Thereupon the drunken cobbler related the story of his life, from his marriage in Cairo to the finding of the ring in the peasant's field.

"Will you permit us to see the ring, Your Highness?" asked the vizier.

Without a moment's thought the foolish cobbler slipped the ring from his finger and handed it to the minister.

"Look at the seal!" he said. "My servant the jinnee dwells within it."

The vizier instantly slipped the ring upon his own finger and rubbed the seal; and the jinnee appeared before him.

"I am here," said the jinnee. "Ask and receive! Would you have me build a capital, or lay a town in ruins? Would you have me slay a king, or dig a river bed?"

"Slave of the ring," replied the vizier, pointing to Maaruf, "take up this rascal and cast him down upon some barren desert where he will perish from hunger and thirst!"

At once the jinnee snatched up the cobbler, flew with him between earth and sky, and finally set him down in the middle of a waterless desert.

"Did I not tell you," said the vizier to the King, "that this dog was a liar and a cheat?"

"You were right, my vizier," replied the monarch. "Give me the ring and let me examine it."

"Miserable old fool," the vizier cried, "do you expect me to remain your servant when I can be your master?"

So saying, the vizier rubbed the ring and said to the jinnee, "Take up this wretch and cast him down by the side of his son-in-law!"

The jinnee carried the old King upon his shoulder, flew with him through the void, and set him down in the middle of the desert, where King and son-in-law sat wailing together. So much for them.

The vizier summoned the nobles and the captains of the army and proclaimed himself Sultan of the city. He explained that he had banished the King and Maaruf by the power of a magic ring, and threatened the assembly, saying, "If anyone dares to resist my rule, he shall join them in the desert of hunger and thirst!"

The courtiers swore fealty, and the vizier promoted some and dismissed others. Then he sent a message to the Princess, bidding her prepare to receive him that night.

"You will be welcome," the Princess answered through her footman.

When evening came, she put on her silks and jewels, perfumed herself, and received the vizier with a smile. "What an honor, my master," she said, and invited him to sit down.

"Now that we are alone, Your Highness," said the vizier, "I pray that you unveil yourself."

The Princess readily complied, but scarcely had she done so than she uttered a cry of terror and started back, covering her face again.

"What is the matter, my mistress?" asked the vizier.

"Would you show my face to that stranger?" she cried in terror.

"Where, where?" exclaimed the vizier angrily.

"There, in your ring!"

The vizier laughed, and said, "Dear lady, that is no man but only my faithful jinnee."

But the Princess screamed louder and cried, "I am terrified of the jinnee! Put him away, for my sake!"

The vizier took the ring off his finger and placed it under the cushions. Thereupon she gave a loud cry, and at once forty slave girls burst into the room and laid hold of the vizier. The Princess quickly snatched up the ring and rubbed the seal; and the jinnee appeared before her.

"Cast this traitor into a dark dungeon," she said, "and bring me back my father and my husband."

"I hear and obey," the jinnee replied; and, carrying the vizier on his shoulder, threw him into the darkest dungeon of the palace. Then he flew toward the desert and presently returned with the King and Maaruf, both half dead with fright and hunger.

The Princess, rejoicing to see them, offered them food and wine and told them how she had outwitted the vizier.

"We will tie him to the stake and put him to death!" the King cried. "But first give me back the ring, my daughter."

The Princess replied, "The ring shall stay with me. I will take care of it from now on."

Early next morning the King and Maaruf entered the council chamber. The courtiers, who were astonished to see them, again kissed the ground before them and gave them a jubilant welcome. The stake was set up in the grounds of the palace and the vizier was put to death in sight of all the people.

Maaruf was appointed vizier and heir to the throne. He governed jointly with the King, and lived with the Princess ever after.

As I ran in pursuit of the creature, stumbling here and there in the dark, I gradually made out at the far side of the cavern a speck of light that grew larger and brighter as I advanced toward it.

The Dream

There once lived in Baghdad a rich merchant who lost all his money by spending it unwisely. He became so poor that he could live only by doing the hardest work for very little pay.

One night he lay down to sleep with a heavy heart, and as he slept he heard a voicie saying, "Your fortune lies in Cairo. Go and seek it there."

The very next morning he set out for Cairo and, after traveling many weeks and enduring much hardship on the way, arrived in that city. Night had fallen, and as he could not afford to stay at an inn, he lay down to sleep in the courtyard of a mosque.

Now, as chance would have it, a band of robbers entered the mosque and from there broke into an adjoining house. Awakened by the noise, the owners raised the alarm and shouted for help, whereupon the thieves made off. Presently the chief of police and his men arrived on the scene and entered the mosque. Finding the merchant from Baghdad in the courtyard, they seized him and beat him with their clubs until he was nearly dead. Then they threw him into prison.

Three days later, the chief of police ordered his men to bring the stranger before him.

"Where do you come from?" asked the chief.

"From Baghdad."

"And what has brought you to Cairo?"

"I heard a voice in my sleep saying, 'Your fortune lies in Cairo. Go and seek it there.' But when I came to Cairo, the fortune I was promised proved to be the beating I received at the hands of your men."

When he heard this, the chief of police burst out laughing. "Know then, you fool," he cried, "that I, too, have heard a voice in my sleep, not just once but on three occasions. The voice said, 'Go to Baghdad, and in a cobbled street lined with palm trees you will find a three-story house, with a courtyard of green marble; at the far end of the garden there is a fountain of white marble. Under the fountain a large sum of money lies buried. Go there and dig it up.' But did I go? Of course not. Yet, fool that you are, you have come all the way to Cairo on the strength of a silly dream."

Then the chief of police gave the merchant some money. "Here," he said, "take this. It will help you on the way back to your own country." From the policeman's description, the merchant realized at once that the house and garden were his own. He took the money and set out promptly on his homeward journey.

As soon as he reached his house he went into the garden, dug beneath the fountain, and uncovered a great treasure of gold and silver.

Thus the words of the dream were wondrously fulfilled, and Allah made the ruined merchant rich again.

The Ebony Horse

A long time ago there lived in the land of Persia a great and powerful king named Sabur. Not only was he rich and wise, just and honorable, but he also surpassed all the rulers of his time in generosity, courage, and kindness. He had three daughters, each fairer than the full moon, and a son called Prince Kamar, who was a gallant and handsome youth.

Every year it was the King's custom to celebrate two feasts in his capital: one at the beginning of spring, and the other in the fall. During these two festivals the gates of the palace were thrown open, and alms were given to the needy and the poor. From the remotest parts of the kingdom people came to lay their presents at the King's feet.

On one of these occasions, the King was seated on his throne, surrounded by all his courtiers, when three wise men presented themselves. They were skilled in the arts and sciences and had invented many rare and curious objects. The first was an Indian, the second a Greek, and the third a Persian.

The Indian kissed the ground before the King, wished him joy, and laid before him a truly splendid gift: the golden image of a man, encrusted with precious stones and holding a golden trumpet in his hand.

"Wise Indian," the King said, "what is the purpose of this figure?"

"Your Majesty," he answered, "if you set this golden figure at the gate of your capital, he will be a guardian over it; for if your enemies march against you, he will raise the trumpet to his lips and with one shrill blast put them to flight."

"By Allah," the King cried, "if what you say is true, I promise to grant you all that you desire."

Then the Greek came forward, kissed the ground before the King, and offered him a great silver basin, which had in it a gold peacock surrounded by twenty-four gold chicks.

"Honored Greek," said the King, "tell us what this peacock can do."

"Your Majesty," he replied, "at the stroke of every hour of the day or night the peacock pecks one of the four and twenty chicks. Furthermore, at the end of every month, it will open its mouth and you will see the crescent moon within it."

"By Allah," exclaimed the King in wonderment, "if what you say is true, you have but to name the price and it will be paid."

Now the old Persian came forward, kissed the ground before the King, and presented him with a horse made from the blackest ebony, inlaid with gold and jewels, and harnessed with a saddle, bridle, and stirrups such as no king ever possessed. King Sabur marveled at the creature's perfection and at the excellence of the workmanship.

"Tell us what it can do," he said.

"My lord," the Persian answered, "this horse will carry

its rider through the air wherever he fancies, and cover a whole year's journey in a single day."

"By Allah," he cried to the Persian, "if your claim proves true, I promise to fulfill your dearest wish and utmost desire."

The wise men were entertained at the palace for three days, during which time the King put the presents to the test. He found, to his great joy, that all the claims were true: the golden image blew his gold trumpet, the gold peacock pecked its golden chicks, and the Persian mounted the ebony horse, turned a little peg near the saddle, and soared swiftly through the air, finally alighting on the very spot from which he had taken off.

"Now that I have seen these wondrous things in action," said the King to the wise men, "it only remains for me to fulfill my promise. Therefore ask what you desire and it shall be granted."

"Your Majesty," the three answered, "these presents are beyond all price and can be exchanged only for things of immeasurable value. Since you have given us the choice of our rewards, our request is this: your daughters' hands in marriage."

At these words the young Prince, who was sitting his father's side, sprang to his feet.

"Father," he cried, "these men are old and wicked sorcerers. They are unworthy of my sisters. Surely you will never agree."

"My son," the King answered, "I have given them my word, and a king's word is his bond. And just think what I can do with this wonderful horse; I *must* have it, whatever the cost. Go and ride it yourself, and then tell me what you think of the exchange."

The Prince vaulted lightly into the saddle, thrust his

feet into the stirrups, and spurred the horse on. But it did not move.

The King turned to the Persian. "Teach my son how to ride it."

The Persian, who had taken a dislike to the Prince because he opposed his sisters' marriage, went up to him and gave him some directions. As soon as he was shown the peg in the saddle that made the horse move, the Prince touched it and, lo! the horse flew into the air, so high and so swiftly that it was out of sight in a few moments.

When, after some hours, the Prince had not returned, King Sabur became greatly alarmed.

"Wretch," he cried to the Persian, "what must we do to bring him back?"

"I can do nothing, Your Majesty," he answered. "He gave me no time to explain the use of the second peg, and went off without learning how to come back."

Beside himself with grief and anger, the King ordered his slaves to beat the Persian and throw him into prison; then he shut the doors of his palace and gave himself up to weeping and lamenting, together with his wife, his daughters, and his courtiers. Thus their gladness turned to sorrow and their joy to mourning.

Meanwhile the Prince had risen happily in the air until he reached the clouds and could hardly see the earth below. For a time he was thrilled with joy at the adventure, but before long he realized his danger and began to think of coming down. He turned the peg around and around, but, instead of descending, he climbed higher and higher until he feared he would strike his head against the sky.

"I am lost," he said to himself. "The magician must have surely meant to destroy me. And yet there must be a second peg to bring this horse to earth again. If only I could find it!"

He felt all over the horse until at last, to his great joy,

he touched a very small screw on the right side of the saddle. He pressed it gently, and at once the horse slowed down. After a few moments it began to lose height as quickly as it had risen. The Prince learned how to manage the peg, the screw, and the bridle; and when he had mastered all the movements and reassured himself, he brought the horse to a comfortable height and journeyed at an easy pace, so that he could enjoy the magnificent views stretching for miles and miles below him.

Seated at his ease, the Prince flew over countries and cities he had never seen before and gazed in wonderment on all the places he passed over. When darkness fell, he found himself circling over a beautiful city that shimmered with countless golden lights, in the midst of which stood a great marble palace flanked by six high towers. He pressed the screw and guided the horse until it alighted on the roof of the palace, at the far end of which he saw a door leading to a flight of white marble steps. Leaving the ebony horse, he made his way down the steps and found himself in a marble hall, lit with lamps and candles, where a black slave lay fast asleep, guarding the entrance to a room beyond. Without a sound, he tiptoed past the slave and, drawing aside a velvet curtain, entered a richly furnished room. In the center stood a couch of ivory and alabaster studded with precious gems. Two young slave girls slept on a carpet near the door, and on the couch reclined the most beautiful girl he had ever looked upon. So beautiful was she that the Prince fell in love with her at sight and nearly fainted as he gazed at her. He approached the couch and, kneeling by her side, gently touched the girl's hand. Her eyes opened, but before she could utter a sound he begged her to be calm and fear nothing.

"Who are you, and where do you come from?" she asked in some alarm.

"I am a Prince," he answered, "the son of the King of

Persia. It is my good fortune that has brought me to this palace, gentle lady. But if your people find me in your private room, my life will be in danger. I therefore beg you for your protection."

The girl, who was the daughter of the King of Yemen, answered, "Have no fear. You will be safe with me."

She roused her slaves and ordered them to give the stranger food and drink, and to prepare a room where he might stay the night. The Prince rested and refreshed himself, and then told her of his adventure.

Princess Shams-al-Nahar (for that was her name) had never met anyone so brave and handsome as the Prince of Persia. She put on her finest robes and adorned herself with her most precious jewels, so that she might be seen in all her beauty. When the Prince came to her next morning, he was even more charmed and dazzled than before. He told her that he loved her with all his heart.

But when it was time for him to take his leave and return to his father's court, the Princess burst into tears.

"Do not cry," he said. "I will come back in a few days and request your hand in marriage from the King your father."

"Take me with you," implored the Princess. "I cannot bear to be parted from you so soon."

"Rise, then, and let us be off!" he cried. "As soon as we arrive in Persia we will celebrate our marriage; then we will return in state to your father's city."

He took the Princess up to the palace roof, sat her on the ebony horse in front of him, placed his arm tightly around her waist, and turned the magic peg. The horse rose into the air, and flew with them at great speed. Halfway through their journey, they alighted for a short rest in an orchard that was shaded with fruit trees and watered by crystal streams. After eating and refreshing themselves, they remounted the enchanted horse and flew onward to Persia. By daybreak they came in sight of King Sabur's capital, and the happy Prince brought the ebony horse to earth in the garden of his summer palace outside the city walls. He took the Princess into the palace and ordered his servants to attend her.

"I will leave you here and go tell my father, the King, of your arrival," he said. "Watch over my horse while I am away. I shall send messengers to bring you in state to my father's court."

Now, when the Prince entered the city he found the people dressed in black and everywhere saw signs of public mourning. Anxiously he hurried to his father's court.

Going up to one of the guards, he asked, "Why is everyone in mourning?"

"The Prince! The Prince has come back!" shouted the guard. "The Prince is alive!"

In a short while the joyful news of the Prince's return spread through the town, and the people's sorrow changed to gladness. King Sabur wept for joy on seeing him safe and sound. He embraced and kissed him, and scolded him for causing such grief and anxiety by his departure.

"Guess whom I have brought with me!" said the Prince.

"Tell me, my son."

The Prince replied, "I have brought to our city the daughter of the King of Yemen, the most beautiful girl in all the East."

And the Prince proceeded to tell his father of his adventure and how he had returned home with the Princess.

"Let her be brought to our court in royal fashion," the King cried. "We will receive her with the utmost honor and entertain her as our guest."

Overjoyed at his son's return, King Sabur gave orders that the Persian sage should be set free and allowed to return home. The magician, who had been expecting to suffer death at any moment, was greatly surprised at the King's pardon, and was no less bewildered by the rejoicing in the streets. Upon inquiry he was told of the return of the King's son and of the Princess who was waiting outside the city gates.

Without losing a moment, he rode off with all speed to the summer palace and, arriving there before the King's messengers, entered the hall, where he found Shams-al-Nahar lying at ease upon a couch.

"Gracious Princess," he said, kissing the ground before her, "the King of Persia has sent me to bring you to his court on the enchanted horse."

The unsuspecting girl was very glad to hear this; she quickly got up and made ready to go with the supposed messenger. The Persian leaped into the saddle of the ebony horse and lifted her up behind him. When he had securely fastened her to his waist, he turned the peg and the horse rose like a bird into the air. After a few moments the Princess, to her great alarm, found she was being carried far from the city and her lover.

"Where are we going?" she cried. "Why do you not obey your master's orders?"

"My master?" the magician echoed with an evil smile. "Who is my master?"

"Why, the King," she cried.

The Persian laughed.

"Do you know who I am?" he asked sharply.

"I know nothing of you except what you have told me," answered the Princess.

"Learn, then," said he, "that what I told you was only a snare to trap you and the Prince. That young ruffian stole my horse from me, the work of my own hands, and the loss nearly broke my heart. Now the horse is mine again, and it is the Prince's turn to grieve. Come with me, gentle Princess, and forget that boastful youth, for I am powerful and rich, and more generous than any Prince. My slaves and servants will obey you as they obey me; I will give you jewels beyond the wealth of kings and grant your every wish and fancy."

The Princess wept bitterly and begged the magician to take her back, but all her entreaties were of no avail. After many weary hours they reached Turkey, where the magician brought the horse to earth in a green meadow, and then went in search of food and water.

Now, this meadow was near the capital. It so happened that on that day the King of Turkey was riding nearby with his courtiers. Hearing the horses galloping past, the Princess screamed and called loudly for help. The King sent his riders to her aid and they seized the magician before he could take off on the horse. She quickly told them who she was and how she had been carried off against her will.

The King was astonished at the sorcerer's ugly appearance and the girl's extraordinary beauty. He ordered his men to throw the magician into prison, and took the Princess and the ebony horse to his own palace.

But Shams-al-Nahar's troubles were by no means over. For no sooner had the King set eyes on her and listened to her story than he became infatuated with the Princess and resolved to marry her himself. He turned a deaf ear to her prayers and entreaties and gave orders for the wedding preparations to begin.

At last, when she saw that nothing would make him change his mind, she devised a scheme to save herself. She refused all food and drink, and began to rave and scream like a woman stricken with madness. So well did she play the

part that everyone believed she was really insane. The King
ordered the wedding to be postponed, and called his doctors
to attend to her. But the more they saw of her, the more they
were convinced that she was past all cure.

Now, all this time the Prince of Persia had been wan-
dering with a heavy heart from land to land in search of his
beloved Shams-al-Nahar, inquiring if anyone had seen or
heard of a Princess and an ebony horse.

One day, at an inn in one of the great cities of Turkey,
he chanced to hear the people talk about the sudden illness
of a Princess who was to have married their King. He disguised himself as a doctor, went to the royal palace, and
begged an audience of the King. He introduced himself as a
physician long experienced in the cure of madness, and
told the King he had heard of the Princess' illness and had
come all the way from Persia to treat her.

"Honored doctor," exclaimed the joyful King, "you
are most welcome." Then he told the Prince the story of
the girl's illness and all that had happened since the day he
had found her with the old magician and the ebony horse.

"I have thrown the villain into prison," he added.
"As for the horse, it is being carefully guarded in the courtyard of the palace."

He led the Prince to the room where Shams-al-Nahar
was confined. They found her weeping and tearing her
clothes. The disguised Prince realized at once that her madness was not real but merely a device to avoid the marriage.

"Your Majesty," he said, "I must enter the room alone,
or the cure will have no effect."

The King left him, and the young man went up to the
Princess and touched her hand. "Dear Princess," he said tenderly, "do you not know me?"

As soon as she heard his voice she turned to him

and in the great joy of recognition threw herself into his arms.

"My beloved Princess," he said, "be brave and patient a little longer. I have an excellent plan for our escape. But first you must make the King believe that you are improved, by talking calmly to him."

The Prince came out of the room and said to the King, "The girl is almost cured. Enter and speak kindly to her, and all things shall go as you wish."

The King marveled to see so great a change in the Princess, and was overjoyed when the Prince told him he hoped she would be fully recovered by the next day. He ordered his women slaves to attend her and dress her in fine robes.

Next morning the Prince advised the King, "Your Majesty, to complete the cure you must go with all your courtiers to the spot where you first found the Princess, and take with you the girl herself and the ebony horse. For you must know that the horse is a devil whose evil power has made her mad. I will now prepare some magic incense to break the spell that binds her; otherwise the evil spirit will once again enter her body, and our cure will work no more."

"I will do as you wish," the King replied, and arranged at once to leave the city for the meadow, accompanied by the Prince, the Princess, and all his retinue. When they arrived, the disguised Prince ordered the girl to sit upon the ebony horse, and placed braziers, in which a sweet incense was burning, all around her. Then, as swift as lightning, and under the gaze of all the people, he leaped onto the saddle behind the Princess and turned the peg. The horse rose straight up into the air, and in a few moments vanished from sight.

The Prince and Princess flew under the blue sky until

they arrived safely in Persia. The King and all the people were overjoyed to see them after having given up hope of their return. Celebrations were held throughout the land, and they were married amid great rejoicing.

When the King died the Prince succeeded to his father's throne, and lived in happiness and peace with Shams-al-Nahar until the end of their days.

The Tale of the Hunchback

Once upon a time, in the city of Basra, a tailor was taking an evening walk with his wife when they met a sprightly little hunchback who was merrily singing and clashing a tambourine. His merriment was so infectious that it banished grief and sorrow and every other care. The couple were so amused by the hunchback that they invited him to spend the evening with them as their guest. He accepted, and when they had reached home the tailor hurried out to the market place, where he bought some fried fish, bread, and lemons, and honey for desert.

The three sat down to a hilarious meal. Being fond of practical jokes, the tailor's wife crammed a large piece of fish into the hunchback's mouth and forced him to swallow it. But, as fate would have it, the fish concealed a large and sharp bone that stuck in his throat and choked him. When they examined him they found, to their horror, that the hunchback was dead.

The tailor lifted up his hands and exclaimed, "There is no strength or power save in Allah! Alas that this man should have met his death at our hands, and in this fashion!"

"Crying will not help us," said his wife. "We must do something!"

"What can we do?" whimpered the tailor.

"Take the body in your arms," she said. "We will cover it with a shawl and carry it out of the house this very night. I will walk in front, crying, 'My child is ill, my poor child is ill! Who can direct us to a doctor's house?'"

Encouraged by her plan, the tailor wrapped up the hunchback in a large silken shawl and carried him out into the street, his wife lamenting, "My child! My child! Who will save him from the foul smallpox?"

So all who saw them whispered, "They are carrying a child stricken with the smallpox."

Thus they proceeded through the streets, inquiring for the doctor's house as they went, until at last they were directed to the house of a Jewish doctor. They knocked, and the door was opened by a slave girl.

"Give your master this piece of silver," said the tailor's wife, "and beg him to come down and see my child; for he is very ill."

As soon as the girl had gone in to call the doctor, the tailor's wife slipped into the doorway and said to her husband, "Let us leave the hunchback here and run for our lives!"

The tailor propped up the body at the bottom of the staircase, and the pair made off as fast as their legs could carry them.

The Jew rejoiced on receiving the piece of silver. He rose quickly and, hurrying down the stairs in the dark, stumbled against the corpse and knocked it over. Terrified at the sight of the lifeless hunchback, and thinking that he himself had just caused his death, the Jew called on Moses and Aaron and Ezra and Joshua son of Nun, and reminded himself of the Ten Commandments, wringing his hands and crying, "How will I get rid of the body?" Then he took up the hunchback and bore him to his wife and told her what had happened.

"You stand there doing nothing?" exclaimed the terrified woman. "If the corpse remains here till daybreak we are lost! Come, we will carry the body up to the terrace and throw it into the courtyard of our neighbor the Moslem."

Now, the Moslem was the steward of the royal kitchens, from which he seldom departed with his pockets empty. His house was always infested with rats and mice, which ate the butter, the cheese, and the wheat; and on fine nights the stray cats and dogs of the neighborhood came down and feasted on the contents of the kitchen. So the Jew and his wife, carrying the hunchback, climbed down from their terrace into their neighbor's courtyard and propped the hunchback up against the wall of the kitchen.

It was not long before the steward, who had been out all day, returned home. He opened the door and lit a candle —then started at the sight of a man leaning against the wall of his kitchen. "So our thief is a man after all!" he thought; and, taking up a mallet, he cried, "By Allah! to think it was you, and not the cats and dogs, who stole the meat and the butter! I have killed almost all the stray cats and dogs of the district and never thought of you and your like, who come prowling around the terraces."

He knocked the hunchback down with the mallet and dealt him another blow on the chest as he lay on the ground. But the angry steward soon found that the man was dead. He was seized with fear, and exclaimed, "There is no strength or power save in Allah! A curse upon the meat and the butter, and upon this night which has witnessed your death at my hands, you wretch!"

He lifted the hunchback onto his shoulders and left the house. The night was already nearing its end. The steward walked with his burden through the deserted streets until he entered a lane leading to the market place, and came to a shop that stood on a corner. There he leaned the hunchback up against the wall and hurried away.

Soon after, a Christian, who was the king's saddler, passed through the lane on his way to the public baths. He was fuddled with drink, and as he reeled along, he kept muttering to himself, "Doomsday has come! The Last Judgment has come!" and staggering from one side of the lane to the other. Suddenly he bumped into the hunchback.

Now, it so chanced that earlier in the evening the Christian had been robbed of his turban and was forced to buy another. So, on suddenly seeing this figure against the wall, he imagined, in his stupor, that it was someone who was about to snatch off his new turban and, taking the hunchback by the throat, felled him with a resounding blow. Then he raised a great outcry, screaming and cursing and calling out to the watchman of the market place.

The watchman arrived to find a Christian beating a Moslem.

"Get up and let go of him!" he shouted angrily. Then he found that the hunchback was dead. "A fine state of affairs when a Christian dares to kill a Believer!" he exclaimed.

Confounded at the swift death of his victim, the Christian began to call on Jesus and Mary: thus, as the proverb has it, intoxication departed and meditation took its place. The watchman took hold of the Christian saddler, manacled him, and dragged him away to the governor's house.

In the morning the governor gave orders for the hanging of the Christian. The town crier proclaimed his crime in the streets, and a gallows was set up in the heart of the city. Then came the executioner who, in the presence of the governor, stood the Christian beneath the gallows and put the rope around his neck.

At this moment the King's steward pushed his way through the crowd, crying, "Do not hang him! It was I who killed the hunchback!"

"Why did you kill him?" asked the governor.

"It all happened," replied the steward, "when I returned home last night and found him in my house, about to break into the kitchen. I struck him with a mallet and he fell down dead upon the instant. In despair, I carried him to a lane adjoining the market place. Is it not enough to have killed a Moslem?" added the steward passionately. "Must a Christian also die on my account? Therefore, hang no man but me!"

Hearing this, the governor set the Christian free and gave the executioner a fresh order. "Hang the steward instead, on the grounds of his own confession."

The executioner led the steward to the scaffold and had just placed the rope around his neck when the Jewish doctor forced his way through the crowd. "Do not hang him!" he cried. "I am the man who killed the hunchback!" And he told the governor his own version of the hunchback's death. "Is my sin not great enough that I have killed a man unwittingly?" he added. "Must another be killed through my crime, and with my knowledge?"

On hearing this, the governor gave orders that the Jew be hanged in place of the steward. But as the rope was being placed around his neck, the tailor came forward and cried, "Do not hang him! No one killed the hunchback but myself!" And he related to the astonished assembly the true circumstances of the hunchback's death.

The governor marveled at the story and commented, "This episode ought to be recorded in books." And he ordered the executioner to set the Jew at liberty and to hang the tailor.

"Would to heaven they would make up their minds," muttered the executioner, understandably impatient at the delay. "The day will end before we hang any of them." He resolutely placed the rope around the tailor's neck.

Now, the hunchback, the cause of all this commotion, was the King's jester and favorite companion. Finding that his jester had been absent from the royal palace all night and all the next morning, the monarch ordered his attendants to look for him. They soon returned to inform him of the hunchback's death and his self-confessed murderers.

"Go to the governor," said the King to his chamberlain, "and get him to bring them all before me."

The chamberlain hurried at once to the city square, where the executioner was about to hang the tailor. "Stop! Stop! Don't hang him!" he shouted, rushing through the crowd. And before the executioner could complete his work, the chamberlain informed the governor of the King's orders and took him to the royal palace, together with the tailor, the Christian, the Jew, the steward, and the hunchback's body.

When they had all been admitted to the King's presence, the governor kissed the ground before him and related all that had happened. The King marveled greatly and gave orders that the story be inscribed on parchment in letters of gold. Then he turned to those who were present and asked, "Have you ever heard a tale more astonishing than this story of the hunchback?"

The tailor came forward, and said, "Of all the tales of marvel that I have heard, Your Majesty, none surpasses in wonder an incident that I witnessed yesterday.

"Early in the morning, before I met the hunchback, I was at a breakfast party given by a friend to some twenty tradesmen and craftsmen of the city, among them tailors, drapers, carpenters, and others. As soon as the sun rose and the food was set before us, our host ushered into the room a handsome but noticeably lame young man, richly dressed in the Baghdad fashion. The young man greeted the company, and we all rose to receive him. But when he was about to sit down, he caught sight of one of the guests and, instead of taking his seat, made for the door. We all expressed surprise and concern, and our host held the young man by the arm and earnestly pleaded with him to explain his abrupt departure.

" 'Sir,' he answered, 'do not try to detain me. If you must know, it is the presence of this obnoxious barber that compels me to leave at once.'

"Our host was greatly astonished at these words, and the rest of us, too, wondered why the young man, a stranger in this city, should have taken offense at the barber's presence. We begged him to tell us the reason.

" 'Gentlemen,' he answered, 'this barber was the cause of a grave disaster that befell me in Baghdad, my native city. Thanks to him my leg was broken and I am now lame. I have sworn never to sit in the same room with him, nor live in any town where he resides. This is why I left Baghdad, yet here I find him again. Not another night will I spend in this city.'

" 'By Allah,' we said, 'let us hear your story.'

"The barber hung his head as the young man proceeded to tell of his adventure."

The Tale of the Lame Young Man and the Barber of Baghdad

You should know that my father was one of the chief merchants of Baghdad and I was his only son. When I reached manhood my father died, leaving me great wealth and a numerous retinue of slaves and servants. From that time I began to live sumptuously, wearing the richest clothes and eating the choicest dishes. But I always avoided the company of women, for I felt shy and uneasy with them.

It so chanced, however, that one day, as I was walking along a narrow lane in Baghdad, a crowd of women barred my way. To get away from them I slipped into a quiet alleyway and sat down on a bench. I had not been there long when a window in the house opposite was flung open, and there appeared a young girl who was like the full moon in her beauty. She was watering the flowerpots on her window sill when, glancing around for the moment, she caught sight of me; whereupon she shut the window and disappeared. I fell in love with her at first sight and sat there forgetful of my surroundings until sunset, when the cadi of Baghdad came riding by, with slaves before him and servants behind him. Imagine my feelings, gentlemen, when I saw him dismount and enter the very house where the young girl lived; for I then realized that she was the cadi's daughter.

I returned home very sad at the thought that I would never be able to make her acquaintance. Presently, however, there entered my room an old woman of my household, who at once understood the cause of my sadness. She sat at my bed-side and comforted me, saying, "Tell me everything, my son, and let me be your messenger."

When she had heard my story she said, "You must know that this girl lives with her father, the cadi, in the strictest seclusion. But I am a frequent visitor to their house, and I will undertake to bring you together. Do not despair. I will go there at once."

I was greatly consoled by her words. The old woman departed on her errand but soon returned crestfallen.

"My son," she said, "do not ask the outcome of my visit. Scarcely had I begun to speak of you when the girl cried, 'Hold your tongue, old woman, or you will receive the punishment you deserve.'"

Seeing that this news had dashed my spirits, the old woman added, "Do not fear—I will shortly approach her again."

My grief was almost too deep to bear until, after a few days, the woman came again and said, "Rejoice, I bring you good news! Yesterday I visited the girl again. When she saw me in tears and asked me the reason for my weeping, I replied, 'I have come from a young man who is languishing with love for you.' Her heart was moved, and she asked, 'Who may he be?' 'He is the flower of my life,' I answered, 'and as dear to me as my own son. Some days ago he saw you at your window, watering your flowers. He loved you from that moment. But when I told him of your harsh response after I mentioned him to you, he began to pine away and took to his bed, where he now lies dying.' 'And all this on

He waited patiently a long time, and then pulled hard on the cords.
When at last he managed to haul the heavy net ashore, he was
astonished to find in it a lame, one-eyed ape.

account of me?' asked the girl, moved with pity and love. 'Yes, by Allah,' I replied. 'Go back to him,' she said. 'Give him my greetings and say that my love is as great as his. Ask him to come and see me on Friday next, before the midday prayers. I will let him into the house myself. But he must leave before my father returns from the mosque.'"

This report filled me with joy and I handsomely rewarded the old woman for her labors. My grief completely left me, and my household rejoiced at my recovery.

When Friday came, I made ready for the great occasion, putting on my finest robes and sweetest perfumes, and then sat waiting for the hour of midday prayers. But the old woman hinted that a visit from the barber might do much to improve my appearance. I called my slave and said to him, "Go to the market place and bring me a barber. See that he is a man of sense who will attend to his business and will not annoy me with idle chatter." The slave went away and brought back with him a barber who was none other than the odious old man you see before you.

As soon as he arrived, the barber said that I looked very pale; and when I explained that I had but recently recovered from an illness, he congratulated me, saying, "May Allah preserve you, sir, from all misfortune, all distress, all grief, and all sorrow!"

"Allah grant your prayer!" I replied.

"Now tell me, sir," he said, "do you wish to have your head shaved? You doubtless know that the famous Ibn Abbas (may Allah rest his soul in peace!) has said, 'He who has his head shaved on a Friday will ward off seventy calamities.'"

"Enough of this talk, old man!" I cried. "Come now, begin shaving my head at once."

He produced from his pocket a large bundle. Imagine my astonishment when I saw him take from it, not a razor or a pair of scissors as one might have expected, but an astrological device made of seven plates of polished silver. He carried it to the middle of the courtyard, and, raising the instrument toward the sun, gazed intently at the reflection for a long time. Then he came back to me and said solemnly, "Know that of this day, Friday the tenth of the second month of the year two hundred and fifty-three after the Flight of the Prophet (upon whom be Allah's blessing and peace), and twelve hundred and thirty-one in the year of Alexander the Great, there have elapsed eight degrees and six minutes; and that, according to the strictest rules of computation, the planet Mars, in conjunction with Mercury, is this day in the ascendant: all this denoting an excellent moment for haircutting. Furthermore, my instrument clearly informs me that it is your intention to pay a visit to a certain person, and that of this nothing shall come but evil. There is also another sign in connection with a certain matter, of which I would rather not speak."

"By Allah!" I cried, "this is intolerable! You weary me with your tedious chatter, and, what is more, your forebodings are far from encouraging. I sent for you to shave my head. Do so at once and cease your babbling!"

"If only you knew the gravity of the impending disaster," he said, "you would listen to my advice and heed the warning of the stars!"

"Doubtless," I cried, "you are the only astrologer among the barbers of Baghdad: but, allow me to tell you, old man, you are also an impudent mischief-maker and a frivolous chatterbox."

"What would you have?" cried he, shrugging his shoulders. "Allah has sent you one who is not only a barber of great repute, but also a master of the arts and sciences: one who is not only deeply versed in alchemy, astrology, mathematics, and architecture, but also (to mention only a few of my accomplishments) well taught in the arts of logic, rhetoric, and elocution. Add to all this the maturity of judgment that can be acquired only through long experience of the world. Your late father, young man, loved me for my wisdom; and it is the memory of his goodness and kind favors that prompts me to render you an honest service. Far from being a meddlesome gossip, as you seem to suggest, I am, in fact, well known for my gravity and reserve; on account of which qualities people call me 'the Silent One.' Instead of crossing and thwarting me, young man, it would be much more befitting to thank Allah for my sound advice and my concern for your well-being. Would that I were a whole year in your service, that you might learn to do me justice!"

Here I exclaimed, "You will surely be my death this day!" But when the old man was about to resume his talk, I felt as though I were about to explode with rage, so I said to my slave, "In Allah's name, give this man a silver piece and show him out, for I do not wish to have my head shaved after all."

"What kind of talk is this?" cried the barber. "By Allah, I will accept nothing before I have shaved you. You must know that I would regard it as a pleasant duty and a great honor to serve you even without payment. For although you do not seem to appreciate my merits, I appreciate yours. I remember one Friday when I was sent for by your late father (may Allah have mercy upon him: he was a man of rare qualities). I found him entertaining a company of visitors. He welcomed me as he might have welcomed an old friend, and said, 'I beg you to cut my hair.' At once I took out my astrolabe, computed the height of the sun, and soon ascertained that the hour was clearly unfavorable for haircutting. I did not hesitate to tell him the truth. He accepted my judgment and readily agreed to wait for a good moment. Incidentally, it might interest you to know that, while we waited, I composed half a dozen verses in his praise and recited them before the company. Your father was so pleased with them that he ordered his slave to give me a hundred and three dinars and a robe of honor. When the awaited hour had come and I had cut his hair, I asked him in a whisper, 'Why did you pay me a hundred and three dinars?' 'One dinar is for your wisdom,' he replied, 'one for the hair-cutting, and one for the pleasure of your company; as for the remainder and the robe of honor, pray accept them as a slight reward for your excellent poem.'"

"Then may Allah have mercy on my father," I burst out, "if he ever had dealings with a barber like you!"

"There is no god but Allah, and Mohammed is his Prophet!" exclaimed the barber, laughing and shaking his head. "Glory to him who changes others and remains himself unchanged! I always took you for a sensible and intelligent young man: now I see that your illness has slightly affected your head. You would do well to remember that Allah in his Sacred Book mentioned with special praise those who curb their anger and forgive their fellow men. I will forgive you.

"As I was saying, neither your father nor your grand-father before him ever did anything without first seeking my advice. You have doubtless heard the proverb 'He who takes good counsel is crowned with success.' Now, you will find no one better versed in the ways of the world than myself; and here I stand, waiting to serve you. What I cannot understand, however, is that you seem to be a little tired of me, when I am not in the least tired of you. But the high esteem in which I hold your father's memory will always make me mindful of my duty to his son."

"By Allah," I yelled, "this has gone too far!" I was about to order my slaves to throw him out of the house when he suddenly began to dampen my hair, and before I knew what was happening my head was covered with lather.

"I will take no offense, sir," continued the wretched old man, quite unruffled, "if you are a little short-tempered. Apart from the strain of your recent illness, you are, of course, very young. It seems but yesterday that I used to carry you to school on my shoulders."

Unable to contain myself any longer, I said solemnly, "My friend, I must beg you to get on with your work."

"And have I, sir, all this time, been engaged in anything else?" was his reply.

Here I tore my clothes and began to shriek like a madman.

When he saw me do this, the barber calmly produced a razor and began to strop it, passing it up and down the piece of leather with deadly deliberation. At length, he held my head with one hand and shaved off a few hairs. Then he raised his hand and said, "I do not suppose you are aware of my standing in society. These hands of mine have dressed the heads of kings and princes, viziers and noblemen. Have you not heard the poet's verses in my praise?"

At this point I interrupted him again. "You have stifled me with your nonsense!"

"It has just occurred to me that you might be in a hurry," said the barber.

"I am," I shouted, "I am!"

"Well, well," he went on, "haste is a bad thing and leads only to ruin and repentance. The Prophet said: 'The best enterprises are those that are carried out with caution.' I wish you would tell me the purpose of your haste, as there are yet quite three hours to midday prayers." Here the barber paused, and then added, "But let me first make sure of the correct time."

So saying, he flung away the razor, took up the astrolabe, and went out into the courtyard. There he observed the sun for a long time, and at last came back, saying, "It is now three hours to midday prayers, neither one minute more nor one minute less."

"For Allah's sake," I cried, "hold your tongue! You have goaded me beyond endurance."

Again he took up the razor and proceeded to strop it as he had done before. Scarcely had he removed a few hairs when he again stopped and said, "I am rather anxious about you, you know. It would be in your own interest to tell me the cause of your haste. For, as you know, your father and grandfather never did anything without consulting me."

I realized that I should never be able to evade his persistent questioning. To cut the matter short, I said that I had been invited to a party at the house of a friend and begged him to stop being impertinent.

At the mention of a party the barber exclaimed, "This reminds me that I myself am expecting a few friends at my house today. But I have forgotten to provide anything for them to eat. Think of the disgrace!"

"Do not be troubled over this matter," I replied. "All the food and drink in my house is yours if you will only finish shaving my head."

"Sir," he cried, "may Allah reward you for your generosity! Pray let me hear what you have for my guests."

"Five different meat dishes," I answered, "ten stuffed chickens finely broiled, and a roasted lamb!"

"Be so good," he said, "as to let me look at them."

I ordered the provisions to be brought before him, together with a cask of wine.

"How generous you are!" he exclaimed. "But what shall we do without incense and perfume?"

I ordered my slave to set before him a box containing aloeswood, musk, and ambergris, the whole worth not less than fifty gold pieces. Time was running short, so I said, "All this is yours; only, for the sake of Mohammed, on whom be Allah's blessing and peace, finish shaving my head!"

"Pray allow me to see the contents of the box," he replied.

My slave opened it, and the barber put aside his razor and sat down on the floor, examining the incense. He then rose and, taking up his razor again, held my head and shaved off a few more hairs.

"My son," he said, with great satisfaction, "I do not know how to thank you. The party I am giving today will now owe a great deal to your kindness. Although none of my guests might be considered worthy of such magnificence, they are all quite respectable. First, there is Zantoot, the bathkeeper; then Salee'a, the corn merchant; Akrasha, the fruit seller; Hamid, the trash collector; Silat, the grocer; Abu Makarish, the milkman; Kaseem, the watchman; and last, but by no means least, Sa'eed, the camel driver. Each one of them is a delightful companion and has a song and dance of his own invention; and is, like your humble servant, neither inquisitive nor given to idle talk. In truth, no description of my friends can do them justice. If, therefore, you would care to honor us with your company, you will have a more pleasant time, and we will all be the happier. In my opinion, one reason why you would do well not to visit those friends of yours is the possibility of meeting some busybody who will split your head with incessant chatter."

I choked with rage, and burst into a fit of hysterical laughter, but calmed down sufficiently to say, "I should be delighted to come some other time. Shave my head now and let me go my way. Besides, your friends must be waiting for you."

"But how I long to introduce you to these excellent

fellows!" he continued. "Once you meet them, you will give up all your friends forever."

"May Allah give you joy in them," I said. "I shall doubtless have the pleasure of meeting them one day."

"Well, well," he went on, shrugging his shoulders, "if you must go to your friends, I will now carry to my guests the presents with which you have favored me. As I do not stand upon ceremony with them I will return without delay to accompany you to your party."

Here I lost all control of myself and cried, "There is no strength or help save in Allah! Pray go to your friends and delight your heart with them, and let me go to mine; for they are waiting for me."

But the barber cried, "I will not let you go alone."

"The truth is," I said, "that no one may be admitted to the house where I am going except myself."

"Aha!" he exclaimed. "It must be a woman, then, or else you would allow me to accompany you. Yet I am the right man for that kind of adventure and could do much in an emergency. Why, you may even get yourself murdered! Furthermore, you know how ruthless the governor is about such secret meetings, particularly on a Friday."

"Vile old man," I cried, "how can you speak so to my face?"

"Did you imagine," retorted the barber, "that you could hide such a design from me? My only concern, young man, is to serve you."

Afraid that my servants might hear the barber's remarks, I made no answer.

The hour of prayer had come and the imams had already begun their sermons, when at long last the barber finished shaving my head.

"Take away this food to your house," I said, "and when you return we will go together to the party."

But he would not believe my words. "You want to get rid of me and go alone," he replied. "Think of the trap that may have been set for you! By Allah, you shall not leave the house until I come back to accompany you and watch over your safety."

"Very well," I said, "but you must not be late."

The barber took all the meat and drink I had given him and left me in peace. But if you think the wretch carried the things home, you are wrong. He hired a porter for the task and hid himself in one of the neighboring alleyways.

The muezzins had now intoned their blessings on the Prophet from the minarets of the city. I rose quickly, flung on my cloak, and ran as fast as I could to the girl's house. Finding the door open, I hurried up the stairs to her apartment. But I had scarcely reached the second story when the cadi arrived. Seized by a great fear, I rushed to one of the windows overlooking the alleyway, and was confounded to see the barber (Allah's curse be upon him!) sitting on the doorstep.

Now, it so happened that immediately on his return from the mosque the cadi took it into his head to beat one of his maidservants. She raised an uproar of wailing and screaming. A slave went to her aid, but the furious cadi fell upon him also, and he joined in yelling for help.

Imagining that it was I who was the victim, the barber set up a great outcry in the street, tearing his clothes and scattering dust upon his head. "Help! Help!" he cried. "My master is being murdered by the cadi!"

Then, running frantically to my house with a great crowd following him, he roused my people and my servants; and before I knew what was happening they all came, men and women, to the cadi's house, with torn clothes and loosed tresses, lamenting, "Alas! Our master is dead!"

The clamor in the street was heard by the cadi, who

ordered a slave to find out what had happened. The slave quickly returned saying, "There is a great multitude of men and women at the door. They are all shaking their fists and shouting, 'Our master has been murdered!'"

The cadi rose in anger and opened the door to find an infuriated mob shouting threats at him.

"What is the meaning of this?" he demanded indignantly.

"Dog! Pig! Murderer!" shouted my servants. "Where is our master?"

"What has your master done to me," asked the cadi, "that I should kill him?"

"You have just been flogging him," replied the barber. "I myself heard his cries."

"But what has your master done that I should flog him?" repeated the cadi. "And who brought him to my house?"

"Wicked old liar," answered the barber, "do not pretend to be so innocent, for I know the whole truth and every detail of the matter. Your daughter is in love with him and he with her. When you caught him in the house you ordered your slaves to flog him. By Allah, the Caliph himself shall judge this outrage! Give us back our master, or else I will have to enter by force and rescue him myself."

Embarrassed and perplexed, the cadi said, "If you are not lying, come and bring him out."

I saw the barber push his way through the door. I desperately looked for a means of escape, but could find none. At length I saw in one of the rooms an empty wooden chest into which I jumped and pulled down the lid. But there was no escape from the barber. He came running into the room, looked right and left, and instantly guessed where I was. He was a stronger man than I thought, for he hoisted the chest onto his shoulder and carried it down the stairs. But as he rushed through the door, he tripped over the threshold, hurling me out of the chest into the crowded street. My leg was broken, but my single thought at that moment was to fly for my life. I took from my pockets handfuls of gold and threw them to the crowd. While they were busy scrambling for the coins I made off, hobbling through the back streets as fast as I could manage.

The barber pursued me, crying, "The blackguards would have killed my master! Praise be to Allah who aided me against them and saved my master from their hands!"

Then, calling out to me as he ran, he continued, "Now you see the fruits of your rashness and impatience! Had not Allah sent me to your rescue, you would not have escaped alive today. I have risked my life in your service; but you would not even hear of taking me with you. All the same, I will not be angry, for you are very young and exceedingly rash and foolish."

Writhing with the pain in my leg and the anguish in my heart, I turned on my heel and threw these words at the jabbering monster: "Is it not enough that you have brought me to this pass? Must you also hound me to my death in the middle of the market place?" Then, quickly entering a weaver's shop, I begged asylum of him and implored him to drive the barber away.

I sat in the back room prostrated with fear. I thought, "If I return home, I will never be able to rid myself of this fiend." I felt certain he would pursue me like a shadow, and I could endure the sight of him no longer.

I sent out for witnesses and wrote my will, dividing my property among my people. I appointed a guardian over them, and committed to him the charge of the young and the aged, and also the sale of my house and other estates. I then left Baghdad and came to live in your city, imagining that I had forever freed myself from this man. Yet no sooner had I stepped into this house than I found him sitting among you as an honored guest. How can my heart be at rest or my stay be pleasant when I am under the same roof as the man who did all this to me and was the cause of my lameness?

The young man (continued the tailor) refused to sit down and went away. When we had heard his story, we turned to the barber and asked, "Is it true what this young man has said of you?"

"By Allah, gentlemen," replied the barber, "I must assure you that had it not been for my presence of mind, resourcefulness, and personal courage, this youth would have surely died. He should, indeed, be thankful that his folly cost him merely his leg, and not his life. This young man has accused me of being talkative and meddlesome—two vices from which, unlike my six brothers, I am entirely free. To prove to you the falseness of this charge, however, I will now tell you a story, and you shall judge for yourselves that I am a man not only of few words but also of great generosity and chivalry."

The Barber's Tale

The little adventure I am about to relate happened to me some years ago during the reign of our former Caliph. (May Allah have mercy upon him: he was a just ruler and a righteous man.)

One day I came across a group of ten men whom (as I discovered later) the Caliph wished to punish as rogues. He ordered his lieutenant to bring them before him. It so chanced that just as they were being taken onto a boat to cross the river Tigris I was taking the air along the riverbank. Drawing close to them, I thought to myself, "This must be a pleasure party. They will probably spend the day in this boat eating and drinking. By Allah, I will be their guest and make merry with them."

I jumped into the boat and sat in their midst. But as soon as we set foot on the opposite bank, the governor's guards took hold of us and put chains around the necks of the men, and around my neck also. However, I uttered not a syllable (which, I submit, is but a proof of my courage and discretion). Then they dragged us away to the Caliph's court and led us before the Commander of the Faithful.

When he saw us, the Caliph called the executioner and said to him, "Strike off the heads of these ten wretches!"

The executioner made us kneel down in a row before the Caliph; then he unsheathed his sword and beheaded the unfortunate men.

Seeing me kneeling still at the end of the row, the Caliph cried, "Why did you not kill the tenth man?"

The executioner counted aloud the ten heads and the ten bodies that lay on the ground—and the Caliph turned to me and said, "Who are you, and how did you come to be among these criminals?"

Then, and only then, did I decide to break my silence.

"Commander of the Faithful," I replied, "I am called the Silent One and my wisdom is proverbial. I am a barber by trade and one of the seven sons of my father." I then explained how I was mistaken for one of the prisoners and briefly outlined my life's history.

When he was satisfied that I was a man of rare qualities, the Caliph smiled, saying, "Tell me, noble sheikh, are your six brothers like you, distinguished for their deep learning and the brevity of their speeches?"

"Gracious heavens!" I replied. "Each of them is such a disreputable good-for-nothing that you almost slander me by comparing me to them. Because of their recklessness, stupidity, and unusual cowardice, they have brought upon themselves all kinds of misfortunes and bodily deformities: the first is lame, the second loose-limbed and disfigured, the third blind, the fourth one-eyed, and the fifth ear-cropped, and the sixth has had both his lips cut off. Were it not for the fear that you might take me for an idle gossip, I would gladly tell you their stories."

Thereupon the Commander of the Faithful gave me leave to relate to him the story of my first brother.

The Tale of Bakbook,
the Barber's First Brother

Know, Commander of the Faithful, that the oldest of my brothers, he who is lame, was in his youth a tailor and lived in Baghdad.

He used to ply his trade at a little shop that he rented from a wealthy man, who himself lived in the upper story of the same building. In the spacious basement below, a miller worked at his mill and kept his ox.

One day, as he sat sewing, my brother chanced to raise his eyes and caught sight of a young woman looking out at the passers-by from an oriel window above his shop. She was the landlord's wife and was as beautiful as the rising moon. Bakbook fell in love with her at first sight. He could sew no more and passed the whole day in trying to gaze at her. Next morning he opened his shop at an early hour and began sewing; but each time he sewed a stitch, his eyes wandered toward the window and his love for the lady increased.

On the third day, she noticed him and gave him a smile. She sent her slave girl to him with a parcel containing a length of red flowered silk.

"My mistress sends you her greetings," said the girl, "and desires you to make her a shirt from this material."

"I hear and obey," replied my brother.

Bakbook set to work, so that the shirt was ready before the evening. Early next morning the slave girl came to him again and said, "My mistress greets you and inquires if you slept well last night, for she herself, she says, could scarcely sleep a wink, thinking of you."

Then the girl placed before him a piece of yellow satin, adding, "From this my mistress wishes you to make her two more shirts and to have them ready by the evening."

"I hear and obey," replied my brother. "Give your mistress my tender greetings, and say to her, 'Your slave prostrates himself at your feet and awaits your will and pleasure.'"

He worked hard until evening, when the young woman looked out from her window, smiling, so that Bakbook persuaded himself that she was deeply in love with him. Presently the slave girl came to the shop and took the two shirts.

Next morning the slave came again and said, "My master wishes to speak to you and desires you to come into the house."

Thinking that this was but a device to further the woman's intrigue with him, Bakbook gladly followed the slave girl, and when he entered, he greeted his landlord, kissing the ground before him. The husband threw him a great roll of silk, and said, "Make me a few robes from this, good tailor."

My brother went back to his shop and worked so hard that twenty robes were ready by the evening. At suppertime he carried them to his landlord.

"How much do I owe you?" asked the landlord.

But as Bakbook was about to say, "Twenty dirhams,"

the young lady made a sign to him that he should accept no payment. And the shallow-pated Bakbook, who did not for a moment suspect that the fair woman of his dreams was in league with her husband to make an ass of him, refused payment despite his poverty.

Early next morning the slave came again and said, "My master wishes to speak with you."

As soon as Bakbook entered, the landlord handed him a roll of stuff, saying, "Make me five pairs of trousers." My brother took the rascal's measurements and went back to his shop.

After three days of drudgery, he finished the trousers; and when he proudly delivered them, the landlord complimented him on his tailoring and loaded him with praises. But just as he put his hand into his pocket to take out his purse, the young woman again signaled to Bakbook to accept no payment. So he feebly murmured a refusal and went back to his shop in exceedingly low spirits.

However, to repay Bakbook for his services, the young woman and her husband decided to marry him to their slave girl. My brother accepted without hesitation and looked forward to becoming, in a sense, a member of the family. On the evening of the wedding they advised him to spend the bridal night at the mill in the basement of the house. Nothing, they assured my brother, could be luckier than such a beginning.

After the marriage ceremony, the credulous Bakbook waited in the basement for his bride. But when she failed to come down he was obliged to sleep in that dreary place alone. At midnight he was awakened by the whip of the miller, who, at the instigation of the landlord, had tied my brother to the grinding stone during his sleep. He heard the miller's voice saying, "A plague on this lazy ox! The corn is waiting to be ground, and the customers are demanding their flour."

Then the miller lashed Bakbook with his whip, crying, "Get up, and turn the mill!"

Yelling and screaming, my brother began to go around and around the millstone, and continued to do so for the rest of the night.

Early in the morning, the slave girl to whom he had been married the night before came down to the basement. Seeing him still tied to the millstone, she unfastened him and said with affected concern, "We have just heard of this unfortunate mistake. My mistress cannot find words to express her grief."

Bakbook was so overcome with exhaustion that he could not answer.

Soon after, the clerk who had drawn up the marriage contract appeared. He greeted my brother, saying, "Allah give you a long and happy life, my friend!"

"Allah confound you!" retorted my brother. "Your contract and blessings have only caused me to turn a mill all night."

When the clerk heard the story of the unhappy bridegroom, he said, "I think I know the reason. Your star is at variance with that of your bride. I can, for a small fee, draw you up a luckier contract!"

But my brother refused to listen to him and told him to go and play his tricks elsewhere.

He resumed his tailoring, hoping to make a little money with which to buy something to eat. But while he was sitting at his work, his landlord's wife appeared at the window. With tears running down her cheeks, she swore she knew nothing of what had happened at the mill that night. At first Bakbook would not believe her; but before long her sweet words won his heart again, and all his troubles were forgotten.

A few days later the slave came to him and said, "My mistress greets you and invites you to come to her at dusk."

Now, you must know that the young woman and her husband had conspired to ruin my brother. The landlord had said to his wife, "How shall we entice him into the house, so that I may seize him and drag him before the governor?" And the wicked woman had answered, "Let me play another of my tricks on him, and he shall be paraded through the city as an example to all."

That evening my brother—a very simple-hearted man, alas—was led by the slave to the landlord's dwelling. The young woman welcomed him in and seated him by her side.

But before he could say one word to her, the husband burst into the room. He gripped my brother, crying, "How dare you annoy my wife? By Allah, the governor himself shall judge this outrage!"

Turning a deaf ear to Bakbook's pitiful cries, he dragged him away to the governor, who had him whipped and then mounted on a camel and driven through the streets of the city. Great crowds watched the spectacle, shouting, "Thus shall evil-doers be punished!"

During the ride Bakbook was thrown off the camel's back and broke his leg. Furthermore, the governor banished him from Baghdad. I took pity on him and carried him back in secret to my house, where I have fed and clothed him ever since.

The Caliph was much amused by my story. He ordered a gift to be bestowed upon me, saying, "You have spoken well, my silent sheikh."

"Commander of the Faithful," I replied, "I will not accept this honor until I have told you the stories of my other brothers; although, indeed, I fear that you may think me a little talkative."

And thereupon I began to relate the tale of my second brother.

The Tale of Al-Haddar, the Barber's Second Brother

My second brother, Commander of the Faithful, is called Al-Haddar and was in his younger days as thin and loose-limbed as a scarecrow.

One day, as he was slouching along the streets of Baghdad, an old woman stopped him, saying, "I have an offer to make you, my good man. You can accept or refuse it as you think fit."

"Tell me what it is," said my brother.

"First," continued the old woman, "you must promise that you will talk but little and ask no questions."

"Speak, then," replied Al-Haddar.

"What would you say," whispered the old woman, "to a handsome house set about with beautiful gardens, where you could eat and drink to your heart's content, sitting with a pretty girl from night until day?"

"How is it, good mother," asked Al-Haddar, "that you have chosen me from all others to enjoy this marvel? What quality of mine has pleased you?"

"Did I not tell you," replied the old woman, "to ask no questions? Be silent, then, and follow me."

My brother followed the old woman, his mouth watering at the delights she had promised him, until they came to a magnificent palace, at the doors of which stood many slaves and attendants. As he entered, my brother was stopped by one of the servants, who demanded, "What is your business here?" But his guide promptly intervened, saying, "He is a workman whom we have hired."

The old woman led him up to the second story and then ushered him into a great pavilion decorated with rich ornaments. He had not waited long before a young woman of striking beauty came in, surrounded by her slave girls. Al Haddar rose and bowed to the ground before her as she welcomed him in a most amiable fashion. When they were all seated, the slaves placed delicate sweetmeats before their mistress and her guest and, as she ate, the young woman jested with my brother and made a great show of affection to him. Although she was really laughing at him all the time, my imbecile of a brother perceived nothing and fancied that the young woman admired him greatly.

Wine was brought in, and ten beautiful girls entered the pavilion, singing to the accompaniment of lutes. The young woman plied Al-Haddar with wine, and while he drank she began to stroke his cheeks, more with violence than affection, and ended by slapping him hard on the nape of his neck. He rose angrily, and would have questioned this behavior and left the house had not the old woman reminded him, with a wink, of his promise. Determined to control himself, he sat down in silence; but no sooner had he resumed his seat than the young woman and her servants fell upon him, slapping and cuffing him until he almost fainted. Upon this Al-Haddar made up his mind that he was not to be trifled with any longer, and resolutely made for the door. But the old woman hastened to prevent him.

"How long," he asked, "have I to sit here? Never in all the days of my life have I been so vilely treated."

Nevertheless the old woman prevailed upon him to stay in the pavilion.

Presently the young woman ordered her slaves to perfume my brother and sprinkle his face with rose water. When they had done so, she called one of her slave girls and said, "Take your master and do to him what is required. Then bring him back."

Not knowing what lay in store for him, my brother allowed himself to be conducted into a neighboring room. The old woman soon joined him and said, "Be patient."

"Tell me," said Al-Haddar, his face brightening, "what does she want the slave to do to me?"

"Nothing but good," replied the old woman. "She will only dye your eyebrows and shave off your mustache."

"As for the dyeing of my eyebrows," said Al-Haddar, "that will come off with washing; it is the shaving of my mustache that I cannot endure."

"Beware of crossing her," replied the old woman.

My brother patiently suffered the slave girl to dye his eyebrows and remove his mustache. But when the girl returned to her mistress to inform her that her instructions had been carried out, the young woman said, "There remains only one other thing to be done: his beard must be shaved off." So the slave went back to him and told him of his hostess' orders.

"How can I allow this to happen to me?" said the blockhead, deeply perplexed.

But the old woman answered, "Be a little more patient, and you will win her."

So my brother hopefully let the slave girl shave off his beard. When he was brought back, the company was so amused by his grotesque appearance that they rolled on the floor with laughter.

The young woman whispered in his ear, "Run after me

until you catch me!" With this she tripped out of the pavilion and rushed in and out of many rooms and galleries, Al-Haddar following close behind. At length she slipped into a darkened chamber, and as he was scampering after her the floor suddenly gave way beneath him. In a twinkling he found himself below in the market of the leather merchants.

On seeing Al-Haddar drop down in their midst, his beard shaven and his eyebrows dyed, the merchants booed him, clapped their hands at him, and thrashed him with their hides, until he collapsed senseless. Finally they threw him on a donkey's back and took him to the governor, who asked, "Who can this man be?"

"He fell down upon us," they answered, "through a trap door in the vizier's house."

The governor sentenced him to a hundred lashes and banished him from the city. As soon as this news reached me, I set out to search for him, and when I found him brought him back in secret to Baghdad and made him a daily allowance of food and drink. Were it not for my generosity and courage, I would not have gone to so much trouble over such a fool.

I now beg you, Commander of the Faithful, to listen to the story of my third brother.

Holding a dagger in one hand, she danced gracefully, to the delight
of all the company, and particularly of the pretended merchant,
who took out his purse to throw a gold coin to her.

The Tale of Bakbak,
the Barber's Third Brother

My third brother, Commander of the Faithful, is the blind one called Bakbak.

One day, as he was begging in the streets of Baghdad, destiny directed his steps to a certain house. He knocked at the door, hoping that he might be given a coin or something to eat. The master of the house called out from within, "Who is there?" But my brother, who knew all the tricks of his profession, would not answer before the door was opened. Again he heard the master of the house call out at the top of his voice, "Who is knocking?" and still he made no reply. Bakbak then heard the sound of approaching footsteps, and the door was opened.

"What do you want?" he was asked.

"Some little thing for a poor blind man, in the name of Allah," replied my brother.

"Give me your hand," said the man, "and follow me."

Bakbak stretched out his hand, and was taken within and then up from one flight of stairs to another until the roof of the house was reached, my brother thinking at every step that he was about to be given some food or money. On the roof the man asked Bakbak a second time, "Now, what do you want?"

"Some little thing," repeated my brother, "in the name of Allah."

"Then may Allah have pity on you," replied the man, "and open a door for you elsewhere."

"Could you not have given me that answer when we were still below?" cried my brother indignantly.

"Wretch," retorted the master of the house, "why did you not tell me who you were when I first asked you?"

"What are you doing with me?" asked my brother helplessly.

"I have nothing to give you," the man answered.

"Then guide me down the stairs," pleaded Bakbak.

"The way lies open before you," answered the man coldly.

Unaided, my brother groped his way down the stairs. But when he was some twenty steps from the bottom his foot slipped, and he rolled down nearly all the way, breaking his skull.

Outside the house, two of his fellow blind beggars heard his groans and went to ask him what had happened. Dolefully he described the treatment he had received, adding, "Comrades, there is no way left for me but to go to our house and take something from our common savings; or else I shall be hungry for the rest of this black day."

Now all this time, the man from whose house my brother had been so rudely thrown out was following Bakbak and his blind companions and overheard all that they said to each other. He continued walking quietly behind them until they reached their dwelling. When the three had entered, he slipped into the house without a sound.

"Shut the door quickly," said my brother to his friends, "and search the house lest any strangers should have followed us."

When he heard my brother's words, the man, who was an accomplished thief, noiselessly caught a rope that was hanging from the ceiling, and, climbing it, held fast until the blind men had inspected every corner. They then brought out their money and, sitting down beside my brother, began counting it; and there were more than twelve thousand coins. This done, one of them took a coin and hurried out of the house to buy something to eat, while the other two put back the silver in its hiding place under the tiles. As soon as their companion returned, all three sat down to eat.

During the meal my brother gradually became aware of a fourth pair of jaws chewing by his side. "There is a stranger in our midst!" shouted Bakbak. He stretched out his hand and groped around him. It fell on the thief.

The three blind men closed upon the stranger, punching and kicking him, and crying out, "A thief! Help, good Moslems! A thief, help!"

When the neighbors and passers-by came to their rescue, the thief shut his eyes, pretending to be blind like the three beggars. "Take me to the governor, good Moslems," he cried out; "for, by Allah, I have important information to give him."

At once the crowd seized the four and led them to the governor's house.

"Who are these men?" asked the governor.

"Noble Governor," cried the thief, "nothing but the whip can make us confess the truth. Begin by flogging me, and then these others!"

"Throw this man down and thrash him soundly," said the governor.

The guards seized the pretender and set upon him with their whips. After the first few lashes, he yelled and opened one of his eyes; and after a few more he opened the other.

"Wicked impostor," cried the governor, "so you are not blind after all!"

"Grant me your pardon," begged the thief, "and I will tell you the whole truth."

The Governor nodded assent, and the man continued, "For a long time we four have pretended to be blind beggars, entering the houses of honest men and cheating them of their money. We amassed a large fortune, amounting to twelve thousand dirhams in silver. But when I demanded my share today they rose against me and beat me. I beg protection of Allah and of you; and if, noble Governor, you doubt the truth of my confession, put them to the whip and they will open their eyes."

"Scoundrels!" roared the governor. "Dare you deny Allah's most precious gift and pretend to be blind?"

The first to suffer was my brother. In vain he swore, by Allah and by all that is holy, that only one of them was blessed with sight. They continued to whip him until he fainted.

"Leave him until he comes to," cried the governor, "and then whip him again!"

The others received similar treatment; nor did they open their eyes in spite of the impostor's repeated exhortations. Then the governor sent his guards to fetch the money from my brother's house. A quarter of it he gave to the thief, and kept the remainder for himself. Furthermore, he banished Bakbak and his friends from the city.

When I heard of my brother's misfortunes I set out to search for him and brought him back in secret to my house, where he has lived ever since.

The Caliph laughed heartily at my story, and said to his attendants, "Give him a reward and show him out of the palace."

"By Allah," I replied, "I will accept nothing, Commander of the Faithful, until you have heard the stories of my other brothers."

The Tale of Al-Kuz, the Barber's Fourth Brother

My fourth brother, one-eyed Al-Kuz, was at one time a butcher and sheep breeder in Baghdad. He catered to the rich and the highborn, so that he amassed great wealth and in time became an owner of many herds of cattle and large estates.

He continued to prosper until a certain day when, as he was attending to his customers, an old man with a long white beard entered the shop and asked him to weigh him some mutton. My brother did so, and when he examined the coins that he received from the stranger he was so struck by their unusual brilliance that he kept them in a separate coffer. For five months the old man bought meat regularly from my brother, who, each time he was paid, put the bright new coins aside.

One day, wishing to buy some sheep, my brother opened the coffer and found, to his astonishment and dismay, that it was filled only with little pellets of white paper. He set up a great clamor, beating himself about the head and calling out to passers-by, until a huge crowd gathered around him. While he was telling them his story, the old

man himself came forward with the glittering coins ready in
his hand, as was his custom. My brother sprang upon him
and, taking him by the throat, cried, "Help, good people!
Here is the scoundrel who has robbed me!"

But this did not seem to perturb the old man, who
calmly whispered to my brother, "Hold your tongue, or I
will put you to public shame!"

"And how will you do that?" shouted Al-Kuz.

"By charging you here and now with selling human
flesh for mutton!"

"You lie, accursed swindler!" yelled my brother.

"None is more accursed," rejoined the other, "than the
man who at this moment has a human corpse hung up in his
shop instead of a sheep!"

"If you can prove this crime against me," said Al-Kuz,
"my life and all my property are yours!"

Accepting the challenge, the old man turned to the bystanders and cried, "Good Moslems, for months this butcher
has been slaughtering his fellow men and selling us their
flesh as mutton. If anyone doubts this, let him enter the shop
and see for himself!"

The crowd rushed in, and what should they see hanging from one of the hooks but the corpse of a man! Struck
with horror, the infuriated mob attacked Al-Kuz, crying,
"Criminal! Murderer!" Even those who were his oldest cli-
ents and dearest friends turned against him and beat him. In
the hubbub, the sorcerer (for such was the wicked old man)
struck my brother in the face, knocking out his left eye.

Then the crowd carried him and the supposed corpse
to the chief of the city's magistrates.

"Your honor," said the sorcerer, "we bring before you
a criminal who for months has been murdering human

beings and selling their flesh as mutton. We call upon you to administer Allah's justice; and here are all the witnesses."

My brother tried to defend himself, but the judge would not listen to him and sentenced him to five hundred lashes. He confiscated all his goods and banished him from the city. Indeed, had Al-Kuz been a poor man he would have been put to a cruel death.

Penniless and broken, he left Baghdad and journeyed many days and nights until he arrived in the chief city of a foreign land. There he set up as a cobbler, making a precarious living in a small shop.

While walking along the street one day he heard the neighing of many horses and a loud clatter of hoofs and was curious to know what was happening. Upon inquiry he was informed that the King was going hunting, so he stopped to watch the procession pass. Chancing to glance over his shoulder, the King caught sight of my brother's face and with a start turned away his head, crying, "Allah preserve us from the evil eye and from the portent of this day!" At once he turned his horse about and rode back to his palace, followed by the troops. As for my brother, he was set upon by the King's slaves and beaten, and then left for dead by the roadside.

Al-Kuz was so perplexed at this stroke of ill-fortune that he took himself off to one of the King's attendants and told him what had happened. The courtier burst into a fit of laughter, and said, "The King cannot bear the sight of a one-eyed man, especially if it is the left eye that is missing. Indeed, in this land, death is the usual penalty for such a disfigurement."

When Al-Kuz heard this he decided to flee the country, and set out at once for a far-off town where no one knew him. Many months afterward, as he was taking a walk, he suddenly heard in the distance the neighing of horses and the clatter of hoofs. He took to his heels in great panic, searching in vain for a hiding place. At length he found himself on the threshold of a great door and, pushing it open without a moment's thought, entered a long passage. Scarcely had he advanced one step when two men sprang upon him, crying, "Allah be praised that we have caught you at last! We have passed three sleepless nights in fear of you!"

"But, good people," cried my brother, "what have I done to offend you?"

"You are the one-eyed ruffian who has plotted to kill the master of this house and to ruin us all!" they cried. "Was it not enough that you robbed him of his property, you and your friends? Where is the dagger with which you threatened us yesterday?" So saying, they searched Al-Kuz and found his cobbler's knife in his belt.

"Good people," pleaded my brother, "Fear Allah and let me tell you my story!"

But instead of listening to him, they beat him and tore his clothes to tatters. His body being uncovered, the marks of whipping could be seen on his back. "Dog!" they cried. "These scars bear testimony to your other crimes!" Then they dragged him away to the governor.

My brother tried to speak out in his own defense, but the governor turned a deaf ear to his entreaties. "Wretch!" he cried indignantly. "One need only look upon your back to see that you have practiced every kind of crime!" and he ordered that he be given a hundred lashes.

Then the governor's men hoisted Al-Kuz on the back of a camel and drove him through the streets, crying, "Thus shall house-breaking ruffians be punished."

When I heard of my brother's misfortunes, I searched

for him until I found him and then brought him back in secret to Baghdad, where he has lived under my care and protection ever since.

That is the story of Al-Kuz. But do not think, Commander of the Faithful, that it is in any way more extraordinary than the tale of my fifth brother.

The Tale of Al-Ashar,
the Barber's Fifth Brother

My fifth brother is called Al-Ashar. In his youth he was very poor and used to beg alms by night and spend the proceeds by day. When our father died, we each inherited a hundred pieces of silver. For many weeks Al-Ashar did not know what to do with his share, and at length he decided to be a glass merchant. He bought some glassware with his hundred dirhams and, placing the articles in a large basket, sat with it at a corner in a busy thoroughfare.

On a certain Friday, while squatting in his accustomed place, he sank into a reverie, and thought to himself, "I have invested the whole of my capital in this glassware. It cost me a hundred dirhams and I will no doubt sell it for two hundred. With the two hundred I will buy more glass, which I will sell for four hundred. I will go on buying and selling until I make a large fortune. With this I will buy all kinds of essences and jewelry, and make a vast profit. Then I will be able to afford a splendid house, with slaves, and horses, and gilded saddles. I will eat the choicest dishes, drink the rarest wines, and be entertained in my own house by the sweetest singers of the city.

"When I have made a hundred thousand dirhams, I will

send for the most knowledgeable marriage brokers and instruct them to find me a wife among the daughters of kings and viziers. I will perhaps ask for the hand of the Grand Vizier's daughter, for I hear she is a girl of incomparable beauty. I will offer a marriage portion of a thousand pieces of gold; and should her father withhold his consent, I will carry her away by force. I will buy ten young eunuchs to attend upon me, and dress myself in regal robes. My saddle will be adorned with priceless jewels, and as I ride through the city to the Vizier's house with slaves before me and servants behind me, men will bow reverently as I pass by, greeting and blessing me.

"When I enter the vizier's house, he will stand up to receive me. He will give me his own place and sit himself down at my feet. Two of my slaves will carry purses with a thousand dinars in each; one I will lay before the vizier as his daughter's marriage portion, the other I will present to him as a gift, in proof of my worthiness and munificence. I will be solemn and reserved, and for every ten words he addresses to me I will answer with two. Then I will return to my house. And when one of my future wife's relations returns my visit, I will give him gold and a robe of honor; but if he brings me a present, I will return it to him, so that he will know how proud my spirit is.

"I will myself appoint the wedding day, and then make preparations for the bridal festivities. On the wedding night I will put on my most splendid robes and, surrounded by my guests, will recline upon a mattress of gold brocade. I will turn my head neither to the right nor to the left, but will look straight in front of me with an air of authority and contemptuous unconcern. When my bride is brought before me, decked with jewels and radiant like the full moon, I will not even look at her. Her women will plead with me, saying, 'Our lord and master, here stands your wife, your slave, waiting for you to honor her with a gracious look.' They will kiss the ground before me. I will cast one glance at her and resume my disdainful air. They will then conduct her to the bridal chamber. I will order one of my slaves to bring me five hundred pieces of gold, which I will scatter among my wife's attendants. Then I will go to my bride; and when I am left alone with her I will neither speak to her nor even look at her. Presently the bride's mother will come in, kissing my head and hand, and saying, 'My lord, look upon your slave girl, who yearns for your favor; speak to her and heal her broken spirit.' I will make no answer. She will throw herself down at my feet, saying, 'Your slave is a beautiful girl. On my knees I beg you to cease humbling her, or her heart will break!' Then the bride's mother will rise and, filling a cup with wine, will give it to her daughter, who will offer it to me with all submission. But I, leaning idly upon my elbow among the gold-embroidered cushions, will take no notice of her. With a trembling voice she will say, 'I beg you, my lord, to take this cup from the hand of your slave and servant.' But I will maintain my dignified silence. She will raise the cup to my mouth, pressing me to drink from it. Then I will wave it away with my hand, and spurn her with my foot, thus—"

So saying, Al-Ashar moved his foot, which kicked against the basket of glassware, knocking over the contents and sending them crashing in fragments to the ground.

My brother began to beat himself about the face, tearing his clothes and wailing, as the people went by to the midday prayers. Some stopped to say a kind word to him and some passed by, taking no notice of his lamentation. While he sat bitterly mourning the loss of all his worldly possessions, a woman rode by on her way to the mosque. She was very beautiful, and as she passed, surrounded by her servants, a sweet odor of the rarest musk hung about her.

Moved with pity for my brother, she sent to inquire the cause of his distress. When she heard his story, she called one of her servants and said, "Give this unfortunate man the purse you are carrying."

The servant took from his belt a heavy purse and gave it to Al-Ashar, who, on opening it, found that it contained five hundred pieces of gold. He almost died for joy and fervently called down Allah's blessing on his benefactress.

Carrying the great purse, my brother returned to his house a rich man. He sat thinking of the happy turn of his fortune, and was on the point of conjuring up another vision when he was roused by a knocking at the door. He opened it and found an old woman on the threshold whom he had never seen before.

"My son," said the old woman, "the hour of Friday prayers is almost past, and I have not yet washed my hands and feet as custom requires. I beg you to let me come into your house, so that I may prepare myself."

Al-Ashar politely invited her to enter. He brought her a ewer and a basin, and retired to delight his eyes with his treasure.

A few minutes afterward the old woman appeared in the room where my brother was sitting. She knelt and bowed twice in prayer, and called down blessings on my brother. He thanked her, took two dinars from the purse, and offered them to her. But the old woman refused the gold with dignity, saying, "Put this money back into your purse. If you have no need of it, return it to the lady who gave it to you."

"Do you know her?" asked Al-Ashar in a transport of joy. "I beg you to tell me how I can see her again."

"My son," she replied, "I have served that lady for many years. I assure you that she has a great liking for you.

Rise, take with you all your money lest a thief should steal it, and follow me to the lady's house."

Bursting with happiness, Al-Ashar rose, took all his gold, and followed the old woman until she stopped at a great house and knocked. The door was opened by a Greek slave girl, and the old woman went in, followed by my brother. Al-Ashar soon found himself in a spacious hall, hung with rich tapestry and spread with rare carpets. He sat down on a cushion, holding his turban on his knees, and had not waited long before a young woman, attired in splendid silks and blessed with more loveliness than the eyes of men had ever seen, appeared before him.

Al-Ashar rose to his feet as she entered, and when she saw him she welcomed him with a sweet smile. They sat talking for a few moments. Then the young woman rose, saying, "Stay here until I return."

While my brother was waiting, the door was flung wide open and there entered a tall slave, holding an unsheathed sword in his hand.

"Vilest of men," cried the slave, "who brought you to this house, and what are you doing here?"

My brother's tongue stuck in his throat and he did not know what to answer. The slave took hold of him and beat him with the flat of his sword until he fell down unconscious. Taking him for dead, the slave called out for the old woman, who instantly appeared.

She took his purse of gold, then gripped Al-Ashar by the feet, dragged him out of the room, and pushed him into a dark cellar.

For two days he remained there unconscious. After he came to, and his strength had returned a little, Al-Ashar crawled on all fours groping for the door. Having at length found it, he made his way, with Allah's help, from the cellar to the vestibule, where he concealed himself. Next morning the old woman went out in search of another victim; and before she had time to shut the door behind her, my brother slipped out and ran home as fast as his legs could carry him.

He now began to plan a punishment for the old woman and her accomplices. Keeping a watchful eye on her movements, he acquainted himself with her daily haunts. As soon as he was restored to his normal health he disguised himself as a traveler from a foreign land. To his waist he tied a large bag filled with glass fragments as though it were bursting with coins, and hiding a sword under his robe went out to seek the old woman.

On finding her, Al-Ashar addressed her in an uncouth foreign accent, "Good mother, have you a pair of scales in which I can weigh nine hundred pieces of gold? I am a stranger here and do not know anyone in this city."

The old woman answered, "One of my sons is a money-changer and has all kinds of scales. He will gladly weigh your gold for you."

My brother followed her until she stopped at the door of the sinister house. The young woman herself opened it for them, and the old servant whispered, "I have brought you a good catch today." The young woman led my brother in, as before, and presently the slave appeared with his naked sword.

"Get up," he roared, "and follow me!"

My brother rose, and as the slave turned his back, Al-Ashar drew his sword, sprang upon him, and struck off his head with one blow.

He next called out to the old woman, and when she appeared he cried, "Black-souled hag, do you not recognize me?"

"I do not indeed," she replied.

"Know, then," shouted my brother, "that I am the man

to whose house you came to wash your hands and feet, and whom you betrayed so wickedly!"

The old woman implored him on her knees to pardon her, but with one stroke of his sword Al-Ashar cut her in two pieces. He then set out to look for her mistress. When he found her, the terrified young woman entreated him to spare her life. His heart was softened, and he pardoned her.

"How did you fall into the power of that cruel slave?" he asked.

"Three years ago," she replied, "before I was imprisoned in this house, I was a slave in the service of a merchant of this city. A frequent visitor at our house was the old woman. One day she invited me to accompany her to an entertainment. I accepted gladly, and, putting on my best clothes and taking with me a purse of one hundred dinars, went out with her. She led me to this house, where that man has kept me and made me the instrument of his crimes ever since."

Al-Ashar ordered her to conduct him to the place where the stolen gold was hidden. He stood dumbfounded as she opened coffer after coffer, all filled with glittering coins.

"You will never be able to carry all this gold alone," she said. "Go and bring some porters to take it from the house."

Al-Ashar left at once and soon returned with ten strong men. But he found the doors wide open and the girl and most of the money gone. He realized that the young woman had deceived him. Nevertheless, he contented himself with what she had left behind. He emptied the closets of their valuables and took everything home.

Al-Ashar slept in great happiness that night. But when he woke next morning, he was terrified to find twenty of the governor's guards at his door. They seized him, saying, "You are wanted by our master."

The men dragged him before the governor, who asked, "Whence did you steal all this money and these goods?"

"Noble Governor," replied Al-Ashar, "grant me the pledge of mercy, and I will tell you the whole truth."

The Governor threw him the white handkerchief signifying pardon. My brother related to him the story of his adventures and offered him a handsome share of the spoil. But the governor seized everything for himself and, fearing that the Caliph might hear of his action, decided to get rid of my brother by banishing him from the city.

Thus Al-Ashar was forced to leave Baghdad. But he had not traveled far before he was set upon by a band of highwaymen, who, finding that they could not rob him of anything except his rags, beat him mercilessly and cut off both his ears.

When I heard of my brother's misfortunes, Commander of the Faithful, I set out to search for him and, having found him, brought him back in secret to my house, where I have provided for him ever since.

That is the story of Al-Ashar. I will now tell you the tale of my sixth and last brother, which, as you will readily agree, is even more extraordinary than the other tales.

The Tale of Shakashik, the Barber's Sixth Brother

My sixth brother, Commander of the Faithful, is called Shakashik. In his youth he was very poor. One day, when he was begging in the streets of Baghdad, he noticed a splendid mansion, at the gates of which stood an impressive band of attendants. Upon inquiry he was informed that the house belonged to a member of the wealthy and powerful Barmecide family. Shakashik approached the doorkeeper and begged for alms.

"Go in," they said, "and our master will give you all that you desire."

My brother entered the lofty vestibule and proceeded to a spacious marble-paved hall, hung with tapestry and overlooking a beautiful garden. He stood bewildered for a moment, not knowing where to turn his steps, and then advanced to the far end of the hall. There, among the cushions, reclined a handsome old man with a long beard, who, my brother saw at a glance, was the master of the house.

"What can I do for you, my friend?" asked the old man, as he rose to welcome my brother.

When Shakashik explained that he was a hungry beggar, the old man expressed the deepest compassion and rent his fine robes, crying, "Can there be a man as hungry as yourself in a city where I am living? It is, indeed a disgrace that I cannot endure!" Then he comforted my brother, adding, "I insist that you stay here and partake of dinner with me."

With this the master of the house clapped his hands and called out to one of the slaves, "Bring in the basin and ewer." Then he said to my brother, "Come forward, my friend, and wash your hands."

Shakashik rose to wash his hands, but saw neither ewer nor basin. He was bewildered to see his host make gestures as though he were pouring water on his hands from an invisible vessel and then drying them with an invisible towel. When he had finished, the old man called out to his attendants, "Bring in the table!"

Numerous servants hurried in and out of the hall, as though they were preparing for a meal. My brother could still see nothing. Yet his host invited him to sit at the imaginary table, saying, "Honor me by eating of this meat."

He moved his hands about as though he were touching invisible dishes, and also moved his jaws and lips as though he were chewing. Then said he to Shakashik, "Eat your fill, my friend, for you must be famished."

My brother began to move his jaws, to chew and swallow, as though he were eating, while the old man still coaxed him, saying, "Eat, my friend, and note the excellence of this bread and its whiteness."

"This man," thought Shakashik, "must be fond of practical jokes." So he said, "It is, sir, the whitest bread I have ever seen, and I have never tasted the like of it in all my life."

"This bread," said the host, "was baked by a slave girl whom I bought for five hundred dinars." Then he called out to one of his slaves, "Bring in the meat pudding, and let there be plenty of fat in it!"

Turning to my brother, he continued, "By Allah, my friend, have you ever tasted anything better than this meat pudding? Now, on my life, you must eat and be merry!"

Presently he cried out again, "Serve up the stewed grouse!" And again he said to Shakashik, "Eat your fill, my friend, for you must be very hungry."

My brother moved his jaws, and chewed, and swallowed, while the old man went on calling for one imaginary dish after another, and pressing his guest to partake of them. He ordered, "Serve up the chickens stuffed with pistachio nuts," and turned to Shakashik, saying, "Eat, for you have never tasted anything like these chickens!"

"Sir," replied my brother, "they are indeed incomparably delicious." Thereupon the host moved his fingers as though to pick up a morsel from an imaginary dish, and popped the invisible delicacy into my brother's mouth.

He continued to enlarge upon the excellence of the various dishes, while my brother became so ravenously hungry that he would almost have given his life for a crust of barley bread.

"Have you ever tasted anything more delicious?" asked the old man, "than the spices in these dishes?"

"Never," replied Shakashik.

"Eat heartily, then, and do not be ashamed!"

"I thank you, sir," answered Shakashik, "but I have already eaten my fill."

"Bring in the dessert!" cried the master of the house to a servant; and to my brother he said, "Taste this excellent pastry, eat of these fritters—take this one before the syrup drips out of it!"

Shakashik helped himself to the imperceptible dainty, and, clicking his tongue with delight, remarked upon the abundance of spice in it.

"Yes," agreed the old man, "I always insist on a dinar's

weight of spice in each fritter, and half that quantity of honey."

My brother continued to move his jaws and lips and to roll his tongue between his cheeks, as though he were enjoying the sumptuous feast.

"Eat of these roasted almonds, and walnuts, and raisins," said the old man.

"I can eat no more," replied my brother.

"By Allah!" repeated the host. "You must eat and not remain hungry!"

"Sir," protested Shakashik, "how can one remain hungry after eating all these dishes?"

My poor brother considered the manner in which his host was making game of him, and thought, "By Allah, I will do something that will make him repent of his pranks!"

Presently, however, the old man clapped his hands again and cried, "Bring in the wine!"

Numerous slaves ran in, moving their hands about as though they were setting wine and cups before their master and his guest. The old man pretended to pour wine into the cups and to hand one to my brother. "Take this," he said, "and tell me how you like it."

"Sir," replied Shakashik, lifting the invisible cup to his lips and making as if to drain it at one gulp, "your generosity overwhelms me!"

"Health and joy to you!" exclaimed the host, as he pretended to pour himself some wine and drink it off. He handed another cup to his guest, and they both continued to act in this fashion until Shakashik, feigning himself drunk, began to roll his head from side to side. Then, taking his host unawares, he suddenly raised his arm and dealt him a blow on the neck that made the hall echo with the sound. And this he followed by a second blow.

The old man rose in anger and cried, "What are you doing, vile creature?"

"Sir," replied my brother, "you have received your humble slave into your home and loaded him with your generosity. You have fed him with the choicest food and quenched his thirst with the most potent wines. Alas, he became drunk, and forgot his manners! But you are so noble, sir, that you will surely pardon his offense."

At these words, the old man burst out laughing, and said, "For a long time I have jested with all types of men, but no one has ever had the patience or wit to enter into my humors as you have done. Now, therefore, I pardon you, and ask you in truth to eat and drink with me, and to be my companion for as long as I live."

He ordered his attendants to serve all the dishes that they had consumed in fancy, and when he and my brother had eaten their fill they repaired to the drinking chamber, where beautiful young women sang and made music. The old Barmecide gave Shakashik a robe of honor and made him his constant companion.

The two lived in amity for a period of twenty years, until the old man died and the Caliph seized all his property. My brother was forced to fly for his life. He left Baghdad and rode into the desert. There a band of roving bedouin took him prisoner and carried him away to their encampment. Every day their chieftain put him to the torture and threatened him, saying, "Pay us your ransom or I will kill you!" My brother would weep and swear that he was a penniless outcast. Finally the chieftain cut off both his lips, then took him on a camel to a barren hillside and left him there to perish.

However, Shakashik was rescued by some travelers who recognized him and gave him food and drink. When news of his plight reached me, I journeyed to him and brought him back to Baghdad. I nursed him in my own house and have provided for him ever since.

When he had heard the tale of my sixth brother (continued the barber, finishing the story he was relating at the tradesmen's party), the Caliph Al-Muntasir Billah burst out laughing and said, "I can well see, my silent friend, that you are a man of few words, who knows neither curiosity nor indiscretion. Yet I must ask you to leave this city at once and go to live elsewhere."

Thus, for no conceivable reason, the Caliph banished me from Baghdad.

I journeyed through many foreign lands until I heard of Al-Muntasir's death and the succession of another Caliph. Then I returned to Baghdad, and found that all my brothers had died also. It was soon after my return that I met this young man, whom I saved from certain death, and who has so unjustly accused me of being talkative and officious.

Your Majesty (continued the tailor), after hearing the barber we were all convinced that the lame young man had been the victim of an exceptionally garrulous and meddlesome fellow. We therefore decided to punish him; so we seized him and locked him in an empty room. Then we sat in peace, eating and drinking and making merry until the hour of afternoon prayers.

When I returned home, my wife received me with angry looks.

"A fine husband you are," she burst out, "to enjoy yourself all day while your wife sits moping all alone at home. If you do not take me out at once and entertain me, I will divorce you!"

We went out together and passed the rest of the day in search of amusement. As we were returning home in the evening we met the hunchback whose untimely death has caused all this company to assemble here.

The King of Basra was much amused by the tailor's story and said, "The young man's adventure with the barber certainly surpasses in wonder the story of the hunchback." And, turning to the chamberlain and the tailor, he added, "Go seek the barber and bring him before me. We will then bury the hunchback, for he has been dead since yesterday."

The two men hurried to the house where the barber was still imprisoned. They set him free and brought him before the King, who discovered that he was an old man past his seventieth year, with dark complexion, a long white beard, and gray, bushy eyebrows; his nose was long, his ears were shriveled, and his manner was lofty. Having looked him over well, the King burst into a fit of laughter, saying, "Silent One, we wish to hear some of your stories."

"First, your Majesty," replied the barber, "I would myself wish to know the occasion for this gathering and why the hunchback's body lies before you."

The King said to the company, "Tell the barber the story of the hunchback's death, and all that befell him at the hands of the tailor, the doctor, the steward, and the broker."

When he had heard all, the barber exclaimed, "By Allah, this is very strange! Lift the cover from the hunchback's body, and let me examine it."

They removed the cover, and the barber, having sat down, took the hunchback's head upon his knees. After scrutinizing the face for a while, he burst out laughing and exclaiming, "Death is one of Allah's mysteries; but the death of this hunchback is a wonder that ought to be recorded for all time!"

The King and all the company were astonished by his words.

"Explain your meaning," said the King.

"Your Majesty," came the reply, "the hunchback is alive!"

So saying, the barber took from his belt a vial containing an ointment, with which he rubbed the hunchback's neck. Then, producing a pair of iron forceps from his pocket, he inserted it into the hunchback's throat and pulled out the piece of fish with the bone. With a violent sneeze the hunchback sprang to his feet. He passed his hands over his face and said, "There is no god but Allah, and Mohammed is his prophet."

The King and all the company marveled greatly. "By Allah," exclaimed the King, "I have never in all my life heard of a stranger incident than this!" Then, turning to the captains of his army, he added, "Have any of you, good Moslems, ever seen a dead man come to life in this fashion? Had not Allah sent him this barber, our hunchback would have now been counted among the dead."

And all those present said, "By Allah, it is a rare marvel!"

The King ordered that the incident be recorded on parchment and that the scroll be kept in the royal library. He bestowed robes of honor upon the Jew, the Christian, the steward, the tailor, the hunchback, and the barber. He appointed the tailor to his court, endowed him with a large annuity, and reconciled him with the hunchback, who again became the King's drinking companion. The barber he also appointed to his court, and conferred upon him many honors, and made him a favorite companion. And they all lived happily until they were visited by the Destroyer of all earthly pleasures, the Annihilator of men.

Ali Baba and the Forty Thieves

Long ago there lived in a city of Persia two brothers whose names were Kassim and Ali Baba.

Though born of the same parents and brought up in the same home, their characters were quite different. Kassim, the elder, was arrogant, shrewd, and greedy, while Ali Baba was unassuming, kind-hearted, and content with his situation. When their father died, they divided all he had between them and started life on an equal footing, but while Kassim married a rich wife and became the owner of a thriving shop in the city's main bazaar, Ali Baba took to wife the daughter of a humble family, and earned a modest living by cutting wood in the forest and selling it in the town.

Ali Baba lived frugally and wisely with his wife, saving as much as his earnings would allow, so that in a few months he was able to buy three donkeys. Every day he would lead his donkeys to the forest and bring them back laden with firewood.

One day, while working at the edge of a far thicket, with his donkeys grazing peacefully near by, he heard the clatter of galloping hoofs in the distance and saw a great cloud of dust approaching. Curious to find out the cause of the commotion, he climbed cautiously into a tall tree that stood on a hillside, giving a clear view of the adjacent plain. From his hiding place he saw a troop of fierce-looking armed horsemen riding toward him. He counted forty of them, and guessed from their appearance and demeanor—their fiery eyes, their black, pointed beards, and the weapons they carried—that they were a band of robbers.

When they came under the tree, the forty thieves dismounted at a signal from the captain and started removing their saddlebags. They carried their loads to a great rock at the bottom of the hill; then the captain went up to the rock and in a loud voice cried, "Open, Sesame!"

Ali Baba was astonished to notice that, at the mention of this word—the name of a cereal commonly grown in Persia—a hidden door in the rock swung wide open. The entire band of robbers filed in. In a few moments they emerged, carrying their now-empty saddlebags in their hands, and the captain cried, "Close, Sesame!" The rock at once shut behind them, and no one could have guessed there was any opening in that solid surface.

As soon as the robbers had mounted and ridden off, Ali Baba climbed down from the tree and went up to the mysterious rock. Finding the surface as smooth and solid as before, he marveled at the magic that had forced it open.

"What priceless treasures must lie within it!" he reflected, and, remembering the captain's words, decided to utter them himself and see what would happen.

"Open, Sesame!" he shouted.

The rock opened, just as it had done before, and Ali Baba walked in. Being a good Moslem, he murmured as he entered, "In the name of Allah, the Compassionate, the Merciful!" He found himself in a huge cave piled up with rich ornaments, chests brimful with gold and silver coins, and great bags bursting with precious stones—which must have taken hundreds of years to accumulate. As he scanned the vast treasures, Ali Baba realized that the cave was the secret storehouse of countless generations of thieves and high-waymen.

Carefully choosing six bags of gold, he loaded them on his donkeys and covered them with brushwood to hide them. Then he cried aloud, "Close, Sesame!" and in a twinkling the door slid to behind him, leaving not a trace on the rock's outer surface.

When Ali Baba arrived home and his wife saw him unload the bags of gold, she was seized with shame and fear.

"Good husband," she said, "do not tell me you have earned all this gold by cutting wood in the forest. Bad luck is sure to enter our humble house if we keep such ill-gotten gains here."

"Fear nothing, I am no thief," Ali Baba quickly inter-rupted. "Rather rejoice, for it was Allah who guided my footsteps in the forest this morning." And he told her of his adventure and how he had found the gold in the robbers' hide-out.

When she heard the story, the poor woman was filled with relief and joy. She squatted before the pile of gold that her husband had poured out of the bags and tried to value the incalculable coins.

"Don't try to count them," said Ali Baba with a laugh. "It would take you days to do that. Get up now and help me dig a ditch in the kitchen where we can hide them. To leave them here would only rouse the suspicions of our neighbors."

But his wife wanted to know exactly how rich they were. "If I cannot count them," she said, "I must at least weigh or measure them. I will go and borrow a measure from your brother Kassim's house, and then I can measure the gold while you dig the hole."

She went over to Kassim's house across the lane and begged his wife to lend her a measure.

"You can have one," her sister-in-law replied. But she wondered at the same time why Ali Baba should need a measure when he was so poor that he could buy only a day's supply of wheat at a time. So the cunning woman, curious to know what kind of grain he was measuring, devised a trick; she rubbed the bottom of the wooden vessel with some fat.

Ali Baba's wife quickly returned home and, after measuring out the gold, carried the measure back to Kassim's wife, not knowing that a gold piece had stuck to the fat at the bottom.

"What have we here?" cried Kassim's wife as soon as her kinswoman had left her. "So Ali Baba is now too rich to count his gold and has to measure it!"

Jealousy gripped her soul. She sent a servant to fetch her husband from his shop, and told him the story in a fit of rage. "We cannot let the matter rest at that," she screamed. "You must go now and force that wretched brother of yours to reveal to you the source of his riches!"

Instead of being pleased that his brother was no longer a poor man, Kassim, too, was overwhelmed with envy. His heart burning with spite, he immediately went over to Ali Baba's house.

"How is it that you dare to deceive us so?" he cried. "You go on pretending to be penniless and humble, when you have so much gold that you cannot even count it. Tell me this moment how you came by it, or I will denounce you as an impostor and a thief!"

He showed his brother the gold piece still smeared with fat, and Ali Baba, seeing at once how his secret had been discovered, confided to Kassim the whole story and begged him to keep quiet about it.

There and then, the greedy Kassim resolved to take possession of the treasure for himself alone. He left his brother and quickly returned home, his head buzzing with a thousand plans.

Early next morning he set out with ten donkeys to find the cave that Ali Baba had described. When he came to the rock under the tree, he stretched out his arms toward it and shouted, "Open, Sesame!" And exactly as his brother had told him, the rock opened to let him in. He tied his donkeys to some trees, entered the cave, then closed the rock behind him with the magic words.

Kassim was dumbfounded at the sight of the robbers' treasure, and his very soul was stirred by the prospect of caravan after caravan carrying the riches home. He gathered twenty of the largest sacks of gold and jewels and dragged them to the entrance. Then he tried to remember the magic words. "Open, Barley!" he cried.

But the rock did not open.

The miserable Kassim, preoccupied with the acquisition of so much gold, has completely forgotten the all-powerful words. Again and again he shouted, "Open, Wheat! Open, Barley! Open Beans!" to the door, which obeyed no sound but "Open, Sesame!"

And as he stood shaking with rage and terror before the impenetrable rock, the forty thieves came riding up to the cave.

When they saw the ten donkeys tethered near the entrance they leaped down from their horses and scattered around in search of the intruder, brandishing their swords and yelling angry curses. Then the captain pointed toward the rock and pronounced the two words that rent it asunder. The robbers were enraged to find a stranger in their treasure house. They swooped upon Kassim with their swords and hacked him into six pieces, then hung the pieces just inside the cave as a lesson and a warning to other would-be intruders.

When night came and Kassim did not return home, his wife grew very anxious. She went over to Ali Baba's house and begged him to go and look for her husband. Fearing that the worst might have happened, Ali Baba took his three donkeys and rode off at sunrise to the robbers' cave.

With a trembling voice he cried, "Open, Sesame!" and when the rock opened, he walked in. He was stricken with grief at the sight of Kassim's body cut in pieces. With a heavy heart he took down the pieces and put them carefully together into two empty sacks, which he loaded onto one of his donkeys. He loaded the other two beasts with more sacks of gold, then commanded the rocky door to shut and led his donkeys home.

On reaching the courtyard of his house, he knocked at the door, and it was opened by the slave Marjanah, who was the cleverest and most faithful of his servants.

"Marjanah, my girl," said Ali Baba, "today you can give us proof of your ingenuity and wisdom. Your master's brother has been killed by robbers and cut into pieces, but no one must know about it. Think of some way by which we can bury him without arousing any suspicions."

Then he went to his brother's house and broke the bad news to Kassim's wife.

"Do not grieve, dear sister," he said. "Allah has given me more riches than I can use. Come and live in our house, and share everything with us. But no one must know our secret."

They unloaded the pieces of Kassim's body, and discreetly told the neighbors that he had died suddenly in his sleep.

Then Marjanah went to the shop of an old cobbler in another part of the town where she was quite unknown.

"We want you to do a little sewing," she said. "Bring your needles and thread with you. Your work must be secret, and I must blindfold you and lead you to the house."

At first the old cobbler refused, but when Marjanah slipped a piece of gold into his hand, he allowed himself to be led along the streets and down into the cellar of Ali Baba's house. There she showed him the pieces of Kassim's body, slipped another gold coin into his hand, and bade him sew them together, adding, "If you work quickly you shall have two more pieces of gold."

The old man set to work at once and sewed the parts so neatly that no one would see the stitching. She led him back blindfolded to his shop, and returned home to make arrangements for Kassim's funeral. Thus Kassim was buried according to the customary rites, and no one outside the household had the slightest suspicion of the way he had met his death.

When the forty thieves paid their next visit to the cave they were dismayed to find no sign of Kassim's body.

"My men," the captain said, "it is clear that someone else knows our secret. We must find out at once who the accomplice of the man we killed is."

Calling one of the robbers, he said to him, "Disguise yourself as a holy dervish. Go into the town and find out the identity of the man whose body we cut to pieces."

Just before sunrise next morning the robber entered the town, and the first shop he saw open was the old cobbler's. He greeted the old man, praised his wares, and engaged him in a friendly conversation.

"I see, good sir, that you begin work before sunrise," he began. "Your eyes must be very good indeed to see so well in the gray light of dawn."

"Allah be praised, good dervish," replied the cobbler. "I can still thread a needle at the first attempt. Why, only yesterday I sewed together the parts of a man's body in a dark cellar without a light."

"Indeed," said the robber, "and who might the man be?"

"That I cannot tell," the cobbler replied, "for I was blindfolded and led to the place by an impudent girl, and brought back the same way."

The robber slipped a gold coin into the cobbler's hand.

"I would like nothing better," he said, "than to be taken myself to that house. I will blindfold you, and you can grope your way along the same route you followed yesterday. Take me there and you shall have more gold."

The cobbler allowed his eyes to be bandaged and, holding on to the robber's sleeve, felt his way slowly to Ali Baba's house; and there he stopped.

"This is most certainly the place," he cried.

The robber was overjoyed at the discovery. He removed the old man's bandage, slipped a second gold piece into his hand, and sent him back to his shop. Then he took a piece of chalk out of his pocket and with it marked the door of Ali Baba's house. This done, he returned with all possible speed to the forest and told his captain the good news.

When, soon afterward, honest Marjanah went to do the shopping, she noticed the white mark upon the door and thought to herself, "This is an evil sign, the work of an enemy plotting my master's ruin."

So she fetched a piece of chalk and made the same mark on the doors of all the houses in the street.

Next morning the thieves came one by one into the town to break into the house their spy had marked for them, and to avenge themselves on everyone who lived in it. But when the robber led them into the street, they were confounded to see that all the doors were marked in the same way, so that it was impossible to tell which was the house they sought. The angry captain sent them back to the forest, with orders to put the foolish spy to death.

"It seems that I shall have to go myself," said the robber chief.

So next day he rode into the city in disguise and went straight to the old cobbler, who led him to Ali Baba's house. But the captain did not mark the door this time. He gazed long and carefully at it until its very image was engraved upon his memory, and then he returned to the forest.

He called the thieves together and said to them, "I know the house for certain now. Tomorrow we shall be avenged. All I require you to do is to bring me thirty-nine earthenware jars, each large enough to contain a full-grown man. One of them must be filled with cooking oil, the rest must be empty."

The thieves, who always obeyed the captain, rode off at once to the market place and returned with thirty-nine large jars. One of these jars they filled with oil, and in each of the others a robber hid himself, on the captain's orders. The chief armed each with a dagger and club, and covered the mouth of each vessel with a muslin cloth, so that the men inside would be hidden and yet breathe freely. Then he loaded his men's horses with the jars, linked the animals together, and drove them toward the city.

When he came to Ali Baba's house, he found the woodcutter seated on his threshold, enjoying the cool evening air.

"Peace be to you, my master," said the captain with a low bow. "I am an oil merchant and have been traveling the road these three days. I am a stranger in this city and do not know where to pass the night. I pray that you will give hospitality, for myself and my horses, in the courtyard of your house."

"You are most welcome, sir," said Ali Baba kindly.

He took his guest by the hand and led him into his house. Then he ordered Marjanah to help with the unloading of the jars, to feed the horses, and to prepare a hot meal for the stranger.

Now, the captain had told his men that when he threw a pebble into the jars they were to come out of the jars and join him. So they crouched there, patiently waiting for the signal.

Meanwhile, Marjanah, who was busily cooking the dinner in the kitchen, found her lamp going out for lack of oil.

"We surely cannot complain of being short of oil," she said to herself, "when there are thirty-nine jars full of it in the courtyard. I will go and take a little from one of them."

She took her lamp and went to fill it, but as she touched the first jar a voice whispered, "Is it time?"

The quick-witted Marjanah guessed at once what was afoot, and instead of screaming with fright, whispered back in as deep a voice as she could, "Not yet!"

As she approached the jars in turn, from each came the same question, and to each she gave the same answer, until she came to the last jar, which she found was in fact filled with oil. After taking what she needed, she returned to the kitchen, lit the lamp, and set to work upon a plan to save her master.

From the last jar she quickly filled a great caldron with oil and set it over the fire to boil. Then she poured the boiling oil into those of the jars in which the thieves were hidden and killed them all.

After dinner the captain of the robbers retired to bed, and at midnight, seeing no light and hearing no sound, he threw his pebble into the yard. But there was no answer, and not one robber appeared.

"The dogs have gone to sleep," he muttered.

When he ran down to the courtyard and looked into the jars, he found that all his men were dead. Realizing that his plan was discovered and that he himself might be in danger of his life, he leaped over the courtyard wall and fled. On and on he ran until he reached the treasure cave, where he sat brooding over the calamitous end of his followers.

Next morning, Marjanah took Ali Babi into the courtyard and showed him the jars. He recoiled in horror when he looked into the first and saw a dead man inside, but the girl quickly told him the whole story. Now he rejoiced to hear that all the robbers were dead and was deeply thankful to Marjanah.

"From this moment," he declared, "you are no longer a slave, but our own beloved daughter."

Ali Baba buried the thieves' bodies in a great pit and lived in peace and contentment with his family for many months.

One day, Ali Baba's oldest son, who by now had become a rich merchant with a shop of his own, said to his father, "I do not know how to repay my neighbor, the merchant Husain, for all the kindness he has shown me since he took the shop next door to mine. I should much like to invite him to our house and give a feast in his honor."

"Invite him, by all means," Ali Baba replied. "He will be most welcome."

But when the merchant arrived, he said to Ali Baba, "You do me great honor in inviting me to your house, but alas, I cannot eat with you. I have made a vow never to taste salt or eat any meat flavored with it."

"That is no difficult matter," Ali Baba cried. "I will give orders that no salt be put into our food tonight." And he hurried into the kitchen to tell Marjanah that she should use no salt in the cooking.

This odd request aroused the girl's suspicions and she looked closely at the guest when she carried the dishes in. Her horror knew no bounds when she recognized the captain of the robbers and saw that he had a dagger hidden in the folds of his robe.

"So that's why the villain would not eat salt with the man he intends to kill," she thought.

When the meal was over, Marjanah entered the room, and Ali Baba and his son were astonished to see the dress she had put on; it was that of a dancer. Holding a dagger in one hand, she danced gracefully, to the delight of all the company, particularly that of the disguised robber, who took out his purse to throw a gold coin to her. As he bent forward she flung herself upon him and plunged her dagger into his heart.

"What have you done, you foolish girl!" Ali Baba exclaimed, aghast at the deed.

"You have killed the kind old man!" cried the son.

"I have saved your lives!" Marjanah cried. And she showed them the dagger hidden in the visitor's robe, and then told them who he really was and how she had found him out.

When Ali Baba realized that the girl had saved him yet once more, he took her into his arms and said, "You shall marry my son and become in all truth my daughter; for you have truly earned this reward."

And so Marjanah was wedded to Ali Baba's son, amid great rejoicing.

For a long time, Ali Baba kept away from the robbers' cave, but when one year had passed he went there with his son and Marjanah. He found the little path that led up to the rock overgrown with long grass, with not a sign of man or beast, and knew that the cave was now perfectly safe. He flung out his arms toward the rock, crying, "Open, Sesame!" and once again the door opened, revealing the secret treasure untouched since the death of the robbers.

So Ali Baba became the richest and most influential man of his time, and lived in tranquillity and joy until the end of his life.

Epilogue

Night after night, for a thousand and one nights, Shahrazad told King Shahriyar strange and wondrous stories; and so charmed was he by her beauty and gentle wit that at the dawn of each day he put off her execution until the next.

Now, during this time she also bore the King three sons. On the thousand and first night, when she had ended the last of her tales, she rose and kissed the ground before him, saying, "Great King, for a thousand and one nights I have told you stories of past ages and the legends of ancient kings. May I now make so bold as to beg a favor of Your Majesty?"

The King replied, "Ask, and it shall be granted."

Shahrazad called out to the nurses, saying, "Bring me my children."

Three little boys were instantly brought in, one walking, one crawling on all fours, and the third held in the arms of his nurse. Shahrazad ranged the little ones before the King and, again kissing the ground before him, said, "Look upon these three whom God has granted to us. For their sake I implore you to save my life. For if you destroy the mother of these infants, they will find none among women to love them as I would."

The King kissed his three sons, and his eyes filled with tears as he answered, "I swear by Allah, Shahrazad, that you were already pardoned before the coming of these children. I loved you because I found you chaste and gentle, wise and eloquent. May God bless you, and bless your father and mother, your ancestors, and all your descendants. O Shahrazad, this thousand and first night is brighter for us than the day!"

Shahrazad rejoiced. She kissed the King's hand and called down blessings upon him.

The people were overjoyed at the news of the King's pardon.

Next morning Shahriyar summoned to his presence the great ones of the city, the chamberlains, the nobles, and the officers of his army. When they had all assembled in the great hall of the palace, he proclaimed his decision to spare the life of his bride. Then he called his vizier, Shahrazad's father, and invested him with a magnificent robe of honor, saying, "God has raised up your daughter to be the savior of my people. I have found her chaste, wise, and eloquent, and repentance has come to me through her."

Then the King gave robes of honor to the courtiers and the captains of his army, and ordered the decoration of his capital.

The city was decked and lighted; and in the streets and market squares drums were beaten, trumpets blared, and clarions sounded. The King lavished alms on the poor and the destitute, and all the people feasted at his expense for thirty days and thirty nights.

King Shahriyar reigned over his subjects in all justice, and lived happily with Shahrazad ever after.

Born in Baghdad, N. J. Dawood went to England as an Iraq State Scholar in 1945 and graduated from London University. He is a director of Contemporary Translations Ltd., and managing director of The Arabic Advertising and Publishing Company, Ltd., London. Mr. Dawood has translated numerous technical works into Arabic, written and spoken radio and film commentaries, and contributed to specialized English-Arabic dictionaries. He has edited and abridged *The Muqaddimah of Ibn Khaldun* and has translated the Koran and an unabridged version of *Tales from the Thousand and One Nights*.